MW01132157

# Kali's *Odiyya*—A Shaman's True Story *of* Initiation

# Kali's *Odiyya*—A Shaman's True Story *of* Initiation

*Amarananda Bhairavan*

NICOLAS-HAYS
York Beach, Maine

First published in 2000 by
NICOLAS-HAYS
P.O. Box 2039
York Beach, ME 03910-2039

Distributed to the trade by
SAMUEL WEISER, INC.
P.O. Box 612
York Beach, ME 03910-0612
www.weiserbooks.com

Copyright © 2000 Amarananda Bhairavan
All rights reserved. No part of this publication may be reproduced or transmitted
in any form or by any means, electronic or mechanical, including photocopying,
recording, or by any information storage and retrieval system, without permission
in writing from Nicolas-Hays, Inc. Reviewers may quote brief passages.

**Library of Congress Cataloging-in-Publication Data**

Bhairavan, Amarananda.
    Kali's odiyya : a shaman's true story of initiation / Amarananda Bhairavan.
       p. cm.
    Includes index.
    ISBN 0-89254-048-6 (paper : alk. paper)
       1. Bhairavan, Amarananda.  2. Kālī (Hindu deity)—Cult—India.
    3. Spiritual biography—India.  4. Priests, Hindu—India—Biography.
    5. Shamans—India—Biography.  I. Title.

BL1175.B435 A34 2000
294.5'092—dc21
[B]                                                                    00–021126

EB

Typeset in 11/13 Galliard

Cover art by Irene Vincent
Cover design by Kathryn Sky-Peck

Printed in the United States of America
07  06  05  04  03  02  01  00
8   7   6   5   4   3   2   1

The paper used in this publication meets the minimum requirements of the
American National Standard for Information Sciences—Permanence of Paper
for Printed Library Materials Z39.48-1992 (R1997).

Salutations to Preemavati, our teacher divine
Who lives in our hearts as heavenly love;
To you we dedicate this work, inspired
by the Shaktis that you awakened in us.

Our profound gratitude to Aghori Narayani,
Supreme mystic of incredible awareness;
Who uplifted us with your acts of power,
Sheltering our hearts at Shakti's feet.

The bands of mystics of selfless compassion,
Who took us into their sacred conclave;
And showered us with their abundant grace,
To them we offer our soulful thanks.

Nishachii our divine protectress and heroic Shakti,
Whose unrelenting vigil and constant solicitude
Carries us through the upheavals of reincarnation,
We enfold you in grateful love.

To Amba our own innermost Self and Supreme Teacher,
We surrender to you all that we are,
Our spirits, a spark of your Cosmic Self,
Pray be a mote beneath your blessed feet.
Salutations again from Sandhya and Shambu!

# Contents

# Acknowledgments

I owe a deep debt of gratitude to my mother and father who brought me into this world and instilled in me divine consciousness, and to my siblings, cousins, aunts and uncles, who fostered a mystic childhood. I salute my matriarchs who taught me the essence of Kali Consciousness.

I am grateful to my wife Irene for her unstinting support throughout this endeavor, and for creating the magnificent cover art. I am grateful to my friend Usha Harding from Kali Mandir,® whose gentle guidance gave coherence to the primitive manuscript. My deep thanks to Kim Saccio-Kent whose diligent and caring edit helped transform the work into its final shape. My heartfelt thanks go to Betty Lundsted, my publisher, whose kindness has made this book possible. I thank the staff of Nicolas-Hays, who gave of their hearts and souls to make this book a success.

# Introduction

The village of Karingkalchuttor nestles in a valley at the bottom of foothills that lead to a chain of mountains in the East—the ramparts of the Ramagiri range. Boulders stud this valley, many of which are incorporated into the buildings in our village. The only manmade structure that stands above every tree in the valley is the imposing tower of the temple. It rises like a majestic granite bastion, dwarfing the banyan trees and coconut palms that clamor around it, themselves set in a waving sea of green paddy.

My village had many homes, principal among which were 108 priestly households of various sizes. These households, called *taravads*, were true matriarchies, as opposed to the more common matrilineal systems prevailing in most villages in that part of the country. My childhood name was Shambu and my life joyful, living among an extended family of fifty-seven people, in a rambling three-hundred-year-old homestead.

Matriarchs headed the households, governed the village through the Tantric Council, and guided the agro-pastoral and religious affairs of our community. The younger generation learned everything about our way of life from the matriarchs. These old ones guided their successors in matters of daily ritual. In our culture, where every aspect of our way of life was taught by word of mouth and through direct apprenticeship, the role of the matriarch was indispensable. Time had distilled much wisdom into the matriarchs, who served as reservoirs of cultural knowledge. The matriarchies of my village gave prime recognition to women in spiritual and temporal matters. This appreciation was most evident in spiritual issues, as women seers and tantrikas enjoyed superior standing compared to their male counterparts. It was not uncommon to find housewives who officiated as family priestesses, liturgists, and as initiators of festival rituals. Female preceptorship thrived in this environment. The tenets of Hinduism, though guided by centuries of tradition, are neither driven by a centralized institution, nor guided by any single prophet or scripture. Hinduism is the collective experiences, realizations, and revelations about the Supreme Being. The younger generation followed the elders in matters of family rituals, communal ceremonies, and household duties. *Shakti* worship, in our matriarchy in particular, fell into this category.

Paddies abounded on the outskirts of our village and groves of coconut palms and fruit trees surrounded the homesteads. The men of these families maintained their *taravads* while working under the guidance of a male elder called the *karanavar*. The *karanavar* was sometimes the oldest male of the family; he was often also the eldest maternal uncle. The *karanavar*, in turn, accounted to the ruling matriarch of the family.

Most men specialized in agriculture. This was a full time job except for two months during summer when their work slackened a little after the rice was harvested, winnowed, and stored. The younger men consulted the grandfathers (the husbands of the matriarchs) on aspects of farming, whose knowledge of the subtle variances in the monsoon was intimate. Our lives depended on these biannual monsoons. Besides agriculture, men maintained the buildings of our homesteads.

The day-to-day life in our village revolved around the early-morning-to-midnight worship performed at our main Kali temple. This temple rose from the center of the village, with the homesteads forming a crescent around it. The crescent opened to the hills in the east. We call the deity of our temple *Kula Bhadra Kali* ("benign Kali of the clans"), and She was central to our daily lives.

The goddess Kali has been described in many writings, both scriptural as well as modern, but in the microsociety of our matriarchy, She assumed a peculiar cosmological significance. Kali is the feminine anthropomorphism of the cosmos, with its plethora of phenomena that, though in constant flux, is eternal. She is movement, or the power that manifests all—as opposed to that absolute incomprehensible neutrality called Brahman, which is also eternal, but unchanging. Kali is the ultimate personification of goodness experienced as the Divine Mother, and She is also the terminal face of evil. She incarnates as *Prakriti*, nature's complex interlocked web of changing relationships that thrive at the cost of one another, yet paradoxically, are mutually nourishing. This is Kali, who in truth is neither pure evil nor good, but cosmic energy itself (*Shakti*). This energy is distributed in all things living and nonliving, in every conceivable and inconceivable space-time, realm, dimension, and plane of existence, powering them all in their individual and collective evolutions toward that ultimate "Face of Good and Evil," beyond which is that Supreme Unfathomable. So Her devotees comprehended Her in two forms, the benign and the malevolent. The former is associated with Her creative and nurturing functions, and the latter with Her

depredatory and destructive roles. The deity of our temple is the benign Kali, sculpted in black granite.

Women officiated exclusively as priestesses in this temple all year
round, except in the month of April, on the day of the ascendance of
a cluster of stars called *Bharani*, when men performed special ceremonies. On this particular night, the elders in every homestead invoked this goddess of our temple along with the spirits of our
ancestors. After special offerings were made to the spirits of the dead,
Kali and these spirits were treated to a sumptuous feast.

Evergreen forests draped the hills and mountains that ranged to
the east of this temple. Within this woodland is a mountain shrine
dedicated to a form of this goddess known as *Kattu Kali* (or Forest
Kali)—also called *Raktha Kali,* after the deep, crimson-black color of
this gory image. In contrast to the benign image in the greater temple, this deity has a ghastly presence. Though She is the same divinity
worshipped at the main temple, on the Night of Kali, She assumed
Her destructive functions. This manifestation of Kali was purposeful-
ly sequestered in this forest, away from all homesteads. In this gruesome form, Kali erupted one night each year, to devour the evil and
the wicked among all life.

While the benign Kali and the ancestors were invoked to a midnight feast in each homestead, the priests performed an impressive
ritual to awaken and honor the Forest Kali. First, they sacrificed a
black, male goat. Its blood was carefully collected and poured over
the Forest Kali. This served to appease the hordes of Forest Kali, as
well as to awaken Forest Kali from Her slumber. As soon as the Forest Kali was aroused with goat's blood, She was offered human blood
to whet Her malevolent energy—Kali devotees, immersed in divine
rapture, struck their own heads with scimitars. The blood that
streamed forth was offered to this Kali.

In the meanwhile at the village, after the ceremony of the ancestors was concluded, and everyone had partaken of the great feast, every family bolted their doors and windows. *Yantras* (mystical,
geometric markings), drawn earlier around their homes, protected
them with a mystical force. Some people stayed indoors, protected
by the emanations from these *yantras*. Pets were brought in, and cattle and poultry, though penned outside, were surrounded with
*yantras* as well. Those who remained outside marked themselves
with the blood from the goat sacrificed at the forest shrine.

The Forest Kali and Her hordes roved the universe that night to
mete out destruction to the forces of darkness. By early morning, intox-

icated by the stupendous blood-feast, She retired to Her forest shrine to sleep, only to be reawakened at the same time the following year.

Mystics of various traditional sects frequented our village, and our household was often host to them. Wandering on foot from village to village, they spread the gospel of the Divine Love and the all-pervasive oneness of life. Abandoning possessions, they opened themselves to the vagaries of nature, reposing completely in the grace of God. These were members of traditional monastic orders.

Then there were those who appeared from the hills—strange beings who practiced bizarre rituals. We knew very little about their ways, yet we have witnessed their extraordinary powers of transcendence over space and time. Many villagers claimed to have seen these apparitions coalescing seemingly out of nothing, sometimes within their own homes. Others have come home shaken, having encountered one of these beings while at work in the hills. Some people who bolted home discovered that they have now been endowed with the ability to heal the sick, or to predict the future.

In contrast to their godly benevolence, these beings also invoked fear because of their mysterious abilities over nature, in turn giving birth to rumors of their dark powers. The villagers' profound reverence for these beings was matched only by an irrational fear of them. We called them *odiyyas*, or sorcerers—adepts of light and masters of benevolent magic.

Odiyyas are masters of body-mind. Having attained the Supreme Experience, odiyyas are similar in this respect to the self-realized sages in traditional monastic orders. But unlike these traditional sages, odiyyas have no inhibition manifesting their supernormal powers and abilities. Traditional mystics consider supernatural powers to be impediments to their ultimate objective, and avoid them. Odiyyas engage in many practices that appear strange, fantastic, or even deviant.

Odiyyas are worshippers of the Divine Mother. Having realized this universe to be the Divine Mother's play, they are playful in life and in death. They experience no barriers, having transcended space-time. They have gone beyond mind and body, therefore nothing limits them; they play, assuming different bodies. As children of the Divine Mother, they romp with absolute volition in the planes of the cosmos.

There are many levels of odiyyas. Some are adepts who have achieved the Supreme Experience many incarnations earlier, and they are so advanced that they can create whole universes with their intent, yet they make their presence in this temporal plane again and again for reasons known only to themselves. It seems that love and compassion for the uninitiated propel them to limit themselves repeatedly. An adept can be likened to a kind person tenderly lifting struggling ants from a puddle of water, while the ants themselves are mostly unaware of their benefactor.

Beginners among odiyyas are those who have just emerged from the cocoon of human experience in this life, and are in the process of ascension into the planes of Divine Experience. Adepts guide them out of human experience like a midwife coaxes a child's birth.

Odiyya novices are fostered in bands. In the early stages of their preparations, odiyyas work with rituals. The adept guides the odiyya novice through rituals that unseat the mind shaped by the novice's life among lay people. At this critical stage in the novice's transformation, the adept and the rest of the band provide cohesion and protection. After the initial rites and practices, the novice experiences one delightful transformation after another in the company of the band, in the seclusion of the woods. A person is fortunate to be watched over by adepts, but to be a part of their elusive group is a rare fortune. To be guided by them is to live with joy, peace, and supreme abandonment.

The odiyyas were once normal people, but have transcended their human nature. During their rare encounters with lay people, most odiyyas restore the human form with which they are born. These sorcerers have mastered the technique of perceiving their physical bodies as energies, and are able to manipulate these energies in order to disassemble and reassemble themselves through pure will. The laws of physics and biology that inexorably govern their lay brethren do not bind odiyyas. By sloughing off human limitations, these beings alienate themselves from human experience. Thus a natural gap develops between them and the common people—a gap of experience like that found between two species, one having evolved out of the other.

The lay people in our society learned elements of mysticism from the prodigious writings of traditional mystics who taught restraint in the development or use of supernormal powers. The elusive odiyyas, on the other hand, revel in manifesting their supernormal powers. When the common people juxtaposed rumors about the doings of the odiyyas with the teachings of the traditional mystics, the odiyyas seemed unrestrained, unpredictable, and powerful.

Odiyyas live on the fringe of our society—they actually exist between two realities, with an unnerving ability to move between these realities. Some of the men and women sorcerers cohabited ritually, performing erotic mystical ceremonies of tremendous power. The adept guided all these ceremonies. The odiyyas lived with deliberate intent with the adepts among them performing every act with unnerving power.

Stories about the feats of the odiyyas were popular in our village. These tales strengthened my mystical background and fanned the embers of my spiritual curiosity. Like children everywhere who play-act the roles that the adults around them pursue with serious endeavor, the children in our community played at being mystics, performing pretend rituals and temple worship. The worship of Kali, the constant presence of mystics, and the acts of the odiyyas, produced a climate of mysticism that made the incredible possible, so much so that we experienced a constant interweaving of the mundane and the superphysical realities. Divine fervor and intuition superseded reason and doubt, making it possible to manifest subjective experiences as sensory realities.

Our village was a sanctuary for the serene, austere, and self-controlled *vallichappads*, who were quite different from the elusive odiyyas. *Vallichappad* means "harbingers of spiritual light," and they interacted intimately with our society. These mystics were devoted to Kali, the benign Cosmic Mother, and explored the Divine Realm through intense mystical love, or *Bhakti*.

Vallichappads functioned in our society as healers, repositories of scriptural knowledge, consultants and interpreters of hoary arts, oracles, and sometimes, as exorcists. They aided households during special ceremonies and during rites of passage. These mystics lived in their cluster of hermitages in an orchard at one end of the village where they practiced different austerities. The grandmasters among them were called *kurukkals*. Their hermitage was a spiritual sanctuary to elderly householders who wished to leave home to embark on their ultimate quest of their Self in the evening of their lives. In a solemn ceremony, any previous obligation to social life was loosened and marital vows were dissolved. The elder was given a spiritual name and welcomed into the company of the vallichappads. Though the vallichappad community harbored both sexes, they lived separate monastic lives. Some joined this commune as children, having been discovered as spiritual prodigies by older vallichappads.

These spiritual wonders had normal childhoods, but showed strong mystical inclinations early in their lives. Such children lived in their natural households and were apprenticed in their early years to a specific elder. In later years, some of these children were initiated and absorbed into the community of the vallichappads, to the great satisfaction of all, with the hope that a rare few of these would eventually become spiritual lights and uplift society by joining an unbroken succession of mystics.

Odiyya adepts also watched these children unobtrusively. Once in a rare while, one or two of these special children disappeared from their homes, having been drawn into the fold of the odiyyas. Highly evolved even at birth, these spiritual powder kegs called out to the elusive adepts. These unusual children found even the highly spiritual vallichappad community too limiting to their immense consciousness. This was a major reason the common people feared the odiyyas——they considered these disappearances as willful abductions.

During the annual Night of Kali, we witnessed the emergence of the pilgrims of Kali, called the *villambadis*, a Paishachii word meaning "Children of Kali." These common people swarmed the temple in hordes, wearing the pilgrim's distinct crimson garb, many carrying heavy scimitars. On that midnight, at the peak of the ceremony, they struck their heads with these scimitars, performing a ritual of self-blood sacrifice. They surrendered to Kali with deep religious fervor. Under that extraordinary state of mind, these pilgrims recovered rapidly from their ghastly wounds.

Now, cracking skulls may not be the most appealing path to spiritual evolution, but to these pilgrims, it was a fulfillment of a vow. This act transported them into feeling they were one with the Universal Being, enabling them to go beyond body consciousness and ego attachments. This behavior can be understood if one sees these pilgrims as products of a culture permeated by Kali-consciousness and daily ritual worship. This was a community whose ideals were such principles as selflessness, humility, and surrender to the all-pervading Cosmic Being, a people whose heroes and heroines were the mystics and the devotees of God. It was such a climate that bred the vallichappads, the children of Kali, and the mysterious odiyyas.

I was raised in this environment where the air I breathed smelled of incense, camphor, flowers of worship, and smoke from fire ceremonies. This kindled my yearnings for mystical experiences. It is my preceptor, Aunt Preema, who first set me upon this path.

Aunt Preema was my mother's cousin, and the mother of my childhood playmate Sandhya. She was one of the principal priestesses of our village temple and our family shrine. Aunt Preema was a powerful sorceress, and she wielded great influence over beings of many realms. I discovered her various and formidable aspects over several years of my discipleship with her. Her contribution to my spiritual growth is immeasurable, and my debt of gratitude to her is cosmic.

The story in this book is derived from childhood memories and adolescent experiences. I have altered the names of people and the descriptions of certain places. As I revisit my childhood experiences, I have interpreted my memories in the light of new understanding, thereby capturing certain experiences through the eyes of an adult. Hindsight is a strange thing, because it interferes with innocent childhood impressions, supplanting those magical experiences with rational descriptions.

The extended family I had experienced no longer exists. The matriarchies, extended households, and landed properties that sustained these homesteads have disintegrated under the impact of modernizing forces. The family shrines and ancient rituals performed there have disappeared with them. Imported cultures and lifestyles have pressured the younger generation to abandon old ways. With no one to train, generations of vallichappads and mystics who had refined their spiritual techniques upon spirited novices have retreated from society. Bereft of a mystical climate to foster divine consciousness, children with mystical tendencies have become rare. Only the main temple and the rituals performed there have managed to survive. Therefore I have decided to narrate these events, before the jagged edge of time frays my memory. May these inspire divine consciousness! May the mystics prevail!

*Jai Jagad Ambae!*
—**Amarananda Bhairavan**

CHAPTER ONE

# The Night of Kali

It was five-thirty in the evening and the sun was about to set. The road leading into Karingkalchuttor brought in the last of the teertha yatris—pilgrims and devotees of Kali —from several outlying villages. Pilgrims had been flocking into my village in cartloads for several days, and they settled in makeshift camps on either side of the road. Many had walked two or three hundred miles to make this special pilgrimage to their beloved Kali. The young often took turns helping the old. For some, this pilgrimage would be the last leg in the long journey of life. The arduous trek and the rigors of the penance undertaken inevitably claimed the most feeble. They came to Kali dead or alive; the dead brought in, carried by loving hands. After the ceremonies were over, the dead bodies were cremated and the remains interred in the burial ground outside the village. For the devotees of Kali, a more blessed exit cannot be imagined.

They came in all ages, wearing the pilgrim's cotton vestures of brilliant red that identified them as Kali's devotees. The rays of the evening sun painted these streaming hordes ruddy, and the road took on the aspect of a river of blood. Hundreds of pounding feet threw up a cloud of dust that hung in the air, lending the twilight a crimson cast.

Devotees thronged our temple tonight for the final hours of their pilgrimage, which would culminate in the ceremony of awakening Kali performed by the mystics of our village. Like little red streamlets pouring into a river, they converged on the road from various encampments. Their fervor increased as they approached the outskirts of the temple. Pilgrims arriving by ox-carts leaped onto the dirt and joined others as they ran into the temple grounds in rapture, jiggling their scimitars over their heads. Dashing down the steep sandy slopes of the temple pond, they plunged into the sacred water by the bathing ghats. After their ceremonial dip in the pond, they scrambled up the slopes and ran toward the outer perimeter of the temple.

Pilgrims streamed past me as I sat observing the activities from my seat upon the low stone wall that skirted the temple grounds. I watched them plummet upon the loose sand outside the temple walls with cries of "Ambae! Kalii!" and begin their arduous, rolling circumambulation of the entire temple complex. This is their first task in the fulfillment of the vows they had taken. Family members followed each rolling devotee, guiding and protecting them from others stampeding around the temple walls while calling hoarsely to Kali. They ran swinging tridents, scimitars, sickles, and swords, clashing them along the low trim of the copper roof-plates. At times, bits of metal broke and flew out of their flailing arms. Some ran carrying half a large cymbal and struck it upon its other half, which was tied to the back of the person running ahead. The clamor that rose sounded like the din of battle. Even though this heightened my religious sensibility, the unnerving devotion made me shiver.

During this Night of Kali some young men went through a spiritual transvestitism and mimicked the dress of female devotees. Wearing crimson saris, they adorned themselves with flowers. Several weeks of abstinence and rigorous preparation gave these men the mental power to enter into a spiritual trance this evening as they entered the temple grounds after the ceremonial bath in the temple bathing ghats. They stood stark naked, their bodies shivering slightly from the ascending transformation, while women dressed them as females. This was the best way to invoke the divine goddess within—they sublimated their maleness and became female. The elders considered this the highest form of tantric worship any male can perform to Kali.

This night was the last day of a mystical year tracked by my people. It culminated in a mystical moment called muhoortham, with the ascendance of the cluster of stars called Bharani. It also marked the beginning of the final war between the forces of Kali and the Demons of the Dark. The learned ones of our village kept track of Bharani's emergence, which was due in the east. A lookout kept vigil from the pinnacle of the temple tower. Upon sighting the star cluster, he would signal the priests below by hoisting the sacred banner. Then the kurukkals would conclude the mysterious ceremony they have been doing for several hours inside the temple's sanctum and in the adjoining secret chamber. Rumor had it that one could enter the secret chamber from the sanctum through a door that can be opened only from within the secret chamber. There were also speculations on the existence of an underground tunnel that connected the secret chamber to a cave in the hills, six or seven miles away.

Pilgrims awaited another divine experience. As soon as the lookout would hoist the sacred flag, a falcon would fly in from the east and circle the temple several times. It would signal an end to the frenzied circumambulations. This falcon's appearance at this exact moment has been recorded for many years now.

I was startled by the blast from a conch blown by a devotee as she dashed past me. My grandfather had explained before that the tumult from the frenzied pilgrims sounded a wake up call, a cry to battle. Twilight will mark the beginning of the final massing of the forces of light. Just then, I heard the drums boom within the temple. The rumble of the temple drums called forth energy from every being, so the elders had explained to us children. Sloughing off slumber, grotesque forms will rise from the embers and ashes of the cremation grounds. This force is prepared to issue from every tree and stone, from everything living and dead, ready to do battle at the side of Kali. The Night of Kali will witness the beginning of a cosmic confrontation; Kali Herself is expected to rise and lead these forces. To my heightened awareness, this power was palpable—but for now, it seethed, constrained, as it waited for Kali to rise.

Somewhere in the distance, I heard the hillsides reverberate with the sound of drums. The village was agog with excitement as people prepared for Armageddon and readied themselves for their great annual worship to their beloved Bhadra Kali, and the goat sacrifice to the crimson-black goddess of the forest known as Raktha Kali.

An ominous gloom grazed the jagged rim in the east. Evening shadows lengthen rapidly in the tropics, and the sky changes color with the twinkling of an eye. With little time left before darkness enveloped the countryside, the men of our village busied themselves with various chores, disregarding the pilgrims. Much remained to be done before nightfall, although we had begun preparations soon after lunch. Darkness would blanket the valley shortly; soon it would be time for the procession to move out of the temple and head into the forest. In the vast grounds of the temple, men created torches by winding long bamboo poles with wads of old cloth, while others dipped these into a cauldron of sesame oil. I saw young men scoot in and out of the temple, busy with some task or the other.

For hours now, the kurukkals had locked themselves into the inner sanctum of the Kali temple, invoking the power of the Black Goddess. I have heard from my elders that it required the combined power of these kurukkals, garnered through intense mystical practices, to perform the secret ritual held in the sanctum this night. Nobody else was allowed to be present in the sanctum or in this sacred, inner quadrangle. The excitement outside the temple walls was contagious. My cousins and I romped the temple grounds, which bustled with the activities of the elders.

Several women prepared large packets of kumkum (a red dust made from mineral compounds) and turmeric powder, Kali's beloved colors, while some plaited tender coconut palm leaves into decorative braids that would be strung along the path leading out of the temple into the hills. Other women sat with heaps of flowers, making long garlands from basil leaves, hibiscus, jasmine, and marigold. Girls brought baskets full of flowers to the women. The villagers worked beneath the sprawling branches of the banyan trees that grew in the spacious territory surrounding the temple. The place resembled a busy nest of ants, but the atmosphere, though festive, seemed to be tainted with an anxious haste that bordered on the ominous.

Tonight is a special Amavasya, the night of celebration of Kali's victory over the demons. Amavasya is the first day of the first quarter of the lunar month when the night is moonless.

I was only 9, an age with little or no responsibilities, but with plenty of energy. I was quickly swept aloft the tides of excitement and anticipation that crackled in the air like electricity. My cousins Sandhya, Meena, and Sreedham were playing near the garland-makers. They used mud and pebbles to build a small structure. I decided to join my cousins in their game.

When I approached them, they were plastering mud over a roof of green twigs.

"Look inside. See, like this," Meena said to me, as she put her head to the ground before the mud house.

"What's in there?" I asked, peeking in through the miniature doorway.

"Can you see Kali?" asked Sreedham.

"I see a stone in the center," I said, putting my right eye against the doorway.

"That is our Kali, you little mongoose," said Sandhya, giving me a shove.

"We could put some flowers on Kali," I suggested.

"Oh! Kali! We forgot. Now we will have to take the roof off!" exclaimed Sreedham beating his forehead with his right palm.

"No, you don't. We can put a flower on a stick and place it on Kali," I said.

"Let's do it!" said Sandhya.

There were plenty of discarded flowers lying around, since the women selected only the best for the ceremony and tossed out the rest. So we collected these and decorated our little Kali. Sandhya and I were straining to reach Kali with a hibiscus stuck at the end of a stick. It was more difficult than I thought. We had to manipulate the stick through the miniature doorway to reach Kali within the chamber.

The shrill bleat of a goat caught our attention. I looked up and saw a few men drag a reluctant black goat past us.

Rituals fascinated me, but I found it difficult to deal with animal sacrifice. The sacrificial goat stood tethered to a betel nut palm with a garland of hibiscus and marigold adorning its black neck. The goat chewed on some palm leaves, oblivious of its fate. Deep compassion for the animal swept over me and dampened my excitement. I sank to the grass and prayed that Kali would be kind to the goat. I left my playmates and sat with the goat for a while, feeding it flowers. Then, feeling somewhat drained, I made my way back home.

At home I found a few women and a handful of my cousins busy with last minute preparations for the ritual this night, since most of my family was at the temple. As I wandered along a corridor inside my home I heard my mother call me.

"Shambu, come here." I hastened to her.

"Come with me, I'll feed you," she said, clutching my arm.

"I am not hungry, Mother," I answered as I pulled my arm free.

"We won't be eating until after the midnight worship, dear. You will soon be hungry. Come with me, dear. Gopalan, Hari, Padman, and Chaya are eating," she said, trying to perk my interest. I joined my cousins at their meal. Eating hastily, I finished and ran out of the dining room before my mother could wipe my lips.

My father and a few uncles assisted the women in preparing the ritual feast to honor Kali and our ancestors. Tonight, every home in our village tended the fires of the sacred hearth because Kali, Her hosts, and our distinguished ancestors would be invoked and served a sumptuous feast.

The feast must be prepared with such purity that my uncles had built a temporary kitchen with a thatched roof in the back yard. I wandered along the perimeter of this construction, watching my father and uncles preparing cauldrons of food over blazing fire pits. It was getting dark, but the fires lit up the yard. The wood smoke and the aroma of spices were pervasive. Earlier, my father had said he would let me witness the festivities that would take place in the forest temple. I approached him to remind him of this.

"Father, can I go with the procession to the forest temple?"

"It's all right with me. But you better tell your Aunt Gauri before you go," he said. I was not enthused about asking her permission;

her moods were unpredictable. However, she ranked high in the chain of command, next only to the matriarchs, and she never missed an opportunity to assert herself or to speak for the matriarchs.

As I moved away from the hearth, I saw a shadowy woman painting figures on the walls of the house. As I approached, I recognized my Aunt Preema. She held a small bucket of kumkum paste in her left hand and, with a brush fashioned from a piece of coconut husk, she hastily painted geometric shapes onto the walls.

"Aunt Preema, can I see the forest shrine?"

She turned around. "Shambu, my dear! Sure you can!"

"But, father wanted me to ask Aunt Gauri. I don't know where she is! Is it okay if I just ask you?"

"Oh, Gauri is at the temple. It's okay—you may go," my aunt replied. Now that I had her permission, I felt relieved. My attention was drawn to the designs she was painting.

"Aunt, what are you painting?"

"These are sacred forms designed for protection, dear. Tonight is the Night of Kali, and these forms will protect our household from Kali's wrath," she replied.

"Why is Kali angry?" I asked.

"Kali is angry at the evil forces. She will eat them all tonight. Anyone who stays outside past midnight, without a sacred mark upon them, will be eaten up by Kali's army," my aunt laughingly answered.

"Are you serious, Aunt?" I was confused. Her expression was lighthearted, but her words frightened me.

"Yes, I am," said Aunt Preema wistfully, but she quickly reassured me saying, "but Kali is kind. She will protect you, Shambu."

"I want to be protected from Kali's wrath. Please put a mark on me," I pleaded.

My aunt peered at me through the darkness, thoughtful for a few moments.

"Yes . . . Yes, you are to be marked," she muttered to herself. "You are to be marked," she repeated. She dipped her right thumb in the red paste, and lifting my upper cloth, squiggled a smudge of red on my belly button.

"There! This mark will protect you," said Aunt Preema. "You are marked! You must be," she continued to mutter to herself. At that instant we heard the shrill sound of brass horns blown in the distance, followed by drumbeats. Soon after, the peal of numerous temple bells floated across to us in the wind.

"Listen! Do you hear? They have spotted the falcon that arrives every year at the precise time the star group Bharani is sighted. Shambu, don't you want to see the vallichappads carry Kali in the procession?" she asked.

"Yes, I do," I answered eagerly.

"Well, then you have to get to the temple quickly! I can hear the procession beginning its journey into the forest."

"I am going, Aunt Preema," I said. I was about to dash away, when she seized me by my arm and kissed me on my head.

"Go carefully!" she said.

I ran through the coconut grove all the way out to the rice fields. Though the thin mud ridges that separated one paddy plot from the other were hard to see in the semidarkness, I knew my way and skipped along the ridges, running east toward the sound of drums and cymbals. Darkness closed in fast and I had to stop now and then to glean the outlines of the ridges ahead, which slowed me down considerably. Meanwhile, the sounds coming from the procession began to fade. The procession must have left the main temple and entered the jungle, I thought.

It was quite dark when I approached the temple grounds. Usually the combined light from hundreds of oil lamps glowing from the granite tower and from the walls of the temple suffused the area with a soft radiance, but tonight the vast spaces were eerily dark, empty, and quiet. I could see vague shapes—scattered leaves, flowers, bits of cloth and rope lying about me, remnants of earlier activities. The granite tower loomed massive—a black silhouette that blotted out the faint light of the stars. I stopped for a moment, seized by a strong desire to peek into the temple that stood strangely empty. I wanted to see if the image of Kali was still within the sanctum. Some said that Kali was taken in the procession, while others claimed that it was only the energy of Kali and not the image itself that went in the procession. Here was an opportunity to lay to rest my curiosity.

I walked to the main entrance of the temple, toward the massive wood and copper doors built into the tower. When I turned the corner, I saw two oil lamps set in niches that were carved into the walls on either side of the doors. They glowed like twin eyes. The massive doors were ajar, but the inner quadrangle was empty. I stepped in through the doors and trembled momentarily as a strong gust hit me. A wave of apprehension coursed through me, but my curiosity and attraction for Kali were stronger. I walked toward the sanctum, and stood before the black stone image of Kula Bhadra Kali. Flickering light from a single lamp illumined Her. Holding my breath, I edged my way up the granite steps. This was the closest I had come to this awesome power. I saw that Kali was shorn of all Her jewelry; She was bedecked simply with a hibiscus garland and a red silk skirt. I stood outside the threshold of the sanctum. Wind blowing through the empty stone corridors sounded like Kali's breathing.

Tonight Kali was not distant, but intimate in Her naked simplicity. In the flickering light, I felt Her gaze. Her face was radiant, and the corners of Her lips appeared to curl upward in a smile. A glimmer in Her eyes caught me off guard. It felt strange to be here, all alone in the night with Kali as my sole companion. She was my friend, this Kali, not a lofty and fearsome goddess as I had heard people describe Her. As I gazed upon Her glistening form, I felt a passion stir in my bosom and I wanted to touch Her.

I wished so much to step across the threshold of the sanctum and hug Her. But rigorous training regarding the sanctum's purity erected an invisible barrier between the image of Kali and me. My heart's desires buffeted against this block. I knew of only a few initiated priestesses who had the fortune to touch Her during their daily worship rituals. I closed my eyes and Kali's image popped into my mind, clear and inviting. Ritual barriers did not exist in this inner space and I could cross this inner sanctum and hug Her.

Opening my eyes, I prostrated myself upon the threshold of the sanctum and I was about to back out of the temple when something shimmered to my left. Startled, I glanced to my left. An open door was cut into the granite wall; in the faint light, I made out an inner granite wall made from stone carved with intricate patterns. Then it happened again, a shimmer of white blur moved across from one end of the room to the other. This apparition scared me—the door was, without doubt, the entrance to the rumored secret chamber. I withdrew from the temple quickly.

I plunged into the darkness, heading eastward into the forest, toward the shrine of the Forest Kali. The sounds from the procession had long since ceased; it was well on its way to the shrine of the Forest Kali. This was the night, when the kurukkals would awaken the Forest Kali with a powerful ceremony. I wondered why I was allowed to witness this year's event, since I had not been allowed before. There were many things about this night that nagged my mind. What did the kurukkals do when they gathered at the main Kali temple before their journey to the forest? I had been told that the Forest Kali slept the whole year, waking only tonight. How was the Forest Kali different from our Kali in the main temple? Questions such as these bothered me as I made my way through the dark forest. My belly button itched from the dried kumkum, but I dared not scratch it, for fear of loosening my protective mark.

As I drew closer to the temple, I could hear the entire forest echo with the rhythm from tribal drums. A cluster of gigantic banyan trees hid the temple from my view, but I caught glimmers of light through the dark foliage. Breaking through the banyan grove, I came upon a primal scene in a large area cleared of vegetation. Young men and women, adorned in palm leaf headdresses and skirts, pounded the ground in a trance. Light from scores of torches cast eerie, fleeting patterns on their undulating bodies. In the background loomed the granite temple set against boulder hills. The temple was an extension of a shallow, but massive cave. Within the cave, I saw the huge, dark image of Kali, nude and unadorned, in a horrific pose. She was at least fifteen feet tall and Her eight arms clutched numerous weapons. Her face was crude and inhumanly angular, and She appeared to glare at me.

In stark contrast to the costumed dancers, the head priest was attired in a simple white dhoti, his dark hair tied into a bun at the back of his head. He was burly. A thick, black beard grew out of his chin and jowls in every conceivable direction. His countenance and gestures were terrifying and barbaric, matching the primal fury of the Kali he worshipped. Several other red-garbed priests were chanting hymns. The head priest climbed onto a stone platform. He held a large buffalo skull as if it were a vessel. Reaching up to Kali's crown, the priest poured blood from the jaws of the skull onto Kali's head. It streamed down Her menacing face, hideously obscuring one eye. The head priest held out the bovine skull for a refill. Another priest appeared with a brass bucket and, climbing the stone steps to the platform, poured its sanguine contents into the skull.

The deep rumble of a conch blasted out from within the sanctum and startled me. Instantly a group of men and women carrying heavy scimitars sprang from the sides of the sanctum. Streaks of sanctified blood dribbled down the corners of their mouths. They howled as if possessed by fiends, their wild shrieks lifting above the din of the drums and cymbals. Their bodies were nude, besmeared with crimson and turmeric paste. Red floral garlands whipped about their necks. Gathering before Kali, they writhed in a sinuous dance, their huge anklets creating a terrifying racket.

Then, to my horror, I saw a woman leap forward, and with a tremendous arching of her body, she swung her scimitar on her head. I heard a dull, sickening thud, and her head cleaved in its center. Rivulets of blood swept down the sides of her temples and ran down her naked body. A horde of older women immediately rushed to her side and stuffed the hole in her head with yellow turmeric powder.

The woman seemed to possess superhuman strength because she tossed aside her helpers and continued to dance. One by one the rest of the scimitar-wielding dancers cracked their pates. Frenzied cries like "Kaliii! My mother!" rent the air. My head began to reel and I tasted my stomach in the back of my throat. As I watched from the edge of the circle, I saw people around me slip into trances and begin dancing wildly. A few women walked among us with small platters of sanctified blood. They dipped their ring fingers into this and applied a dot of blood to the mid-brows of the onlookers.

No sooner did one of these women impress the blood mark onto my forehead, than I felt goose bumps spring all over my body. To my amazement, my whole body began to undulate uncontrollably in rhythm with the drums and the chant. Every breath I took caused a deep sensation inside me. I cast a quick, surreptitious look at the people around me, but they were immersed in their own ecstasy. Their bodies shook as they moved in rhythm to the beat of the drums. Their open eyes seemed to see nothing of their surroundings. Something was happening to all of us—the part of me that was still objective was unnerved.

A group of women came among the bystanders and began to pull us into the stomping crowd in the center. Men and women who were standing with me a moment ago threw themselves before the scimitar-waving group. The women were dramatic—with a violent toss of their heads, they loosened their neatly bundled hair and offered their heads to the nude dancers. The dancers hacked at the women's heads with their scimitars and blood gushed out, matting their hair. They showed no sign of discomfort! I backed out of the ring of people and ran from the banyan grove, leaving the temple behind. I ran along the dirt track that led to the village. Pitch darkness enveloped me.

The sounds of the ritual were far away, but now a cacophony rose around me from the dense, tropical jungle. It seemed that I had exchanged one terror for another. Though I was familiar with the jungle, in my current mental state the jungle was frightening. I stumbled with my hands extended ahead of me, pushing my way through the overgrowth in the intense blackness of the moonless night.

Very soon my peripheral vision came into play, compounding my fear. I was sure I could see fleeting shapes next to me, but they evaded my direct eye. I decided to stay put in one spot, hoping that someone from the forest temple would come and accompany me back to the village. As I stood still, the sounds from the jungle magnified. Paralyzed with fright, I stood rooted to the ground. I felt danger from all sides, and all sounds were suspect.

Though the ritual at the forest temple was gruesome, I regretted leaving human company. The myriad sounds from the jungle seemed to linger, strangely suspended. Images played in the periphery of my vision. Specks of color and effervescent shapes seemed to dart into existence from the stygian blackness.

My mind was in turmoil. Strange and nameless fears seethed up from my deep unconscious like monstrous sea serpents. To calm myself, I began to sing aloud chants from our evening prayers. Suddenly I felt a tingling sensation in the back of my neck. Among the multitude of forms that impinged upon my peripheral vision, one shape seemed to hold its identity. Stifling terror choked my breath. Very slowly, I turned my head, first to the left, then to the right. Unlike other images that moved with my eyes, thus remaining at the edge of my vision, this form stood where it was. I stared at it in terrified fascination. The form I saw was a tall column of faint white and amorphous luminescence that stood in the space among the trees that was pitch black a moment ago. Time passed, but the object stood unwavering. Even though it glowed, it did not illuminate any part of the surrounding forest. The bushes and trees were merely silhouetted against it. It had an indistinct outline. A peculiar shimmer defined a nascent edge, as if the glow it exuded waged a constant battle with the surrounding blackness, making innumerable advances and retreats. As I peered, it seemed to grin at me. The Amorphous Being was at least a hundred feet tall; its smirking face crested top branches of the trees. For a moment, a peculiar buzz filled my ears. A cold wave pulsed up my calves, into my groin, buttocks, and my back.

As I gazed at it, the sounds of the jungle faded into a distant rumble, and I was enveloped by a silence that was more perturbing than comforting. Sheets of luminescence bellowed upward from the ground where the Amorphous Being hovered, enveloping its body. This was either a demon from the dark or one of Kali's hosts, I thought. The Amorphous Being stared at me for a while, and then faded into the blackness.

At once, the jungle exploded around me, and I felt an intense rush of heat all over my body. With a terrific burst of energy fueled by terror I fled from the spot. Gone were my fears of stumbling and running into a tree trunk. Though my eyes could not see, my feet found their steps perfectly, as if fear lent sight to my feet.

When I reached home I crept into my bed, shivering with fright. I slept fitfully, my body burning with fever and my mind in torment. In the early morning hours I had a fearsome dream: a tiny ball appeared and began rolling toward me, growing in size. About half the

distance from me, the ball reached gigantic proportions and transformed explosively into the Amorphous Being of the jungle. I managed to roll out of its way and felt myself sailing through the air.

I woke up to the dull sound of a thud and, when I opened my
eyes, I was staring at the anxious faces of my mother and five of my
aunts. They inspected my head and torso with such concern that I
thought something terrible had happened to me. Muttering to myself, I raised my head to inspect myself and I saw that I had landed on
the cement floor.

"Feel Shambu's brow—the boy seems to have a fever!" exclaimed
my mother, all flustered and groping about my forehead and my hair.
I winced in pain as she passed her fingers over a sizable bump at the
back of my head.

"Let's get him back on the bed," said Aunt Gauri, my oldest maternal aunt. She took command of situations and I always thought
she would make a tough matriarch.

"Poor dear, you must have had a nightmare," she said. "If nothing else, this should at least teach you not to wander around the
neighborhood on your own at night," she commented. Although I
did not reply, I bristled hearing her remark.

I felt myself lifted gingerly by numerous pairs of hands, and I
sailed back up to lie on the bed. My older cousin Chandra and his sister Meena peeked into the room.

"Children, you both go and get some boiled rice ready for Shambu," said my mother and she gently guided them out of the room,
but not before Meena could poke her tongue out at me. I lay in bed
the whole day, seized intermittently by the fever like a mouse at the
whim of a cat.

We kids often thought fevers were good times since we got the
best of attention from everyone. The exception was the food, which
was usually either bland or bitter. My oldest grandmother, Paru, gave
orders to all family members that I should not be fed any food other
than that cooked by herself and her two sisters. All three women were
household waidyas, or medicine women. They also reigned as matriarchs, commanding respect from the elders (my aunts and uncles).

"Don't you give him any fried foods or pickles secretly!" warned
Grandma Paru, wagging a crooked and bony finger at the crowd of
curious cousins at the door. "He needs to get his fever down and his
little tummy won't digest pickles with this fever," she admonished
them, as she puckered my belly with her bony fingers.

The matriarchs cooked bitter medicinal foods on a separate
hearth and prepared pastes and oils which they rubbed me with be-

fore bathing me. I hated these medicinal baths because of their bony hands and the poking.

I lay in bed with fever for three days and nights. On the fourth day, my aunts moved me into the recuperation room, a small, airy chamber with a window facing east and a door that opened into the corridor adjoining the center courtyard. This room provided privacy and much needed isolation from the rest of the family.

At first my father was angry that I got a fever. He said that I brought this on myself by playing recklessly in the family pond and not drying my hair. Moreover, I had been out in the jungle during the Night of Kali ceremonies. He scolded me, saying that I had put the entire family under undue pressure, and that my matriarchs had to toil to prepare expensive medicines at their advanced age. As he continued to chide me, I broke into a fit of wailing and my uncles came to my defense and led him out of the room. I wanted my aunts and my elder female cousins to come in, to cuddle and comfort me. Sure enough, six aunts and thirteen cousins stormed into my room, shooing out my uncles.

Sandhya was my favorite girl cousin. The only living child of Aunt Preema, she was older than me by a year and a half. I had heard that Aunt Preema lost a baby boy. He was stillborn a year before she gave birth to Sandhya. Normally my boy cousins and I played together, or we played with the neighbors. I didn't like to play with any girl cousins except for Sandhya. She and I had a special bond.

Sandhya sneaked me the forbidden food! She knew I wanted my favorite foods—deep-fried salted chili, and pickled mango slices. I was sick of the bland and bitter medicinal food that my grandmas made. They prepared a special type of medicinal gravy called kashaya—nothing could equal it in bitterness. My grandmas fed it to me three times a day; each time, they gave me a small lump of brown sugar to help mask the bitterness. The moment they left my room, I would slip my hand under the pillow for the small packet of banana leaf that contained mango pickle.

I suffered with this intermittent fever for six days. Several times I dreamed vividly of the Amorphous Being, who spoke to me. But every time I woke up, I forgot what it said. I told my mother and Aunt Gauri about the apparition in the forest and about the recurring dreams. My mother dismissed them by explaining that it was the fever that caused these dreams. Aunt Gauri pooh-poohed my experiences as products of my overactive imagination. She called them attempts to evade the fact that I brought the fever onto myself by my carelessness. So I stopped mentioning it to them. I wondered if Aunt

Gauri was angry with me for not asking her permission before embarking on my jungle trip on the Night of Kali.

Sandhya visited me several times a day. I confided in her in detail about my experiences at the forest Kali temple and about my encounter with the Amorphous Being. I know she believed me.

"You must have seen a yakshini or a yaksha," Sandhya said after some thought. "These beings are typically tree dwellers; that is what I have heard from Grandfather Madhavan. Tell me, is it male or female?"

I searched her eyes, puzzled by her question.

"It had a glow all over," I said. "The only features that were clear were its eyes and its grinning mouth. I was too scared to note any details, Sandhya."

"But it is important, Shambu. Think hard," she urged. "Do you remember if it wore some kind of dress?" she probed.

Lying on the bed, I gazed at the rafters, trying to remember the form of the Amorphous Being. Among the rafters, I spotted a lone spider patiently weaving a silk cocoon around what seemed to be the vestiges of a pearly moth. With its hind legs, the spider kneaded strands of silk from the tip of its abdomen. The rhythm of its movements was mesmerizing. I remembered the effulgent light that mushroomed from the ground where the Amorphous Being stood.

"Now that you ask, I think there were some folds in the light that reached all the way to the ground," I said.

"Aaah! That is a yakshini!" Sandhya exclaimed. "It is most auspicious if a boy sees a yakshini and a girl sees a yaksha. In a sense you are lucky Shambu," she declared. I noted a serious look on her face.

"In what sense?" I asked, mystified as to how she concluded the being to be a female merely from my meager descriptions.

"Well, I have only heard stories of yakshinis and yakshas. I have never seen one myself," said Sandhya. "Yakshinis only appear to those whom they like to protect. And a yakshini, I am told, is more powerful than a yaksha. Grandfather Madhavan told us that there are other beings, like the brahmarakshas for instance." (A brahmaraksha is the soul of a Brahmin who has become a ghost because of his deviant former life.)

Sandhya stayed by my side for some time. After a while, I began to doze, and vaguely remembered Sandhya pulling the covers over me before leaving. It was close to evening twilight when I woke up. The chills had begun again. I shuddered under the many sheets, as I lay curled on my side. My eyes burned when I opened them even a little. Presently, I heard a commotion in the hallway. A few moments later, I felt a hand on my brow.

"His forehead is burning!" a voice murmured.

"Deepam . . . Oomm, deepam!" another voice announced.

I struggled to open my eyes, but it was as if thick glue held them shut. Even though I made desperate attempts to move, I felt imprisoned within my body. Then I saw the faces of my matriarchs and aunts in the glow of the kamakshi deepam. This lamp is lit every evening from the eternal flame of the nitya deepam located in our central shrine.

I could not keep my eyes open and when I woke up, an unfamiliar face floated into focus. She looked as old as Grandma Paru, and a thick cloud of white hair floated around her head like a halo. A huge vermilion dot adorned the center of her forehead. She wore a crimson sari. Leaning over me, she used the index and middle fingers of her right hand to press my fluttering eyelids closed. Her touch was soothing, and I felt instantaneous relief, as if some cool medicinal waters were washing away the thick glue from my eyes. After some time, I opened my eyes, and saw the odiyatthi Ahalya Mata, a famed sorceress.

Ahalya Mata ran her fingers through my hair, and a kindly expression played upon her face. I felt uplifted in her presence. I wanted to tell her everything, from the experiences at the forest shrine to the presence of the Amorphous Being. Ahalya Mata roved her open hand over me. Suddenly, her body stiffened as her palm froze over my heart. She dropped her kindly expression and her face became stern.

"This is no ordinary fever!" said Ahalya Mata. "This boy has seen something, and his frightened spirit has jolted out of its place." Her voice was low and melodious in spite of her age. Her statement took me by surprise, but I felt relieved. Who would dare question Ahalya Mata's assumptions? I would have loved to see the face of Aunt Gauri at that moment.

"Prepare the child for ahuthi, there is no time to waste," she commanded.

Ahalya Mata moved from place to place followed by her band of disciples. Nobody knew where and how she spent her time, or when she would make an appearance. She never married, but devoted her life to Kali worship and magical practices. She was called upon as a last resort when medicine failed. The entire village held her in the greatest reverence and awe, and her fame as a great healer was common knowledge. She had been known to transfer venom from cobra bites to plants or trees. However, she was best known for her ability to counteract the effects of black magic. In this respect, she was even held in fear.

The women led me to a seat on one of two grass mats spread on the sand in the center of the courtyard. From my seat, I saw three elders performing the evening services at the family shrine. There was a makeshift altar for Kali assembled before me. A huge bronze lamp stood in the middle of the second mat. Two brass bowls—one holding freshly ground fragrant sandalwood, the other holding saffron—were placed on either side of this lamp. Metal bowls of various sizes were arranged on large plantain leaves. An elaborate design was painted with rice powder on the sandy floor of the courtyard enclosing the altar area. I could see the elders trying to keep my cousins and children from the neighboring homes away.

A group of young men and women stood at the other end of the courtyard. They wore bright golden-yellow dhotis, and in the abundant hair that crowned their heads were pieces of mango leaves and hibiscus flowers. They were Ahalya Mata's novices. They performed a trancelike chant, swaying from side to side and stomping their feet upon the earth in a metronomic beat. At the sight of these swaying people, I began to shiver and my teeth chattered. I felt a gust of energy and wanted to rough them up—I was amazed at my own thoughts. A sudden burst of strength overpowered me. I lunged out of my seat, scattering a tray of sesame seeds.

A rumble of murmurs broke out in the courtyard. I heard somebody beating upon the sand with a coconut-broom, as if they fended off an invisible intruder. Two of my aunts rushed forward and held me in place.

"Sit down, you little devil," shouted Aunt Gauri, thrusting me down onto the seat.

I was perplexed at her allusion to me as the devil. How can she be so rude, I thought? Then, I felt the fury rise again. I felt my arms swing outward in wide circles, throwing Aunt Gauri and Aunt Susheela to the sand. Aunt Gauri's face was distorted with anger as she picked herself up, her hair disheveled. I looked at her discomfort gleefully. Almost immediately, I felt remorse. My spasms grew in strength and so did my embarrassment. I was aware of my fury, my clattering teeth. Pure rage assailed my mind, but toward what? On one hand, an uncontrollable surge of power commandeered my faculties and rebelled at being put through this ceremony, and on the other, I was aware of my rebelliousness and felt bad. Meanwhile, Aunt Gauri stood up and prepared to throw herself at me again.

"I will brand the kid with fire if I have to—to throw you out!" she flew at me screaming. Ahalya Mata intervened immediately.

"Let him be. Stay back!" she ordered everyone. I saw my mother and Aunt Preema help the sorceress hold Aunt Gauri back. By this time, I felt my fury subside into a simmer, but my thighs trembled, as if ready to spring into a fight.

"Is the talam ready?" Ahalya Mata asked.

"It's right here," said Aunt Gauri diffidently.

"Leela, you take it to her," whispered my aunt to my mother as she thrust the large flat brass tray into her hands. In the tray, a lump of camphor burned on a leaf floating upon a red liquid.

"Yes, it is only right that the mother of the child should bring it forward," remarked Ahalya Mata. My mother held the talam for the sorceress as Ahalya Mata went over me with this flame, frequently grabbing the flame in her fist and roving her fist over my skin.

Ahalya Mata did not allow any men to get near us. I saw my father and uncles standing behind the women of the house as she began a rite to purify the ground and the air. Muttering ritual incantations, she walked clockwise around the mat and me, all the while her fingers worked on a large knot at the end of her sari. Her disciples started stomping the ground faster, and their chants increased in pitch. On her third circumambulation, Ahalya Mata produced a quantity of tiny petals from her sari. This she threw in the sixteen directions. I heard my aunts and uncles mutter, "Kalii! My mother!" as the petals fell over their bowed heads.

There was a commotion among the matriarchs.

"Is it time to bring in this kalasham?" asked Matriarch Paru in a faltering voice, holding a brass pot. Her two sisters, Sathya and Chandra stood close to her. Ahalya Mata did not reply. She was in a trance, mumbling incomprehensibly. Perturbed, the matriarchs stood askance, with the brass pot in their trembling hands.

Ahalya Mata approached me and, with a swift move of her left hand, held me by the hair at the nape of my neck. She thrust the crumbled petals in her right palm into my mouth. I chewed involuntarily, simultaneously pushing her hand away from my face. A peculiar, mild, burning numbness spread around my mouth. An intense buzz followed this sensation. My ears felt warm and wet. I wiped them with the palms of my hand, but to my surprise, I saw no moisture.

At some point someone brought the brass pot because I saw it on the sand before me. A melodious chant rang in my ears, and the phrases made great soothing sense to me. The chants came from within the pot. I had this amusing feeling that the pot was singing. No sooner did this thought occur to me than the mouth of the brass pot began to move and form the words of the chant. I was entranced by this and began to reach out with my fingers to feel the movements of the "lips" of the pot. I had to reach over to do this and happened to glance directly into the pot. To my utter amazement I saw the reflection of the Amorphous Being emerging in the water as I looked over the edge. Instantly, I lost sight of my surroundings. Everything seemed insubstantial. I felt that I tumbled along in a moving body of water. After a few minutes, I began to hear voices.

I heard Ahalya Mata's voice ask, "Who are you?"

"Nishachii," said a hoarse female voice from within the pot.

"Nishachii! The night dweller from the underworld! That's impossible!" I heard Ahalya Mata exclaim.

Without warning, Ahalya Mata's saffron-stained palm flashed into my vision. Speckles of tumeric-stained raw rice sprinkled out of her palm as she threw them at me in wide swaths. As these grains closed in, they ceased to be plain rice grains. Instead, flying at my face, neck, and torso were flaming characters of a strangely familiar language. To my utter amazement and horror, I felt a searing heat engulf my body. I let out a shriek and a powerful force propelled me to my feet. It lifted me upright, as if I were a mere feather! I was perplexed to feel my arms and feet twirl in a graceful fluid motion. For a brief instant, I saw Ahalya Mata double over and clutch at her belly, and I saw her novices fall to their knees. Then the pot disappeared and my bladder let go involuntarily. I felt a sense of warmth and moist relief spread through my loincloth. The firestorm abated as suddenly as it had sprung up, drenched as if by a downpour. The next instant I felt myself pulled back into the state of partial sensory suspension I was in earlier.

A disciple of Ahalya Mata stepped toward me crying, "Ashuddham! Ashuddham!" That prompted the women to cry out, "Oh Kali!"

"Stop this ceremony! It is blemished!" urged others.

There was confusion among the disciples and they stopped their trancelike dance and broke formation. I was bewildered by this commotion for a moment. At once Ahalya Mata shouted, "No! Get back. Don't stop," she commanded.

The disciples regrouped, but I still heard murmurs from the onlookers. Something had interfered with the ritual. But my consciousness flipped between normal awareness and partial perception. Then it dawned on me that the Amorphous Being had forced me to urinate, which, aside from being impious, is also debilitating to the exorcist. It disrupted the sanctity of the ritual. Ahalya Mata's astral edifice of exorcism, invoked through ritual, protected by the icons of ceremonial purity and fortified by the combined wills of her novices, was disrupted by the Amorphous Being. The mystical gauntlet, constructed out of the elaborate ceremony and energized by the combined will of the band of mystics, crumbled under the impact of the Amorphous Being's force. This nullified the barrage of scorching spells.

The chanting became frenzied. Mysteriously, the brass pot re-emerged.

"Why do you trouble this child?" I heard Ahalya Mata ask.

"The gates of this spirit were wide open, so we entered," explained the voice from the pot. "As for your complaint of troubling this child, we are here to plug the gap, for a while, until the Big One comes for him. Hee! Hee! Hee! Hee! Heee!" A gale of laughter contorted the pot.

Ahalya Mata was unamused. "We? How many of you are in there?" she asked.

"Irrelevant!" the entity replied.

"This child is in torment. Your presence overwhelms his spirit," Ahalya Mata argued.

"This spirit is living its destiny. We cannot avoid our presence in him!" the entity replied.

"You must leave immediately; you must not interfere with his life," commanded Ahalya Mata. "I can draw you out and nail you into the trunk of the mango tree!" she warned.

"Aii! Hee! Hee! Hee! Ooh! Ho! Ho! Ho!" the voice cackled. It appeared to me that the mouth of the pot contorted so much that it might shatter with mirth.

"This energy is more than you can handle, old one," cautioned the voice from the pot. "Besides, you would then surely interfere with his destiny. Her footprint is on his spirit," came the mocking and enigmatic answer.

"We want the child to be safe. Tell us what your needs are and we shall try to fulfill them," said Ahalya Mata in an effort to bargain. "In return you must promise not to torment this child any more."

"Time is no barrier between this child and us. Be comforted! Our presence is no torment to this child. The child is safe with us. This fever is only his body adapting to our presence; it will subside soon," the Amorphous Being replied. "Hold the child, now," the entity whispered a command. Ahalya Mata rushed toward me. A look of awe spread upon her face.

An uncontrollable fit of shivering came over me. I could no longer see any faces, nor could I hear the pot speak. I felt Ahalya Mata support me just as I slumped down upon the sand.

▼ ▼ ▼

I woke up smelling the subtle fragrance of jasmine. My eyes opened to fleeting glimpses of the crescent moon through the window, as tendrils of wispy clouds obscured its white gleam. I was lying on my rope bed. The rafters appeared to move as the shadows shimmered in the pale and flickering light of a lone oil flame. A crow or two crooned in the trees outside. A mynah scolded elsewhere. The shrill chirrup of crickets and the occasional croak of a bullfrog filled the night. From somewhere within the corridors of the rambling house came the sound of snores.

Throwing the sheets to the bottom of the bed, I swung my legs out and stood up. My head reeled as I walked toward the window. I felt weak, but glad to be rid of the fever. Standing by the window, I took in the many smells of the night. The fragrance from jasmine was the strongest. As I peered out the window, I wondered about the strange happenings of the previous two weeks, culminating in last evening's experiences. Ahalya Mata's arrival was a mystery to me. Who could have sent for her? It would be puzzling if the elders had summoned the sorceress, especially in the light of the fact that they had slighted my experiences as the product of an overwrought imagination. Sandhya was the only one who took me seriously.

Who was this Amorphous Being? It called itself "Nishachii," but had alluded to itself as "we." I wondered if the Amorphous Being was a group of entities. I remembered vividly the struggles and the debate between Ahalya Mata and the Amorphous Being. I suffered intimately with their struggles. I carry the footprint of the Big One, said the Amorphous One. Who is this Big One? I must consult Sandhya. She knew many things. As I stood by the window, I heard a breeze rustle through the trees and within minutes it swirled through the room. I thrust my head out the window, breathing in the cool and fragrant air. The night sky was clear, and I watched the many stars twinkle. I looked at the trees that grew near the house; their trunks swayed gently as the wind caressed their leaves and boughs.

A large shadow hit the ground in front of the window and swiftly swept over the undulating terrain. The frogs fell silent. Even the crickets ceased their constant chirruping. The shadow clamped an unnatural and heavy silence over the nightscape. I looked up just in time to see the magnificent silhouette of a horned timber owl glide silently above the roof and beyond the treetops. The smooth glide was broken only by a couple of momentary flaps of its enormous wings. It disappeared into the darkness, in the west, like a spectral nemesis from the crypt. A few minutes later, the hillsides reverberated with the deep booming of two owl hoots. As if on cue, the night erupted into a discordant babble of relief.

CHAPTER TWO

# *Children of Kali*

 The news of my exorcism spread in the village, along with rumors that the sorceress, Ahalya Mata, had discovered a powerful guardian spirit who shadowed me with a coterie of beings. These spirits, the villagers believed, had come from among the hordes of the "Fierce One who slumbers in the jungle," as the Forest Kali was often alluded to out of fear and respect.

The elders from neighboring households had been giving advice as to how to prepare herbal treatments for my strange fever. Now they came to have an audience with me. They spoke with awe and with an uneasy respect. For example, Bhavani visited at tea time one day. She was the reigning matriarch of the House of Puttuparambu, a rambling household of forty-seven members situated toward the southwest. She came in with her favorite daughters. My mother asked me to pay my respects to her, but when I approached her to touch her feet, she hastily moved away, breaking into a fit of polite fumbling and incomprehensible stammering. This was very strange—the elders usually enjoyed this customary respect paid them.

"Oh! No! That's okay! Shambu, don't! Oh! Kali! Here, this is for you." Saying that, Bhavani turned to her daughter Heemavati. "Bring the basket, dear."

Heemavati and her sister Kastoori brought a bamboo basket filled with wild, golden-yellow bananas that looked deliciously ripe and smelled of pollen and nectar.

"Ooh! Mother Kali!" exclaimed my mother. "This was not necessary, Elder Bhavani!" she politely remonstrated.

"Juicy bananas, we can bake 'em," exclaimed my pudgy younger brother Padman as he came to the rescue of all. He darted in eagerly and pulled free a banana, to my mother's embarrassment.

"Will you have tea with us?" asked my mother. "It's boiled and ready."

"Yes. Thank you, Leela. I'd like that. Please tell me about Ahalya Mata's visit. It will be a blessing to hear from you. You know, Leela, that this has been the topic in our village lately. I wish to hear from you firsthand," said Bhavani.

Soon they gathered on the porch at the east end of the courtyard, where Aunt Ananda joined them. Amid sips of tea and bites of crunchy fried jackfruit peels, my mother and aunt launched into an embellished description of the war between the sorceress Ahalya Mata and the "mighty minion of the Forest Kali," as they called the entity Nishachii.

Over the past few days, my mother, my aunts and my grandmothers had worked through several editions of this account, and I heard subtle variations creeping into the fabric of the narrative. Even though my experiences were firsthand, curiously, my own version was never solicited by anyone except Sandhya. The sounds of their conversation faded as I slipped away from the group.

The elders appeared to be pleased over the recent happenings. I thought that they saw the hand of Kali Herself in the recent events. They convened meetings and astrological consultations with the valli-chappads, and I felt elevated from the lowly rank of a boy to that of a power unto myself, thanks to the entity Nishachii.

In the days that followed, elders from other households visited us—I was always the subject of conversation. Jettisoned into the limelight, I became perturbed by my newfound status within my community. Until this time, I had lived a carefree life. But now I was apprehensive that all these events might trigger a cascade of irreversible decisions by the elders. I did not know what these would be, but I was afraid that the simple pleasures and irresponsibility of childhood would soon come to an end.

It was midmorning when I sought out Sandhya. I found her sifting grains of rice in the company of Reevati, the daughter of Aunt Gauri and Uncle Aravinda. They sat on the floor of the east verandah. The family property extended over an enormous space here; vegetable gardens and coconut palms thrived among a multitude of fruit trees. A large artificial pond occupied the southeastern corner of this area and served as a communal bathing pool for the family.

I stood by a pillar for a moment, hesitant to approach. Reevati sat facing the yard and Sandhya faced the wall. Reevati was a fair-skinned girl two years older than me. My aunts groomed her to be one of my family's priestesses. Being the second daughter of Aunt Gauri, she would be the chief priestess some day. She was an excellent ritualist and knew many Vedic chants, which she chanted every morning. Though I took delight in listening to her, I sometimes envied her melodious voice and her dexterity with the rituals.

This morning she wore a pretty green ankle-length skirt and Sandhya was dressed in a light purple loose cotton garment (called the angavastra) tied into a knot at her chest. I moved out of the cover of the pillar, and Reevati saw me approach.

"Hey, Shambu! Little brother! How do you feel?" asked Reevati.

"I feel well," I replied with delight as I hastened toward them.

"Shambu, come, sit here by me," Sandhya invited me with a smile, and she patted a spot beside her. I felt at ease, and rejoiced to see such delight in her eyes. She dropped the wicker grain grader and threw her arms out to receive me. I launched myself at her in my usual style, tumbling her off balance. With a deft move she rolled to one side, pinning me with her hip and elbow. Sandhya held me down while Reevati tickled me. Out of breath, and choking with laughter, I begged them to set me free.

"So, you feel better this morning?" asked Reevati.

"Yes I do, but I still feel weak," I replied.

"A week of fever can do a body in. You sit by me and do nothing, okay?" instructed Sandhya solicitously and she gave me a hug.

They resumed their work after a few moments. I watched as they whipped rice grains into the air with the grain grader. As the grains fell back onto the grader, the heavier mud clots and little grains of stone settled to the curved end and the rice grains separated at the top. Once in a while Sandhya and Reevati flicked these onto two heaps. The grains were heaped on the right and a small pile of mud clots and stones built steadily on the left. As I sat by her side, I thought of several questions I wished to ask Sandhya. I sought answers to questions that nagged me ever since the fever. I watched her as she rhythmically whipped the grains into the air and deftly sorted them. I placed my palm timidly on her knee.

"Sandhya, you were there when Ahalya Mata fought with the entity Nishachii. Did you hear the pot that was brought before me speak?" I asked.

Sandhya stopped grading the rice and turned around.

"Yes, I was there, but it was you who spoke, not the pot!" she answered with a perplexed expression. "You were there Reevati, weren't you?" she asked.

"Oh yes, I was there. I agree; it was you who spoke to Ahalya Mata, Shambu," Reevati concurred. "But your voice was so different," she added.

I felt stupid and at once regretted starting this topic. I slid my arms along the floor and stretched out on my back. I wondered what they thought of me—maybe I had a screw loose! Now I could only think of some way to get away.

Sandhya placed the grain grader down beside her and crouched near me: "Did you really hear the pot speak?" she asked sympathetically, as she rubbed my chest with her right hand.

"I am telling the truth. It was the pot that spoke, not me. I watched every word that it mouthed," I asserted. "You do believe me, don't you?" I asked her earnestly as I gripped her hand.

Sandhya did not answer, but turned to Reevati, who nodded back at Sandhya as if in some conspiratorial agreement.

"There is not much grain left to clean. I can finish this," Reevati said.

"Thanks, Reevati," she said, touching Reevati's hand, and with that she turned around and looked at me with a smile.

"Well, it seems that my little brother has some questions to ask." She puckered her brows and brought her eyes close to mine affectionately. "Let's go," she said, as she rose from her seat, yanking me up by my elbow.

We leapt from the verandah onto the sand.

"Let's sit by the pond. We can be by ourselves there," Sandhya suggested, pulling me to a sprint.

She whipped around and held both my palms, "Is that fine with you Shambu?" she asked. I was trotting beside her in silence.

"Yes. Yes, Sandhya, I like that," I beamed at her.

"Do you think Reevati would feel left out?" I asked, feeling some guilt for not inviting her.

"Reevati? Nooo! She understands that you always talk to me about things. It's okay—she will not mind," Sandhya assured me.

We trotted gaily along, leaping over several irrigation canals built upon mud embankments among the trees and vegetable plots. After a little while, the edge of the pond came into view. Shrubs of mailanji and sponge gourd grew profusely. The young women of my village extract a red dye from the leaves of the mailanji shrub that they use as a cosmetic to decorate their hands and feet. The sponge gourd contains a bitter alkaloid that works as a bactericide, and when dried, it is used as a body scrub.

We pushed through the leaves and arrived at the pond. Sitting at the edge of the pond, we slid down its bank. Halfway down the sandy slope, we came to a gentle stop, our downward slide arrested by the gnarled root of a jackfruit tree.

"What do you say . . . It is good here, isn't it?" I asked Sandhya between gasps for breath.

"Yes this feels . . . good. Like it here," she gasped alongside me.

We leaned back on the sand, flung our arms across each other and just lay there for a while. Our knees were pulled up as our feet held us against the root. Sunlight warmed our bodies; within minutes I felt myself itch gently as sweat began to break. I was elated; Sandhya and I were friends again, and it felt good to be carefree with her.

Sandhya turned her head and blew at me. I closed my eyes instinctively as sand particles whipped about my face. She pulled herself up on her elbows. "Tell me about your experience with Ahalya Mata; I want to hear it in detail."

I described my experiences; I told Sandhya how I was surprised to see the face of the entity Nishachii reflected inside the pot as I peeked over its rim.

"I saw the entity Nishachii in the pot. It was She who spoke; but as She spoke, the mouth of the pot moved," I explained animatedly.

"You realize that you were possessed by this entity for a week?" Sandhya asked.

"Yes," I concurred. I grabbed my knees and rocked myself onto my bottom. Down in the pond, a dragonfly hovered over the tip of a black stick that poked out of the pond.

"Somehow the pot appeared to speak to you, Shambu. But we saw and heard you speak. Both you and I are right. The Amorphous Being had possessed you," Sandhya explained, then she added, "but it does not matter who spoke. Some of us feel that She is an entity from your past life. That is what I overheard Grandmother Sathya say to the others at the council." Then in a hushed voice she added, "Even Aunt Gauri and Aunt Susheela couldn't hold you down—I mean the Amorphous Being who was in you. She was too strong. Everybody now feels that this being is a good one."

I felt much better, hearing her speak these words. Sandhya had a way of making me feel good. I knew about the council meeting, but I was forbidden from listening to the council's deliberations.

"Did Grandmother Sathya use the words 'from a past life'? I thought that the entity Nishachii was from Forest Kali's group," I asked.

"Right. Everyone said so, but Grandmother Sathya alone thought that the being was from your past life. Nobody agreed with her, though."

"Who else was at the council?" I asked.

"Our grandmothers, Aunt Leela and Uncle Bhaskaran, Aunt Ananda, Aunt Tara, Aunt Gauri, Vallichappad Agnimitra, Vallichappad Shankari, and Vallichappad Chinna."

"How did you listen in to them, Sandhya?"

"I took food to them from the kitchen, remember?" she said smiling.

"You took food to them and stayed there?" I asked, and she nodded. "You fox!" I ribbed her.

"Sandhya, before Ahalya Mata came, none of our elders believed my experience was true. Even my mother did not. So who informed Ahalya Mata? Nobody knew where she was!"

Sandhya placed her elbow on my shoulder. "When I heard Aunt Gauri put you down, I became angry. None of the medicines given to you by Grandmother Paru were working. So I told my mother and we both spoke to my father. Then my mother decided to go look for Ahalya Mata."

"Aunt Preema? She called Ahalya Mata?" I was surprised. "But how did she know where to look for the sorceress?"

"Don't ask me," she said. "But my mother got into trouble with Aunt Gauri," she said with a pout.

"How?"

"When Aunt Gauri came to know that my mother went looking for Ahalya Mata, she was not happy. She said that my mother should have consulted Grandmother Paru."

At once, certain things seemed to fall into place.

"Now I understand why Aunt Gauri jumped at me, calling me a devil. She was so angry. I think she took some of her anger out on me that day."

"Could be true," Sandhya commented.

"I am sorry to cause Aunt Preema so much trouble."

"Not your fault, Shambu. I am glad my mother could help."

"The Amorphous Being said that she was Nishachii. Does the council know what that means?" I asked.

"I don't think they have figured that one out yet, and the Council of the Vallichappads have not met so far. The kurukkals are still in their period of silence, as usual, after their work on the Night of Kali. But once they convene, between them and the astrologers they will find out for sure. The only one who knows something about this is Ahalya Mata, and she thinks that this Nishachii is from the under-world. But I heard that Ahalya Mata has vanished back into the hills. My mother disagrees with Ahalya Mata. She thinks that Nishachii is from a divine realm," Sandhya explained.

"Underworld, like the dark demons?" I asked.

"She didn't say anything like that. I don't know," she said.

"I wonder why. If Ahalya Mata is correct then this is terrible. I don't want to be possessed by a demon, Sandhya!" I cried.

"Don't worry, Shambu. Just before Ahalya Mata left, Grand-mother Paru asked her if you were safe."

"What did she say?"

"She just said, 'Don't worry, Paru. The entity is strong and you leave Shambu alone.' Listen, my mother doesn't think Ahalya Mata is correct in thinking that the entity is from the underworld," Sandhya assured, holding me close to her. "Do you know that the elders are very happy about all this? About you in particular?" she asked. "They think that what is happening to you is auspicious. They feel that Kali has something to do with all this," she added. Hearing her, I felt better.

I picked some flat shards of tile and began hitting the water at an angle. The first two sank, but the third skimmed half way over the pond surface and dove beneath, leaving pockets of algae-free water where it hit. I took Sandhya's hand in mine.

"What do you feel, Sandhya? Are we friends as usual?" I asked with some hesitation.

Sandhya pulled her angavastra up her ankles and sidled close to me. "You are my best friend, Shambu," she said, and wove her fin-gers into mine. "What is happening to you is so special to all of us because we are all Mother Kali's children. Now we know that Mother Kali has touched our family with Her grace."

I was overwhelmed hearing her words. I hugged her.

"I feel that Mother Kali came into your body for a week. Now you are more special to me than ever before," she emphasized slowly with deep feeling.

"I know that we are all taught to keep our link with Mother Kali through our sacred traditions. My mother once said that Mother Kali has a special purpose for each one of us," I said.

"Yes, I know that," she asserted; then in a far away voice she add-ed, "I have many dreams of Mother Kali."

"You have? I didn't know this! How does She look?" I asked, excited.

"She has skin that shines with light and She wears a golden dress," Sandhya described with her eyes closed and said, "She has a pretty face like an oval and has long dark hair that comes down to the back of Her knees. She has a purple rod in Her hand with a shining, copper colored lotus on its end. Once She said to me in a dream, 'Sandhya you are mine,' and She picked me up. I cried so much in my dream that I woke up immediately and I found that I was really crying!"

Hearing Sandhya, I felt a strange, indescribable emotion. When my breathing became heavy, I knew that I was going to sob. So I put my head between my knees and began to breathe slowly. Sandhya rubbed my back in slow circles.

"You never told me this, Sandhya?" I complained.

"I have not told anyone, and now only you know," she said biting her lower lip.

I felt mollified, but I was unhappy that I had not seen Mother Kali in my dreams. Sandhya stared at me, and then she put her arm across my shoulders and pulled me close. I thought she felt my unhappiness. She began to rock me, so I laid my arm across her shoulders and rocked with her. Very soon I felt at ease and was happy again.

I saw a small, oval pebble beside me, and I picked it up with my free hand. As we rocked forward, I quickly slipped the pebble into the back of Sandhya's angavastra. With a wild shriek she squirmed as the pebble passed down her back, tickling her all the way. I jumped aside in glee, but Sandhya grabbed my sleeve with one hand and with the other she swept a handful of sand into my cloth, then she burst into mirth. I stood up to get the sand out of my back while Sandhya lay convulsing with laughter.

"Sandhya, do you know why the men worship our Kali and the Forest Kali only on the Night of Kali, and why do they do it with blood?" I asked as I dropped down beside her.

"I don't know, Shambu, but my mother knows a lot about rituals and celebrations. We could ask her," she said sitting up abruptly, "Let's go and ask her," she urged. She looked at me waiting for a reply.

"All right, let's go," I agreed, jumping up and pulling Sandhya to her feet.

We went straight to the family shrine, for it was close to noon and our aunts would be busy getting the altar ready for the midday worship. Reaching the doorway, we wiped the dust off the threshold with the fingers of our right hands and applied it to our crowns. The dust of a threshold, such as that of a shrine, is considered sacred. Applying this dust to one's head connotes loving surrender of the ego to the supreme spirit within the sanctum of one's being.

We found our Aunts Tara, Susheela, and Bhanu organizing the immense altar. The deities were hidden behind a red silk cloth strung before them. Without waiting to talk to our aunts, we turned on our heels and ran to the kitchen.

A delicious spicy aroma wafted down the hallway. The kitchen was at the northeast corner of our home, a large rectangular brick structure outside the house, but linked to it by the east corridor. As we approached, I saw faint blue smoke issue from the doorway.

My mother turned around at our approach.

"Sandhya, sweetie! Shambu, dear! What's the hurry, children?" she asked with a smile, pulling us both close to her, and tousling my hair.

"Did you see my mother?" asked Sandhya.

"We want to ask her about the significance of Kali Puja," I blurted.

"Are you two making little temples and playing Kali worship again?" asked my mother with a smile.

At that point, thick white smoke belched out of one of the earthen hearths. We looked around to see frothing lentil soup skim over the large pot and drip into the wood fire. Releasing us quickly, my mother pulled her sari tight around her shoulders as she stooped down and dipped a mango-wood ladle into the pot and stirred. As the frothing subsided, she threw half a cake of dried cow-dung into the fire, and the flames once again lapped the black pot. She looked around for more dried dung, but there was none.

"Shambu, get me a bundle of dung."

I ran to the back of the kitchen where we stored flat cakes of dried dung in neat bundles. The surface of the wall here was covered with cow-dung cakes left to dry in the sun. I took a bundle into the kitchen.

"Your aunt is at the main temple. Don't you know that it is her day as the priestess there?" she asked as she relieved me of the bundle.

"Ah! That's right. She's at the temple today!" exclaimed Sandhya, "I forgot all about it.

Sandhya and I wandered about our home. By noon the men took a break from their chores, and some joined the noon worship. Aunt Preema brought home a large platter full of divine food offerings from her service at the village temple. Aunt Tara mixed this with the offerings from our home shrine and distributed it to us during lunch. Then after lunch it was time for a siesta. Some men rested with their women to escape the heat of the afternoon before setting out for work. Others sat on the low wall that skirted the courtyard and chewed betelnut and betel-vine leaves as they engaged in small talk. It was late afternoon before we were able to seek out Aunt Preema.

Sandhya and I found her in the "women's room" at the south end of the house. Men rarely came in this room. They were not prohibited, but it was generally accepted that this was a place for women to come to do the "woman's thing," according to Sandhya. She did not say anything more when I had earlier pressed her for an explanation as to what this "woman's thing" was. But I felt that this was a room for women to just be. We kids came in here, nevertheless, and sometimes women visitors from the neighborhood homes met here and chatted.

Aunt Preema was a beautiful woman with long, curly dark hair that seemed to billow from her head. Her curls fell in ringlets around her forehead and down the sides of her cheeks and ears, much like Sandhya's. In this respect they both were very much like the paintings of Mother Kali we had at home. I always felt self-conscious in Aunt Preema's presence, and I stuttered when she spoke to me. Aunt Preema was very fond of me, and knew that her daughter and I were buddies. She and her husband, Uncle Raghavan, would tease me playfully whenever I came asking for Sandhya. They would send me off where Sandhya was, saying that I would find my "girlfriend" if I looked for her in this place or that.

When we entered the room, we saw Aunt Preema stitching coconut-shell buttons on a cotton totebag. Her fingers were stained red from the kumkum she handled during Kali worship at the temple.

"What are you two butterflies up to?" she asked, hugging us both. She set aside her needlework.

"Mother, we have some questions about the Night of Kali celebrations," Sandhya asked for both of us, while I watched the lovely ringlets of hair that curled their way down Aunt Preema's fair cheeks. Unconsciously, I stared at her long lovely eyelashes as they flicked up and down.

I felt a sudden tug on my arms as Aunt Preema pulled me close to her.

"Hey! What are you staring at?" she asked, and then gave me a soft peck on my nose.

I was embarrassed and my cheeks felt warm.

"Look, Mother! Shambu's ears are red!" Sandhya laughed as she pulled my ear.

"Indeed they are. Look! His cheeks are red, too!" joined Aunt Preema.

I hated it when women made fun of me. I pulled the shoulder end of Aunt Preema's red sari over my head, while Sandhya gleefully tried to extract me from my cover.

"Aunt Preema, why is Forest Kali fed blood on the Night of Kali? Why do they worship Her only once a year? Why do the villambadis split their heads on that night?" I asked. In Aunt Preema's presence, I was either tongue-tied or spoke things in a torrent.

Aunt Preema smiled as she adjusted the cotton pillow behind her.

"Shambu, go fetch the lamp from the shelf; Sandhya, you light the wick." She pointed to the rectangular indentation in the brick wall where shelves of teakwood sat on forged iron brackets.

Sandhya and I leapt to our feet to fetch the lamp. The lamp was made of fired clay, and it contained a half-burned wick that lay submerged in oil. Sandhya grabbed a box of matchsticks.

"Come, sit close to me, here," Aunt Preema pulled me to her right and Sandhya to her left. Sandhya lit the lamp and placed it before us on the grass mat.

"Now let me begin at the beginning," said Aunt Preema as she stretched out her legs. She closed her eyes and began to sing softly.

"Kali, Kali, Maha Kali," [Kali, Kali, Supreme Kali] and we joined her in prayer:

| | |
|---|---|
| *Bhadra Kali namoos tu te;* | Kali O! Auspicious protectress, obeisance to thee; |
| *Kulam cha kula dharmam cha,* | This family, and the dharma of this family, |
| *Mam cha palaya, palaya.* | And us please protect O! Please protect. |
| *Bhadra Kali namas tu bhiyam,* | O! Auspicious Kali, our salutations to thee, |
| *Bhadrae kama roopini;* | O! Beauteous one of desirable form; |
| *Rudra neetragni sam bhoote,* | You who sprang from the flames of Rudra's eye, |
| *Bhadra mam tu prayas cha mae.* | Bestow upon us your grace O! Benign one. |

My aunt closed her eyes for a few moments. "The Night of Kali is the most powerful of all the celebrations in our village," began Aunt Preema, "for on this night we awaken and worship the Forest Kali. In order to understand why we awaken Her with blood, you must know Her true name. She is also called Samhara Rakta Kali," Aunt Preema lowered her voice into a husky whisper as she uttered this name. She explained that the name meant "Kali of the blood of cosmic disintegration." Seeing Sandhya pull her knees up to her chest, I snuggled closer to Aunt Preema instinctively.

"This Kali is quite a different manifestation than our Bhadra Kali in the main temple," she explained.

"Are they different?" I asked, confused.

"No, they are not different; they are one and the same. But on this Night of Kali, our Goddess wakes up in the body of the Forest Kali. That is why on this particular day, the regular worship in our temple is over by afternoon. The male kurukkals perform the worship to Kali on this night inside the closed temple. They perform a special mystical ceremony to extract the *Shakti* or the power of Kali from the image at our temple," she explained.

"Tell us about this mystical ceremony, please, Aunt Preema."

"I cannot, my dear, because I do not know it," confessed Aunt Preema.

I was amazed that Aunt Preema did not know this ritual; in my mind, she was the repository of all rituals.

"Only a few male kurukkals know this ritual, and then they pass it down only to a few. The reason for this strict control and secrecy is that this ritual is from the forbidden scriptures. Only the odiyyas practice these rituals from these scriptures," she explained almost in a whisper. I felt a slight tremor pass up my spine. I noticed that Sandhya gripped Aunt Preema's belly tighter.

"Why can't we practice this ritual? Who decided that only the kurukkals can do it?" asked Sandhya, emboldened for a moment.

"Householders with families like us neither have the time nor the will to practice tapas (severe, mystical austerities). By performing tapas all year, these kurukkals gain much spiritual power, which is necessary to keep the mind focused for the safe performance of this ritual," said Aunt Preema.

"How would this ritual harm them? And how does the power protect them, Aunt?" I was fascinated by this power stuff.

"By performing the ritual, the kurukkals extract the great cosmic force we call Kali from the stone image in our temple. This energy is used to being worshipped as a goddess. With elaborate rituals, we women worship Her four times every day. The rituals we perform collect and focus Maha Prana (cosmic astral energy) upon this deity, building Her power throughout the year," she detailed.

With powerful worship such as this, four times a day for a whole year, I thought it would build up explosive power.

"Of course, this power would not build up to tremendous proportions. With devotees standing before Her image with prayers every day, they absorb this power as blessings, thus diminishing it. Even then there is considerable energy within the sanctum," explained Aunt Preema as if she read my thoughts.

"When the kurukkals initiate the mystic ritual in the late noon of the Night of Kali, the Goddess, along with the collected power, issues from the stone image. I have heard that this ritual has two parts; one of extraction called Maha Preeta Nishkarshana Mantram, a mantra that extracts the Cosmic Spirit, and the other of transference called Maha Preeta Samkramana Mantram. As soon as the extraction is completed, the chief among the kurukkals seals the image by signing potent mystical symbols and slapping them to different parts of the body of the image," she explained.

I thought of the time I spent before the image in our main temple, on the evening of the Night of Kali. If I had known this, I would not have had the courage to stand close to Her alone at night. Unfortunately, my imagination was vivid and I visualized an immense pillar of blinding light birthing out of the image, like one emerging out of a solid wall, and vaulting within the sanctum amid the hapless kurukkals. I squirmed as I imagined this violent spectacle.

Aunt Preema hugged me close and she continued, "Now, with the image sealed, the mighty being looks around for a body. Remember that She is used to being in the stone image. This is when the kurukkals, with their combined power and will, allow Kali into their bodies. They have to combine the power of their tapas now, or their bodies will not be able to bear this force.

Even with all their willpower combined, they cannot keep control of their bodies. They start leaping and dancing as if in a fit. These men are not in their prime of age; some of them are in their 90s. But when Kali gets into a person, even groups of young men are thrown about by a mere sweep of the hands of a 90-year-old kurukkal.

Meanwhile, the vallichappads are waiting outside the sanctum, continuously chanting hymns of appeasement to this benign force that would turn malevolent in a few hours. The person on the temple tower would have informed them of the ascendance of the asterism Bharani. This is a time of great anxiety for the entire village."

"That's why the matriarchs of every house chant Maha Preeta Sammoohanam without a break!" exclaimed Sandhya in a flash of understanding. Maha Preeta Sammoohanam or "Enticement of the Supreme Spirit" is a devotional chant.

"That's very true," said Aunt Preema with an approving nod. "They chant this so that this deity is kept appeased until the transference is completed safely."

"You said that the vallichappads stand anxiously outside the sanctum. Then what happens?" I asked impatiently.

She pulled my head close to her side with a smile, and running her fingers through my hair, she continued, "As soon as the vallichappads hear the kurukkals leaping inside, they throw open the doors of the sanctum shouting with relief, 'Ambae Bhagavati! Kalii jagadambae!'—Mother, Supreme Divinity! Kali, Mother of the Universe! They know that the kurukkals have succeeded in getting Kali into their bodies. Next the drums and the brass horns announce the beginning of the procession. The kurukkals leap in supreme trance along a human avenue made by the vallichappads by linking themselves together and they proceed to the shrine of the Forest Kali.

"Who rings these bells?" I asked.

"The vallichappads, of course. Who else is allowed inside the temple this night, aside from the kurukkals? The villambadis follow at a safe distance, carrying heavy scimitars and chanting Kali's name. Some of them would begin to get into mild trances as they step upon the footprints of the preceding kurukkals," she explained.

"The Kali in our temple is the compassionate Mother. All through the year, She grants us the necessities of living, keeps us in good health, and bestows upon us peace and happiness. It is only one night in a year that She wakes up in Her other body in the jungle. On this night She becomes a bloodthirsty behemoth in order to consume and terminate the Demons of the Dark. It is a chore this mother of all things living and nonliving performs at the end of a cycle in cosmic time, symbolized as a year in our village. In this chore She sets about consuming her creation. Then she gives birth to a new universe at the beginning of a new cosmic time cycle," my aunt said.

"But that is most dreadful, mother!" exclaimed Sandhya, "Kali eats Her own children! How horrible!" she cried.

Aunt Preema took Sandhya's head onto her bosom and said, "For 364 days in a year your Kali is the mother, the sweet nourisher, the giver of all boons, a mother who breaks out into tears at the sight of suffering. But, just this one day, She takes on a gruesome persona to do something that is most important, something that all of us women do, and you brand Her as horrible?" Aunt Preema asked kissing Sandhya's eyebrows.

"What do the women do, Aunt Preema?" I asked puzzled.

"We sweep and clean the entire house every evening before sunset, the time of the evening twilight. We sweep away the dirt and get the house ready for a new day. To do that we have to take down the fixtures and move the furniture in the house. All this dismantling creates a brief disorder. In my example, the house is the universe and the women are Kali," she explained animatedly.

"Now let me tell you what Kali's day and night is. To us life is light, growth, and organization, like the sun that gives us light and nurtures us with food, warmth, and growth. Therefore the day is connected with living, growing, and enjoying life. We associate the forces of life with light and the day. The Kali of our temple is like the women who nurture the household during the day. She gives birth to and sustains this universe. As the universe gets very old everything in it gets disordered."

"Just like in a house by evening time!" Sandhya interjected.

"Correct. Night is like the terminator of all life, as the absence of light connotes, for activities of living and organizing cease at night. Demons of the Dark are cosmic forces that bring disorder to life. They wear down the structure of order created by Mother Kali. The forces of darkness are at work both day and night. But during the night they go unchecked without the forces of light to balance them," explained Aunt Preema.

"These demons appear gruesome to us because we associate darkness with the cessation of activities of living. Now at the end of a cosmic day there is too much disorder in Her universe. Mother Kali assumes Her terrible form and demolishes Her universe and creates a new one, just like the same household women who, close to nightfall, pull apart the furniture and extinguish the fires of nourishment in the kitchen. They, too, clean everything in preparation for a new day."

Sandhya pulled Aunt Preema's chin to face her and asked, "But this is one day and night, but the Forest Kali wakes up once a year. How is this related?"

"The night I am talking about now is the Night of Chaos. The awakening of Kali in Her other body once a year is symbolic of the end of one cycle of space-time." My aunt used the word "prapancham."

"We see light, life, and growth of our universe, 364 days of our year. Kali the nourisher remains in our temple all these days. As the universe grows older, disorder creeps into everything—living and nonliving—perpetrated by the Demons of the Dark. During the end of space-time, disorder is rampant and the universe is all but taken over by the forces of darkness. Now the dark Kali manifests along with Her hordes to become the nemesis of the infernal forces.

"The Divine Mother Kali of our temple wakes up one night in the year—the 365th night—in Her fierce body in the jungle to annihilate these forces of disorder and initiate a new universe of order and righteousness. And for us in our village, it is the beginning of a new year of righteousness, life, light, growth, love, and peace," she explained with a flourish.

"But there is light even on the 365th day just as on other days, Aunt?" I asked in doubt.

"Yes sweetheart, I failed to explain to you that the light we speak of is a different kind of light. It is the light of the Spirit, the light of Dharma that gets clouded during the end days of the universe." She stared at us, then continued, "It is difficult to understand what all this means. It. . . ."

"It is like the love and compassion that we have for all things?" Sandhya interjected excitedly.

"Yes . . . Yes my darling. When the universe comes into its primordial existence, it is filled with love, compassion, truth, and humility. These are the qualities of the atman. This atman is everywhere and we recognize and worship this atman as Mother Kali. In you both, this atman resides as a witness, in the innermost core of your being. Atman in you is the Divine Mother Kali Herself. Whenever you are full of love, compassion, and humility, you should know that your mind has moved close to atman, or the Light of Mother Kali."

"Tell us about atman, Aunt? Is that what leaves the body when we die?"

My aunt closed her eyes for some moments. When she opened her eyes, a smile lit her face.

"I will try my best to explain this to you, dear, but I am not sure if I will succeed.

"The atman does not leave or come. It is all-pervading. The atman is subtler than the subtlest, yet it is greater than the greatest. In you and me this atman is subtle. It is the Supreme Presence that overarches everything. Atman is "chit"—absolute consciousness and absolute awareness. Its splendor is the Light of Divine Knowledge, and its being is Bliss. It is the only unchanging Truth there is. It is one and it is all.

"It is not a being, it is not a form, it is not a thought, a theory, or imagination. It is not a feeling, like love. It is not even Divine Love. But it generates divine qualities and feelings in those who are alert to its presence.

"This atman is Brahman, the Incomprehensible Supreme. If Brahman is the greater atman, then atman is the lesser Brahman.

"Normal people try to grasp it with their thoughts, imagination, and feelings. Thus they call it the Divine Mother or Divine Father. They call it the creatrix; others consider it the Supreme Matriarch or Patriarch. The truth is atman and Brahman is all these and beyond.

"Tainted by duality, the minds of normal people see absolute good and absolute evil as two contending extremes. They establish the Divine on the good end of things, thus ascribing absolute good to the Divine Mother and absolute evil to the Forces of Darkness. They are unable to grasp the inseparability of both, that good and evil are functions of the same Absolute Divine. By creating and nourishing this universe, She is Divine Mother, the Kali of our temple. By destroying and assimilating, She is Kali of the Dark Night of Dissolution, the Kali of the forest." Aunt Preema paused for a while.

"I have a feeling that all this has gone over your heads," she said and tousled my hair as I stared at her wide-eyed. "But do not fuss over this. In time, a single divine experience will remove all the confusion I have created today with my words," she said.

"Now, as time goes by and the universe grows older, the Forces of Darkness begin to rise," explained Aunt Preema.

"But, Aunt, when the universe was born there were no Forces of Darkness, only light, right?"

"Correct, dear."

"Then how did these Forces of Darkness originate? Who gave birth to them? When do they appear? When you say that Mother Kali is everything and everywhere including our spirits, then how can She have darkness in Her?" I was a torrent of doubts. My aunt gave me a dazzling smile, and I snuggled up to her.

"The Divine Mother is everything. It may be difficult to understand now, but She is both "good" and "evil." Divine Mother is Maha Prakriti, Great Nature. Parts of nature survive by consuming other parts of nature. Do you agree with this?"

"I am not sure," I said.

But Sandhya shook her arm saying, "Yes. Like we build houses, but worms and ants eat our houses, and birds eat worms!"

"Excellent. Using your example, when the house is newly built, are there any worms and bugs eating it?"

"I don't think so," I said, quite uncertain.

"Then how did they get in, and when do they start destroying the house?"

"I don't know, Aunt."

"I know," said Sandhya. "They are in the woodwork as eggs and they hatch after some time."

"Correct. The forces of darkness are part of the infant universe, only they are latent. They appear along with the infant universe as tiny blemishes. As the universe ages, they grow and manifest. They reside at every level of every structure in this universe. When this prapancham or space-time gets into its middle age, these initial blemishes grow into the Demons of the Dark.

"The Forces of Darkness are Kali's forms, too. Without them there would be perpetual living and growing of the original lifeforms. How then, could new lifeforms be brought into being?" asked my aunt. "Without decay, disintegration, and death new forms cannot be born. Besides, death is a chance to reenter the time-stream, to cast off the old lifeform and regain a new one. Herein, lies the inherent compassion of the Divine Mother, giving us chance after chance to take on new forms, to make fresh choices, to reexperience the time-stream," she elaborated.

"Is that why we are born again and again, to reexperience life, Mother?"

"That's a good reason—to gain opportunity to better ourselves, opportunity to redeem or reclaim our Self.

"Disorder is a precursor to a new manifestation—for new life and opportunities. Without new opportunities to take form again, all lifeforms will stultify, wither away in perpetual living, or stagnate into a dreariness of everlasting existence in one form," my aunt expounded.

"What is wrong in wanting to keep my form forever, Aunt?"

"The only 'form' that can remain unchanged is the formless atman. This is who you are. By clinging to your earthly form, you deprive yourself of your true nature. How many experiences can you have through your body? It is limited even if the body lasts forever. But imagine how many experiences you can have if you can assume different bodies, in the process of birth, growth, decay, death, and rebirth of each of these, along different points in the universal time-stream. Imagine how much you can grow in compassion, in peace, and in awareness, with all these experiences. Experiences give you growth, and it is through growth that you can redeem your true nature."

"What nature, Aunt?"

"Atman. To be merged in Kali!" She said. "This space-time changes constantly. This change is brought about by the perpetual transformation of the structures within this space-time with the aid of the Demons of the Dark. As structures transform, the space around them changes. Now, with space changing, time itself flows. It flows inexorably into the jaws of Maha Kali. Thus, this space-time issues out of Kali's womb and flows back into Kali's mouth. What Kali creates, She eventually eats, just like nature.

"One cannot go back to yesterday, to do a certain thing better, or be more noble. Without the Forces of Darkness doing their work, we will all be doomed to live our lives in these forms forever," she said as she roved her fingers over Sandhya and me. "But with their help we are able to break the perpetual flow of our lives through this time-stream," she added.

"Mother, would you not feel sad if I died?" asked Sandhya.

"Yes darling, I will feel sad if you die, or anyone for that matter," said Aunt Preema, cupping Sandhya's face in her palms. "To not feel sad is to deprive oneself of that experience to grow. Sadness comes with a feeling of oneness with other forms. Now can you imagine what the Great Mother goes through when She has to lose all her children?" she asked. "Do you know that Maha Kali also means "The Great Manifestor of Time"? Kali is the origin of space-time, and Kali is the annihilator of space-time. Kali brings forth the Forces of Darkness so they can do their work of building disorder out of order," she said, looking at me.

"Toward the end of the life of this universe, symbolized as a year in our village, the Forces of Darkness will have become so rampant that the light of the atman will be clouded over," she said with a sweeping gesture with her hands.

"Then the Divine Mother will become increasingly furious. On the Night of Cosmic Dissolution, symbolized in our village as the Night of Kali, the Cosmic Mother takes on a terrifying form. She produces hordes of Her gruesome minions to help Her with the grisly chore of mopping up the universe of darkness. This is when Ma Kali opens Her great maw and devours space-time," my aunt explained, laughing.

"This is like the men fighting fire with fire!" exclaimed Sandhya.

"Quite right, my child. So does Kali manifest an army of blood-thirsty demons who swarm the dying universe, engaging and mopping up the Demons of the Dark along with their byproducts—disorder and chaos—at the end of this universal time-stream."

"But why does Kali have to destroy the universe along with the evil forces, Aunt?"

"Since disorder and chaos are emergent with the birth of the universe, and therefore are in the very structure of Order, chaos and disorder grow with the evolving universe. At the end, disorder becomes the very fabric of space-time. Therefore, Kali and Her hosts absorb the universe itself," Aunt Preema revealed.

I had seen paintings in which Kali gives birth to and eats her own children. In the light of my aunt's explanation, it flashed in my mind that once the Demons of Kali have eaten up the Demons of the Dark, Kali eats Her demons, too. Somehow the expression on my face betrayed my thoughts, because Aunt Preema pulled my ear and asked, "Can you share that insight with us, Shambu? You are smiling to yourself."

I explained my flash of insight to them and my aunt said to me, "Now, do you know, Shambu, that this darkness is due to the light of the spirit inside us being obscured by the clouds of disharmony and chaos?"

At that point, the flame in the clay lamp brightened as the wick drained the last drop of oil. In a flash Sandhya slapped a gust of air toward the flame with her right palm. It is considered inauspicious to let a lit flame die unattended. A stream of curly white smoke went up to the rafters.

"Well, my dears, it must be close to tea time. Let us get together after supper tonight," said Aunt Preema. With that, we parted for tea.

▼ ▼ ▼

I eagerly awaited the time I could visit with Aunt Preema again. The women had their meals last. Sandhya and I peeked in the dining hall once in a while to see if Aunt Preema had eaten. At last our impatience was rewarded, when Uncle Raghavan came looking for us, saying that Aunt Preema was waiting for us in the courtyard.

The courtyard was a pleasant place at night; it was open to the night sky but kept out the wind. It was also a busy place, as most of the household gathered there to socialize. A three-foot high brick and cement wall bordered the edge of the verandah that skirted the entire perimeter of this courtyard. Kerosene lamps hung from several beams that supported the roof overhanging this wall.

As we entered the courtyard we saw several groups seated, relaxing, along different places on this short brick wall. A moderate amount of conversation was taking place. Several of my cousins were moving about or were playing in the fine sand. The tulasi altar that adorned the center of this courtyard had its four oil-lamps lit; each added to the meager light.

"Where do you think she is?" asked Sandhya.

I pulled her along with me and stepped into the courtyard.

"Aunt Preema!" I called out.

"There she is! Over by the tulasi," said Sandhya as she pushed me toward the altar.

"I'm here, Shambu," Aunt Preema called back. We saw her seated by the tulasi, her back against one of the corners of the stone altar and partially hidden from our view. We took turns greeting her as she hugged us. A brass platter, the tambulam, sat beside Aunt Preema. It held fresh betel-vine leaves stacked on one side, three husked betel nuts, and a small brass vial containing some moist and fragrant lime (calcium carbonate). My aunt began trimming the ends of a couple of the betel leaves with a short folding knife. Most of the elders chewed betel leaves after meals because it aided in digesting food, besides removing the odor of the spices we ate.

"Now, what was I explaining?" asked my aunt.

"The darkness of disharmony clouds the light of the spirit," we both choroused as we gathered close to her.

"But when Kali and Her hordes eat up the universe, She protects her children, She protects the spirits in you," she said tapping her fingers on our chests, and added, "but you will have to help Her do this."

"What should we do, Mother?"

"Keep Kali in your heart at all times. Then your heart will manifest love, compassion, and humility. That is why we put Kali's mark upon our houses and our properties on the Night of Kali. Seeing this mark, Kali blesses us as She and Her mighty hordes sweep through the universe."

This specter of the hordes of Kali sweeping over the universe reminded me of the horned timber owl sweeping over the trees some nights ago.

"Now at the end of one time cycle, She destroys space-time itself," she emphasized.

"Will all of us who die with Kali in our heart be saved?" I asked.

"Yes. You will be untouched," said Aunt Preema, smiling.

"Then what form will we have?" asked Sandhya, voicing my next question.

"This outer form is part of space-time, but your spirit will have Kali's 'imprint' upon you by virtue of Her grace. When you love Kali, She is bound to you by Her Divine Love," she explained.

I felt a thrill hearing her words. Sandhya and I exchanged glances and I noticed her smile in the flickering light. It had now become somewhat clear to me what "Her footprint" meant, as spoken by the Amorphous Being. Aunt Preema took note of the exchange of glances and said, "Yes, Shambu, Kali's grace will follow a person from life to life until the end of Time, when the great cosmic dissolution will take place. We should never slacken on our spiritual path," she said as she squeezed both our shoulders.

"I explained earlier that the Demons of the Dark are Her forms, too, and without them it is not possible to recycle the universe. With no recycling, no change is possible and a universe without change will lead to ultimate stultification—a state of stagnant death. Look upon these forces of darkness as the termites, ants, cotton moths, wool moths, and wood worms in our home. They work incessantly to pull our house and our belongings down and turn them to dust. These are the minions of destruction and chaos that gnaw at the foundation and structure of order, be it in the shape of our humble home or in the grand design of the universe. They give us the motivation to adapt, to change, to rebuild and thus renew life," my aunt said.

"I haven't spoken to you about the blood sacrifice," she reminded us. "We homesteaders cannot awaken the Forest Kali because we cannot muster the heroic feelings needed to do a bloody battle—like terror, fear, and rage. We worship Kali as the loving Mother.

"Once the kurukkals reach the forest shrine, they purify the image there and begin the transference ritual. Odiyyas from the forest officiate as priests, past midnight. From here on only these beings have the power to handle the awakening ceremonies of the Gory One. The head priest sacrifices a goat and gathers its blood. At a critical time during this ritual, the image is bathed with this blood. The smell and feel of this sacrifical blood as it flows over Her body awakens the mighty Samhara Rakta Kali. The transference is now complete. Now that this Great Being is awake, She has to be fed blood. The villambadis partake of the sanctified goat-blood, giving them great courage. These dedicated men and women perform a sacrifice, offering their own blood to feed this Being. The ceremonies go on late into the night, awakening Kali's hordes."

A great wave of strange feelings swept through me, like some mighty gale tearing through my heart. I felt my body shudder in fits and starts. As I began to fade out of the present, I felt my aunt and Sandhya holding me close. Brief scenes of the Night of Kali flashed through my mind.

"Thus, on this night, the kurukkals worship Her at our temple and then the entire village proceeds to the forest for the Great Awakening. Then the odiyyas worship Her at the forest shrine the entire night," whispered my aunt.

"The Great Awakening," I mused aloud.

"Yes, to "Awaken She Who Slumbers." That is the prayer they chant at our temple each morning!" added Sandhya excitedly.

"That is correct. From the Heralding the Mystical Light of the Dawn collection of chants," agreed Aunt Preema. This is a group of chants called Pratha Smaranam Sree Shakti Piitham, chanted at the first light of dawn worship ceremony at our temple.

"So the women worship Kali at our temple because they have the motherly qualities awakened in them, as opposed to the baser heroic ones in the men," elaborated Sandhya in a flash of insight. My aunt looked at her and nodded. Then she fell silent.

"Why do men among the pilgrims dress up as women, Aunt?"

"The shortest way for a man to attain Kali is by invoking his own feminine qualities through special austerities. Once he has invoked his feminine nature, he lets his female qualities assimilate his maleness. Now, when he worships Kali, the will of the Great Goddess takes over his being. He gains Shakti Bhava, a sublime state of Kali consciousness and intense divine ecstasy. It requires total surrender. The atmosphere and the mood generated on the Night of Kali festival helps normal men attain this divine state of mind for brief periods."

"Why doesn't every man go through this ceremony, Aunt?

"Sexual identity is very strong in most people. They cling to their maleness or femaleness as if their very lives depend on it. Even though Shakti Bhava is the shortest path to the Divine Mother's heart, it is difficult for most men. To be willing to lose your male identity for the Divine Mother's love requires a very special love for the Divine Mother. So most men choose other ways to worship Her. Even in the case of those who undertake spiritual transvestitism during the Night of Kali festival, only a handful may retain this state for the remainder of their life as part of deeper karmic transformation. The rest come out of the trance and go about their masculine ways." My aunt explained.

"Aunt, won't people make fun of me if I act like a female all my life?"

"Oh my sweetheart! This ceremony is not about a male changing into a female. When a male is able to summon his female qualities, for the sole purpose of joining with Kali, he transforms from being a mere human to become Divine. Such a person's self-identity soars beyond body consciousness. That's the purpose of this ceremony and it has nothing to do with permanently changing a masculine body to a woman. The Divine Spirit in you is neither male nor female. It is sexless. The process of awakening this non-sexual spirit identity is by arousing the female within a man and the masculine in a woman."

"I want to have this special love for the Divine Mother, Aunt,"

"I know, sweetheart. I know. I know your heart," she said, hugging me.

"Well, it's time for you to go to sleep. Tomorrow, I will take you both on a trip into the hills. Now that you know the cosmic significance of our rituals, it is time for you two to learn a mystical secret that pertains to both of you." Aunt Preema hugged us both good night.

CHAPTER THREE

# *Guardians of the Boundary*

Mid-morning the next day, Aunt Preema herded us out of the house. We wound white cotton turbans on our heads to ward off the increasing heat as we wended our way along the thin mud and grass ridges that bordered the rice fields. All around us was a mosaic of green paddy. Ramagiri range loomed in the east, clothed in hues of green and blue with streaks of reddish brown where the earth showed through. A series of hills intervened in between.

Sandhya and I were excited, and she competed with me at taking the lead. After leading for fifteen minutes, I acquiesced to her. Aunt Preema was in the rear. We carried cloth shoulder bags with ample lunches packed in banana leaves. Our gait was slow, as my aunt insisted on walking at a leisurely pace. Sandhya and I had to halt frequently and wait a minute or two for Aunt Preema to catch up with us. She seemed absorbed. Sometimes, I thought that I heard her mutter to herself. My aunt did not speak much; if Sandhya and I came upon a fork in the trail, we waited for her and watched the direction she took before resuming the lead, for the trail branched at every mud ridge that intersected our path.

As we walked, we passed by a number of our kinsfolk and several neighbors working in the fields, stooped over the paddy in ankle-deep water. Uncle Raman and my father called out to us; we waved back to them. A light breeze rustled through the paddy in waves of green, and a musky smell pervaded the whole area.

One hour later we arrived at the eastern edge of the rice fields and climbed up the gentle slopes of the first hillock. A well-worn foot track started where the mud ridge terminated. Thick, hip-high grass grew on either side of the trail; beyond that, shrubs and large trees thrived. Sandhya and I were excited. We frequently darted ahead to explore the land that lay around a bend in the track. Then we waited for Aunt Preema to come upon us. Soon the sounds of the villagers subsided and the paddy fields disappeared from view. Walking for another hour or so, we approached a densely wooded area. Clumps of large trees clustered together, their branches intermingling.

"Let's get to those trees," said Aunt Preema, pointing to a group of large tamarind trees growing to our right.

"From now on keep close to me," she said. "And listen, you two, this is not a time to play," she warned as she shook free her turban. Sandhya and I sobered at once. We gathered close to the base of one of the trees. The cool shade was a welcome relief, and we stood there feeling our perspiration dry in the breeze. Aunt Preema stood to my right and Sandhya to my left.

Not more than ten minutes passed when a large raven flapped down upon a branch above us. It cocked its head and looked at us, first with its right eye and then with its left. Seemingly satisfied, it let out an ear splitting caw and settled down to peck at the branch. Its feathers shone deep blue-black with hints of purple iridescence. I picked up a small dry twig to throw at the raven. But, in a flash, my aunt caught my arm in a firm grip and whispered,

"Don't disturb her; she is one of them. Be still you both."

Her words were like a kick in my groin. The twig fell from my limp fingers. My curiosity was unbearable, but fear made it difficult even to look at the raven. Aunt Preema motioned to us to take off our turbans and sit down. Sandhya slipped close to me, and the three of us slid our backs down the bark of the tamarind tree. I tilted my head ever slowly upward and to the side. The corner of my vision caught the hazy impressions of the raven's movements on the branch. I felt Sandhya's sweaty hand wiggling into mine. She had noticed my foxy antics and began to copy me.

Then we saw Aunt Preema pull a black satin pouch from the folds of her sari near her waist. As she loosened the pouch's drawstring, she started to hum a chant in a low voice. I felt a sudden apprehension, and my right thigh began to tremble. I put my palm on Aunt Preema's thigh, which was next to mine, and she assured me with a fleeting squeeze of my hand. That assuaged my agitation a little. Sandhya began to wedge herself between the tamarind tree and me. I felt her hot frightened breath on my neck.

Aunt Preema gently moved aside the twigs and leaves on the ground and cleared a large circular area in front of her. Then, with her right index finger she drew two separate half circles facing each other. Between them she drew two triangles, overlapping each other at their apices, the remaining corners touching the circles. Next she poked a dot in the center of the interlap of the triangles, all the while humming the chant.

From the black pouch she drew out colored beads of barley and threw a bead each on Sandhya's and my head. Five beads she placed carefully in the four corners of the triangles and one in the center dot within the interlap. At that instant, the raven let out three piercing caws. It then flapped down to a lower branch. I did not see this directly, but the peripheral image became larger and the rustling was louder, giving the impression that the raven was only a few feet from our heads.

My aunt stopped chanting abruptly. Then something incredible happened: we heard a tremendous flapping and swishing above us. We looked up and saw five large ravens descend swiftly upon a branch. The ravens sat still for several moments. Sandhya and I stared at them, fascinated. Moments passed; then a sixth raven appeared and glided down onto a higher branch. This raven was white, with touches of bluish gray on its wings and rosy claws. My aunt interlocked her fingers in a peculiar way and began her chants.

The first raven dropped down to the ground in front of us and began to prance around. It was then that we noticed its unusual size. Sandhya drew herself very close to me, squishing me against Aunt Preema. Now both my thighs began to tremble. Then suddenly, all seven ravens took off. They circled the tree and flew to the east.

"Get up, we must follow them," commanded Aunt Preema.

"What is happening, Mother?" asked Sandhya in an agitated voice, as we lashed our turbans around our heads and made our way into the forest.

"Listen, these are beings from the other realm. I cannot describe to you both how auspicious this is. This is unprecedented—it's a blessing and an invitation to their boundary."

"What boundary, Aunt?"

"Do you remember me explaining to you about the odiyyas who live in the hills?"

"Yes, those people who can take any form," answered Sandhya.

"Yes. They are not human anymore; they live in a dimension of energy beings. This universe we live in is only one among an infinite number that exists. The odiyyas have mastered the technique of crossing into and out of the universe that exists adjoining our own world of matter. Energy beings, called shuddha pranis, guard these portals. Just now they visited us, I think. They are the keepers of the mystic seal I drew on the ground."

"But how do you know that these are the beings, Mother? They could be just ravens," asked Sandhya, as we made our way toward the east.

"You are right. I don't know, sweetie. But I have a feeling that we are moving with the flow of astral energy. The future will tell what we are headed into."

"Aunt Preema, why did you draw the mystic seal?"

"When I was about your age, my aunt Sathya, your grandmother, brought me into this forest. She was instructing me in some of the invocation techniques, when the wind gusted strong, and seven ravens appeared all of a sudden and landed around us.

Aunt Sathya drew this mystic seal and one of the ravens flew up into the tree and dropped a pebble into the seal. Then they flew away. You see there are the confused ones, too, who have fallen into the clutches of the dark powers, who can also take on the form of a raven. But they cannot survive the power of this mystic seal and will not get close to it, unlike these."

Aunt Preema probed about her pouch and produced a smooth white stone that looked like quartz, with a few red veins bulging on one side.

"That is why I have a strong feeling about this. There is energy guiding us on. Whatever happens will happen today; later I will take you to the mystic well," said Aunt Preema.

We walked in silence for two or three hours, with the foot track constantly inclining upward. Squirrels and sometimes mongooses ran across our path. The sun was almost overhead. Occasionally the thick forest gave way to open spaces where shrubs grew in clumps.

Aunt Preema had taken the lead since our encounter with the ravens. The foot track ran ahead of us for about a mile. It disappeared amid a cluster of trees that grew in profusion toward the north, where they seemed to end abruptly against granite studded hills. Aunt Preema stopped suddenly and surveyed the hills. We stood by her in suspenseful silence.

"I don't feel that we should follow this track anymore. Here, let's cut through this grass," she said.

Both Sandhya and I followed close behind, Sandhya clutching my arm tightly. We walked through dense vegetation, pushing branches out of our way, taking care not to hit the one following behind. Our progress was slow. There were no tracks evident, and it appeared to me that my aunt was making her own way through the forest. We walked beneath a cluster of peepul trees, when my aunt veered toward one and said,

"This seems a good place to sit and eat. What do you think, children?"

Sandhya clung to me and we anxiously scanned the branches above in silence. My aunt saw us inspect the branches.

"I know . . . but they are good beings. And you see we are protected. There is nothing to fear. Trust me," Aunt Preema assured us as she held us both close to her.

"Are we going to eat now? I thought you said we have an appointment with the ravens!" said Sandhya.

"Oh, let's eat first," I said, feeling hungry at the mention of food.

"Yes, dear, we have an appointment to keep. They will meet us when they want," my aunt said.

We sat beneath a large peepul tree. Sandhya and I began brushing aside the leafy debris. When we cleared a large space, about three feet in diameter, Aunt Preema drew a circle on the soil with a twig.

"Let us place the food in the center," she instructed.

We took the banana-leaf packets out of our bags and placed them in the center of the circle. My aunt pointed out three spots around the circle, marking them with her twig. "Sandhya, you sit here; Shambu, you over here. From now on you must allow things to happen. Do not question anything either loudly or in your minds, as that will only stir up the physical mind. Do you both understand?"

"Can we just chant in our minds?" asked Sandhya.

"Yes, you can. To feel fear is okay, dear," she said pulling us to her. "We are close to the boundary, and things are not as they appear. Keep your hearts and heads open to any experience. Your everyday minds will be upset when they cannot understand unusual experiences," my aunt said with a faint smile. "Sandhya, open the food packets; let's offer them to the unseen beings."

Savory aroma hit my nostrils, and my mouth watered instinctively at the sight of cooked rice with yogurt and mango pickles. I felt bad—food should be offered with a spirit of true giving, I thought, and not with a salivating mouth. We held our hands as we sat around in a circle, and my aunt began to chant, her eyes half closed.

"To the unseen beings!" my aunt said, and picking up a little food from her packet, she threw it into the forest beyond.

"To the guardians of the energy boundary!" she spoke aloud and threw some food from my packet. I looked with concern at how much she was pulling out of my packet to feed the energy guardians, and at once suppressed my thoughts guiltily.

"To the masters of the twin realms!" she uttered aloud, collecting some food from Sandhya's packet and throwing it behind her.

Sandhya was sitting with her eyes closed. A moment later the top branches rustled with a strong gust of wind, and both Sandhya and I looked up startled. My aunt surveyed the surrounding branches. Our tension began to wane, as we saw nothing out of the ordinary. My aunt handed me my food blessing me, "Consume this energy food and may your boundaries open," she placed her palm upon my forehead and slid it over my crown and the back of my head. She did the same to Sandhya as she handed her food to her.

"Start eating, children," she said with a smile.

I fell upon my food like a starving wolf, oblivious to the surroundings. My aunt ate sparingly and packed the remaining food in the packet. In between mouthfuls, I had this vague thought that there was something odd about the way Sandhya sat, but I did not look to verify. Then, for some inexplicable reason I had an urge to look at her.

She sat wide-eyed with a morsel of food in her right hand. She was staring just over my head. A jolt of terror hit the pit of my stomach. Then she called out in a chilling whimper, "Mother! Mother! Mother! Behind . . . Shambu!"

I sat there petrified, with a lump of food in my throat. I looked at Aunt Preema and was confused to see her incongruously serene face. A faint smile played about the corners of her lips as she gazed beyond my head.

"Shambu, dear, do not be frightened," she spoke gently without looking at me. "Turn around . . . slowly. Do not be afraid," she reassured me, still not looking at me. It was eerie the way she said it.

I pivoted my body around slowly. Two large limbs of the peepul tree grew almost horizontally about fifty feet before me, and approximately eight feet from the ground. A smaller branch from the lower limb grew slightly below it and straight out in our direction. Five large ravens were perched upon this branch. A limb below supported the enormous raven. The branches were swaying gently in a slight breeze.

A movement in the upper branch caught my eye—a beautiful white raven sat upon this limb. They sat there, all seven of them, watching us in silence. They made no sound, nor was there the slightest movement of their bodies, apart from them swaying with the branches, and an occasional ruffle of a feather or two in the breeze.

I gazed at the white raven above, and I noticed that its eyes were red. My elemental fear was inexplicably gone, and in its place was a feeling of quietude. There was something about the raven gently bobbing in the wind that put my mind at ease. Or it could be the monotone of my aunt chanting—almost in a whisper. I could not take my eyes off the white raven. It was like I was feeding through my eyes. Something was giving me a strange satiety. Some celestial nourishment poured into me from the white raven. The surroundings became a blur in my sensorial fringes, sensory distinctions faded. The movement of the leaves in the breeze, the swaying of the grass, the shafts of sunlight as they flirted with patches of shadow—all these and more began to give out a tone or a chime. Musical notes emerged—here and there, at first. Then there were entire melodies—the sweetest of sounds, so pure and sublime—just by the slightest move from a simple leaf. I felt Sandhya creep up beside me. I could feel her dark, curly locks touch my cheeks with lyrical pleasantness. Then the white raven unfolded its wings slowly. One by one the rest of them opened their wings.

I do not remember seeing them leap off the branches, but suddenly they were floating down from the trees. We watched dumfounded as all seven ravens began to elongate vertically as they fluttered down. I felt Sandhya embrace me . . . Oh! The music of the embrace! I felt Aunt Preema's body behind me; her left hand slipped down over my arm and into my palm, triggering gentle peals of bells.

There stood before us a tall and slender being, very fair, swathed in golden folds of luminescence that reached down to the ground, but not quite touching it. This glowing raiment seemed to replenish itself from the ground up. She had an unusually elongated head with long, black tresses. She held a purplish, translucent wand that had a copper-colored lotus as its head.

The other five beings were taller than her, and robed in shimmering, deep blue luminescence. They were arrayed on either side of her and slightly behind. The seventh one was enormous—a giant. This one stood behind them all, its head and torso reaching above the upper branches of the peepul trees.

The fair one advanced toward us, followed by the others. I felt my aunt prod us to stand up. An intense feeling of love erupted in my chest. Without thinking, I walked toward the fair one, pulling Sandhya along with me. I fell at her feet. My feelings of love were so overwhelming that they shut out all other sensations.

When I opened my eyes, I found Sandhya and myself being held close by the fair one. We reached only to the bottom line of her breasts. As she held us, she looked down at us; her irises were whirling wheels of amber.

She began to call gently, "Neela . . . Neela." Looking at me, the others took up the call. Then she looked at Sandhya and began to call softly, "Sveeta . . . Sveeta." The others took up the call again. They began to alternate the names.

The fair one released us from her embrace and turned us to face each other. I gasped in surprise at the beautiful lady who stood before me. She had an expression of delighted recognition as she looked at me.

"Neela!" was all she could say as she fell into my arms.

I clung to her, afraid that she might disappear. I could smell the fragrance from her hair, as I buried my face in her tresses. Space-time barriers melted and I experienced an intense ecstasy. A gentle hand ran through my hair, over the back of my head and down my back.

When we opened our eyes, we found Aunt Preema holding us both. Sandhya was deeply anguished at seeing me. She would not stop running her palms over my arms as if she was searching for something. I looked around, but the beings were nowhere in sight—neither were the ravens.

The place had undergone a strange and subtle transformation. A supermundane forlornness pervaded the area like a mushy fog. The breeze had died down, and the branches and the leaves drooped with a listless melancholy. I was dazed, and I felt pensive. However hard I tried, I could not remember her face—the face of that beauteous lady who I thought was Sandhya.

"Mother! I cannot bear this. Why am I feeling this?" sobbed Sandhya.

"Breathe deep and fix your gaze here," instructed my aunt as she pressed the center of our brows with her thumbs. I closed my eyes and focused my vision at the center of my brow and began to breathe in and out slowly. My aunt kept pressing firmly upon my brow with her left thumb, rocking me gently back and forth. She did the same to Sandhya with her right thumb. She started singing an old lullaby, sung commonly in every household in our village.

I was amused at first, but then I found it soothing. Within a few minutes, Sandhya and I were able to smile and talk about our incredible experience. I started walking toward our food packets.

"They ate it all, Shambu. When you two were lost in each others' memories," said my aunt laughing. Indeed, the food packets were empty, cleaned out, every morsel—including even the spicy hot mango pickle.

"Did they eat our food, Mother?" Sandhya asked, more amazed than disgruntled.

"Yes, dear, they accepted our offerings. This is unprecedented. The guardians of the boundary took our offerings in person!" she said in a muted voice.

My aunt instructed us to remain silent. She said that we were not able to assimilate the magnitude of what was happening to us; it was imperative that we keep our mouths shut and walk with her to the next rendezvous with Shakti (divine power).

Though my mouth was closed, my mind was seething with a million thoughts, and I was sure the case was the same with Sandhya.

We changed directions several times; moving east sometimes, and at other times north. I espied the sun occasionally through the trees; it appeared to have fallen somewhat to the west. My aunt had kept the lead all along, followed by Sandhya. She felt safe between us, not that I was a great source of protection.

After about forty-five minutes of walking, we arrived at a hillside. It was actually a tumble of gigantic boulders, overgrown in places with thick vegetation. My aunt came to a halt.

"Dears, now I know more than ever that you are both marked out for kundabhisheekam," she said solemnly. I wanted to ask her what kundabhisheekam was, but caught myself as I remembered her injunction to keep our mouths shut.

My aunt worked her way through the outlying boulders where trees and vines grew in profusion, the roots and branches grabbing these rocks like giant fists holding mere pebbles. We stopped in front of a thick outgrowth of tall bushes.

"There! This is the well, the Yoni kumbham, the pot of union," announced my aunt, parting a few branches with her left hand and beckoning us to enter with her right. With overwhelming curiosity and apprehension Sandhya and I edged closer.

"What well is it, mother?" asked Sandhya, peeking into the gloom. She wound her arms tight around me and I felt her tremble.

"It is the well of union, dear, just as I said, the well of Divine Union," she replied cryptically.

At that moment a powerful wave of fear hit me, and my knees buckled. My vision became blurry, and a strange sweat broke out over my forehead and temples. In a flash my aunt was by my side. I felt a strong thrust at my belly button. A vigorous surge of alertness spread out of my midsection, giving me great strength. My vision cleared in a few seconds and I saw my aunt remove her right thumb from my navel.

Together, Sandhya and I stepped through the parting in the bushes. I peered into the gloom and saw a clearing that was approximately forty feet in diameter. The place was dark; few shafts of sunlight came through the canopy of leaves.

"Let's step in, children; there's no time to waste," she urged, pushing us as we faltered at the entrance.

As soon as I got accustomed to the level of light within, I saw a triangular well in the center. The sight of the well reminded me of how parched my mouth was. A four-foot high stone wall edged this well. A dark shape in one corner of the clearing attracted my attention; a platform was cut into a projecting boulder; seven serpent figures stood upon it. Attracted by a pale gleam on the platform I stepped closer. On the rock was a small brass pitcher, with a rope around its neck. The serpent figures loomed large and seemed to stare at me. The place was damp and smelled of decaying leaves. Gingerly, I picked up the pitcher and walked away.

The well itself seemed deep, but I was unable to fathom its depths beyond a few feet because of the dense blackness within. But from the numerous coils that the rope made as it lay on the ground, I presumed the well to be very deep.

"Mother! Come here. There is a pot buried in the ground!" cried Sandhya as she stooped over something on the ground.

"I know, my dear. Don't touch it." Aunt Preema admonished. I watched Sandhya withdraw her hand stiffly as I approached her. She was hunched over a brass rim in the ground. When I reached her side, I saw a large brass pot set into the ground in the middle of a small brick triangle. The triangle had its apex pointed to one of the sides of the well. I hunched down beside her.

I looked for my aunt and saw her collecting pieces of dry twigs from the edges where the clearing met the forest.

"That is the Yoni kumbham, dears. It's the sacred pit. This is the pot of the female receptacle," my aunt explained in a whisper. "Spread your head-bands on the ground and sit."

We pulled off our turbans, spread them on the ground, and sat upon them. I could see the whites of Sandhya's eyes. I was beginning to be afraid. My aunt, in the meanwhile, drew some water from the well and came to where we sat. From her cloth bag she produced a box of matches, a lump of camphor, and two small coils of red silk cord. She had collected a large bundle of dry twigs.

She gave us both a long and penetrating look. Then, with great deliberation, she pulled off her turban and laid it on the ground. She undid the knot in her hair slowly, and shook her head, allowing her tresses to tumble down in great curly spreads.

Suddenly, she asked me to take my clothes off. I was taken off-guard and hesitated. She repeated in an insistent tone, "Take your clothes off, Shambu. You, too, Sandhya."

My stomach went into knots. I hastily removed my dhoti. She then sprinkled some water upon us while muttering an incantation. Arranging some twigs a few feet from the base of the little triangle, she lit them with the match. The flames cast a pleasant warmth. The resinous twigs made an aromatic wood smoke.

"Get close to the triangle, children," instructed my aunt. "Shambu, get your legs over here, like this," she said, pulling my legs apart, so that I sat naked with my legs spread astride the triangle, its apex hitting my groin. She ordered Sandhya to sit likewise, facing me. Her thighs crossed over my thighs with the triangle straddled between us.

Aunt Preema wiped clean the brass pot and threw aside the leafy dirt within it. She took our right hands and placed them in the pot, pouring water over them and into the pot. She began to chant in a comfortable pitch and very soon her chants became a monotonous drone that receded into the background.

Sandhya's gaze was directed to our entwined fingers in the pot, the leaping flames lighting up her eyes like twin stars. Presently, I became aware of a strong breeze that rustled the canopy above us, occasionally revealing the sky.

A sudden pressure in my buttocks shook me out of my distraction and brought my gaze back to our hands. With her fingers entwined in mine, Sandhya began to push my fingers into a pattern. I looked at her for some clue, but I was perplexed to see that she bent backward, away from me, her back arched, her left hand on the ground supporting her. Her mouth was slightly open and she gazed upward, with only the whites of her eyes showing. Her chest heaved as she breathed in great gulps of air.

She gripped me tight with her thighs, her heels digging into my buttocks, pulling me closer to her, but the apex of the triangle began to press uncomfortably into my groin. The pressure became intense, escalating my anxiety. Beads of sweat dripped from my forehead. My aunt changed her pitch, the chanting sounded louder, and the words became clear:

| | |
|---|---|
| *Vata vriksha mridu patrakaree* | (Shaped like a tender peepul leaf,) |
| *Roomalamkruta bhooshitae;* | (And adorned with tufts of curly hair;) |
| *Uorvor madhya nivasae Devi* | (Goddess, thou reside in a woman's pubis,) |
| *Yonii linga namoostutae.* | (We worship thee joined with thy Astral Self.) |

She kept repeating the chant.

I felt an almost imperceptible throb under my seat by my tail-bone, and heard a hum. This hum seemed to interfere with my normal perception of my surroundings. The sharp flicker of the flames now appeared as if they were smeared. I felt Sandhya press and relax her heels and for a while I thought that this was what caused me to experience the pulsatile feeling. I looked at Sandhya and noted that her eyes were still glazed. Suddenly, for just an instant, my perception of her became unfocused. I was instantly alarmed and fought to regain clarity. Curiously, I no longer felt the painful pressure in my groin, although Sandhya kept constricting me.

It became a struggle to retain my normal physical awareness intact. Sandhya faded out of my sight again, and my power to regain my normal perception began to falter. The flicker from the leaping flames, the drone of Aunt Preema's chant, the surroundings, and even the smell of the smoke diminished. A thick fog of slumberous haze permeated my senses. My eyelids closed as I gave up my final, futile effort to retain my control. A voice whispered in my left ear, "Drop, your obtuse self! Drop down now!" The voice was shrill, but sweet like that of a girl.

I felt my body jerk as if in the throes of a spasm; I was overcome by dizziness; I began to collapse. Helplessly I expected my head to hit the ground. Moments later a musical sound came, a sound like that of millions of particles of sand tumbling down a metal chute, or perhaps rain drops pattering on dry leaves. Then, from the wispy brume emerged a magnificent cobra, full-hooded, in its entire splendor.

I caught telltale hints of its presence, as its form revealed and hid with the movement of the fog. In great confusion, I lifted my hands to my eyes and felt that my eyelids were still shut. But there was this cobra, still swaying before me. I tried several times to cup my palms over my closed eyelids, but the vision persisted. The cobra's body was a fascinating mixture of white, rose, and golden sheen, sometimes bordering on red.

My disorientation was acute. Then the little girl spoke again, "Drop your fear."

I wanted to ask how. But before I could voice this query, I saw the cobra loom up close, and in an instant it had its coils around me. The feel of the cobra's body slithering upon me was exquisite. It undulated and I rocked with its movements. With sheer pleasure, I put my arms around it. As we twisted and swayed together, the cobra opened its mouth wide and blew straight into my face. As its breath washed over my face, I experienced an exquisite smell, like jasmine, and that ochre-yellow flower we call champakam. As its breath passed over me, I also had a sensation of something peeling off.

One moment I felt intensely female; the next, I experienced masculine pleasure. For a while this dual experience alternated. Then the rocking stopped and I felt a mild glow all around me. It was diffuse, as if emanating from everywhere. There was no sign of the cobra. Not even my body was evident. It was as though I had vision without eyes.

Gradually the glow faded and darkness closed in. A soothing unconsciousness began to prevail, as the darkness embraced my vision.

When I opened my eyes, I saw Sandhya staring at me. I had my head on Aunt Preema's lap. I sat up instantly and looked around for the cobra.

"Aunt Preema, did you see the cobra?" I asked casting about in the gloom.

"Indeed, I did. Not one cobra, but two," said my aunt, bursting into a peal of laughter. "Why, did you see only one?" she asked, still laughing.

Sandhya joined in her laughter. I was puzzled but smiled inanely, a bit out of sorts. That only made Sandhya giggle more, and made my aunt fall back on the ground clutching her quaking belly. I looked around for a clue. The place was the same as before. Behind me was the well; the stone serpents were still there upon the boulder platform.

As I surveyed my surroundings, I could hear my aunt and Sandhya laugh uproariously with some indescribable glee. Then I looked down at the brass pot and the triangular pit and screamed in dismay. Here I was, naked from waist down, wearing Sandhya's blouse. The shame was too much—I put my face on my knees and began crying loud. The sight of me sitting with my face on my knees made their mirth even more uncontrollable. My aunt said that even my penis looked morose because it had its head down like me. Hearing that comment I became curious, and stopped my wailing for an instant to look down at it. Indeed, there was something comic about it—I cracked with laughter.

At length, our mirth abated and Sandhya and I exchanged clothes. Aunt Preema reeled out the red silken chords, knotted them into two circles and placed them around our necks saying that now both our "bottoms" are awakened.

"Kundalini? Is she the cobra?" Sandhya asked.

"Yes. She is the Queen of the Soul. She is awakened," my aunt replied. She whispered a mantra in Sandhya's ears and one in mine, then asked us both to repeat them mentally several times. As we did this, she broke the lump of camphor into two roughly equal parts, placed each lump on two flat stone chips, and gave it to us.

"Hold them out in your right palms, with your left under the right," she instructed.

We stood up and held them out as she told us. She pulled out a flaming twig from the glowing embers and lit the camphor lumps. Aunt Preema began to chant as we waved the flames at each other. Suddenly, I was overcome with a deep love and veneration for Sandhya. I set aside the flaming camphor and prostrated myself at Sandhya's feet. Sandhya pulled me up and hugged me. There was an exquisite smile on her face and tears streamed from her eyes. She touched my feet. Then, as if reading each other's unspoken thoughts, we picked up the flames and waved them around Aunt Preema. Dropping the flames into the embers, we prostrated at her feet. My aunt pulled us up and held us close to her sides, her palms upon our heads. I felt supremely blissful. There were no words spoken, for the great serpent of pure love transcended all thoughts.

# CHAPTER FOUR

# The Clan of Matriarchs

 It was quite dark by the time we descended the last hill and set our feet upon the rice field ridges. We caught glimpses of the temple tower, glowing with hundreds of lamps. My mind was unsettled with strange feelings. Earlier, Aunt Preema explained to us that the mystical ceremony of Kundabhisheekam was complete. According to her, kundabhisheekam meant "ablution to the sacred pit"; she explained that the brass pot was a physical token to help us visualize the astral pit at the base of our spines. The place had great power from many previous awakening ceremonies, including her own, she said. She gave us both instructions on preliminary spiritual practices that we were to do with our mantras.

With the passage of a few hours, my mind began to rebound back and take control. The encounters became dreamlike, pushed into the realm of the unreal; but my good fortune was that I had two witnesses. The spellbinding transformation of the ravens, followed by the transfiguration of Sandhya into an enchanting nymphet, and the tantalizing experiences with the serpent that bordered on the erotic, all threw my mind out of sync. Then Sandhya asked a question that shook my very being.

"Mother, why did I see Shambu as a different person when the White One embraced us?"

My aunt walked in silence for a while. Then she answered in a soft, thoughtful voice, "The veil was lifted for a brief moment, dear."

"What veil, Mother?"

"The veil that separates the current incarnation from the past, sweetheart."

At that point, my feelings became unbearable. "I saw you differently, too, Sandhya." Tears sprang into my eyes as I said this.

"The veil of forgetfulness is a merciful one, and is rarely sundered," continued my aunt. "But when it is rent, memories from the past will disrupt and uproot the being to the core. Life is an experience of playful growth. Often, beings grow in groups, merging and separating from incarnation to incarnation."

"Are we friends from the past, Aunt Preema?" I asked amazed.

"Not only were you friends, you are both joined through spiritual practices. And there are others of your group looking out for you."

She revealed to us that she had been observing Sandhya and me for several months and had come to the conclusion that our lives were forged together from many previous incarnations. Then Sandhya asked my aunt why we were separated from our group.

"You both have karmas to be fulfilled. Your lives are entwined karmically, as you yourselves have some inkling by now. But, this is not the time to explain to you why or what these karmas are. The deity of the mantra will guide you both, and the future will reveal even more explicitly how far you will journey together. Your minds are tender and unprepared to assimilate the import of this miracle today," she explained with a serious look.

We walked in silence. A warm breeze carried in voices from the distance. Midway through the rice fields, my aunt broke the silence.

"Our household will be gathered for the welcoming ceremony. They will honor your awakening, but only a few will know that you two are joined. This you should keep to yourselves."

"Yes, Mother," Sandhya agreed, nodding her head, and she glanced at me.

"You, too, Shambu," my aunt looked at me.

"I promise, Aunt Preema," I vouched.

"All of them know about the joining ritual intellectually, but only a handful are awakened enough to empathize with this experience. If this is revealed to the rest, you two might face devastating criticism," she warned.

The awakening ritual is common, but a joining of two aspirants is rarely coupled with an awakening ritual. Everyone knew of the Kundalini awakening, and some were aware of this rare joining ritual. But most people, bound by a rigid morality, could not accept this practice as a legitimate spiritual path. This spiritual dichotomy and inhibition in the general population required that the joining ritual become a secret practice. I was 9 and Sandhya was 10½ years old. In later years I realized that only a rare combination of karmas and events induced a sorceress to initiate a joining ritual among two aspirants at such an early age.

The awakening ceremony helped set in motion physical, mental, and emotional changes that allowed a playful child to set forth on a journey of self-discovery. It was an initiation into a mystical transition that might someday result in full-fledged spiritual awakening. A culture rooted in mysticism nourishes and supports many mystically inclined souls. The awakening ceremony served to discover these souls and set them on their path to enlightenment. This ritual was particularly suited for those born to experience worship of the Divine Mother and who are to practice Tantra, or power invocation.

Aunt Preema led us through the village. Diffuse spots of light filtered through the trees, marking the presence of houses. Frequently, people went by us, most chanting hymns to the Great Goddess. We passed each other exchanging ritual blessings, "Ambae Bhagavati!" and "Jai Jagad Ambae!"

At the entrance to our homestead, we saw two of our aunts and two of our maternal uncles waiting for us. A few yards from the house, Aunt Preema began to chant aloud. It appeared as if she signaled them with her chants, for the two women instantly cupped their palms over their mouths and began the welcoming ululations.

"Take the children to the water jar, Preema," instructed Aunt Ananda. A large copper pitcher stood to the left of the doorway and Aunt Preema guided us to it. Uncle Bala, who was the eldest maternal uncle and the karanavar, poured water over Sandhya and me. My cousins were conspicuously absent. Uncle Ramachandran wrapped a red silk drape across each of our shoulders and led us to the threshold of our house. The kuttuvilakku cast ample light in the hallway that led to the courtyard.

I followed Sandhya into the hall, reverently touching the threshold step, while Aunt Preema and the rest brought up the rear. It was a thrilling sight to see the entire family gathered in a circle in the courtyard. Except for some of my youngest cousins, everyone wore red silk. During our absence, my family had built a large makeshift ceremonial fire pit, or homa-kuntta, at the east end of the courtyard. A fire blazed in this pit and the matriarchs sat around this with their husbands, chanting hymns and pouring oblations of ghee into the hungry flames.

I saw Uncle Raghavan emerge from a group to the left and join Aunt Preema. My mother and father came up behind me. I felt somewhat self-conscious with all this ceremony, even though I had witnessed a similar ritual two years ago when our household honored the awakening of Padmini, Rati, and Raghu, three of my elder cousins.

I wanted to get close to Sandhya, for I badly needed her support. I wondered how she felt, whether she experienced the same turmoil as I did. She walked a step ahead of me with her parents close on her heels.

"Come forward; come close to the fire," called Grandmother Paru. She motioned us to sit on two grass mats placed before the fire pit. The fire ceremony began as the grandfathers chanted the mantras and I repeated after them. When the matriarchs chanted, Sandhya repeated after them.

*Om agni prajvalitam vandae jata vedam hutashanam;*
*Suvarnam amalam, samiddham visvatoomukham.*
*Sree yajna purushaya namaha . . .*

*(Om. O Agni, foremost among the shining ones, creator of the*
*vedas, Blaze forth thine pure golden flames and cast thy*
*splendor in all directions; We worship thee, O eater of obla-*
*tions, salutations! Hail! O lord of the fire ritual.)*

We scooped clarified butter with mango wood ladles and poured it into the flames. Sandhya and the matriarchs chanted, "Ardram jvalati jyoti aham asmi" (I am that Supreme Light shining as this cosmic light).

The grandfathers and I chanted, "Jyotirjvalati Brahma aham asmi" (I am that Supreme Light of Brahman shining as the innermost light).

Sandhya and I chanted together, "Yo aham asmi Brahma aham asmi" (I am that Brahman, I am indeed Brahman). The Poornahuti, or culminating chant, was performed next. Sandhya and I stood up, holding a mammoth mango wood ladle, with its open end tipped into the fire. We chanted the following:

"Brahmarpanam Brahma havir Brahmagnau Brahmanahutam Brahmaiva teena gantavyam Brahmakarma samadhina." (The offering is Brahman, ghee offered is Brahman, the priest is Brahman, the fire is also Brahman. Into Brahman will merge one who cognizes Brahman in every action.)

The matriarchs poured entire buckets of ghee down the ladle's spout. The fire blazed mightily and the heat was intense. My throat felt parched as I intoned the incantations. The entire household, beginning with our parents, circled us slowly, each one coming near to throw a handful of yellow ceremonial rice akshatam upon us and into the flames. This ritual of blessing welcomed us as newly initiated beings into our immediate society, the extended family. I fell at the feet of my mother, who blessed me with tears in her eyes, filled with joy and pride in seeing her son fulfill this profound step in his life as an evolving being. Our clan of the matriarchs was indeed sustained by awakening beings such as Sandhya and me. We were like new growths on an old tree, sprouting fresh currents of spirituality around the aging core. We served as vital links between old and new. The old were on the threshold of eternity, ready to say their farewells, to make their final flights into the arms of the Divine Mother. The new, yet-to-be-born beings, prayerfully waited in the wings of space-time for an opportunity to incarnate so that they, too, could chart their lives among wise beings and make their way to full enlightenment.

When I touched my father's feet, he helped me up and gave me a hug, adding a benediction for divine life. In the meanwhile Sandhya's parents blessed her. I heard Sandhya and Aunt Preema sob. In the background, the entire family stood in a circle chanting lyrics from the Sree Devi Mahatmyam (Dialogues on the glory of the Divine Mother by Sage Markandeya to his disciple Krasustuki).

The elders guided me to Aunt Preema and Uncle Raghavan, and Sandhya to my parents. Aunt Preema did not let me touch her feet, but swept me into a tight embrace, while Uncle Raghavan put both his palms upon my head and blessed me cheerfully. Aunt Preema guided us to the rest of the family and we received blessings from everyone.

Aunt Preema steered us to the group of cousins who had previously undergone the initiation of awakening. They blessed us by whisking us with tender coconut palm fronds. Our male cousins blessed us with sheaves of rice stalk. After we were blessed by all who were older than us, it was our turn to bless those younger than us. Uncle Jaya guided the group of cousins, who wore cream-colored ceremonial silk, called kasavu, toward Sandhya and me. Cousin Reevati brought a platter of akshatam. One by one, our younger cousins fell at the feet of Aunt Preema, who blessed them, they bowed down to Sandhya and finally me, both of us sprinkling the rice over their heads.

With the completion of the ceremonies, the elders herded the children into the dining hall by the kitchen, where the feast would be served—the much-anticipated feast at last! The atmosphere was festive. With the rigid formality imposed by the ritual having been lifted, general pandemonium was in progress. Some of the elders were busy trying to get my younger cousins to relinquish their new ceremonial dress for ordinary cotton clothes, while other elders headed toward the kitchen to kindle the flames anew and warm the cauldrons of food.

At length, Sandhya and I were seated at a special place on the floor, with our cousins arrayed on either side. Aunt Preema sat with us, to my right; as our preceptor, she, too, was honored. Fresh-cut banana leaves were spread before us to use as dinner plates, and a miniature kuttuvilakku was lit. The matriarchs and their husbands sat facing us. A brass platter was brought and placed between Sandhya and me. My mother brought before us a second brass platter containing a sampling of all the dishes cooked that night. The matriarchs and their husbands then commenced the worship of the divine fire Vaisvanara by invoking the pranas. Sandhya and I followed their cue. We invoked each of the five pranas by variously combining the thumbs and two other fingers of each hand. Then we plucked parcels of food from the brass platter and offered them into the second platter with the following chants:

*Sradhayam pranae nivisto
    amritam juhomi,*
*Sradhayam apanae nivisto
    amritam juhomi,*
*Sradhayam vyanae nivisto
    amritam juhomi,*
*Sradhayam udanae nivisto
    amritam juhomi,*
*Sradhayam samanae nivisto
    amritam juhomi,*
*Brahmani ma atma
    amritatvaya."*

With reverence and faith, I offer
    ambrosia into prana,
With reverence and faith, I offer
    ambrosia into apana,
With reverence and faith, I offer
    ambrosia into vyana,
With reverence and faith, I offer
    ambrosia into udana,
With reverence and faith, I offer
    ambrosia into samana,
May my self be united with the
    Supreme; may I attain
    immortality.

The dining hall reverberated as the elders intoned along. Then the feast commenced.

▼ ▼ ▼

The following morning, Aunt Preema awakened me before dawn. I rose up with a dizzy, surreal feeling.

"Ambae Bhagavati! Arise, to the morning light, Shambu," she greeted me.

"Kalii Jagadambae! Namastae!" I greeted her, touching her feet.

"Sandhya is up already and waiting for you," she said, picking up a new red dhoti and a red shoulder spread from the wardrobe.

"I am coming, Aunt," I said, gathering my fresh-cut neem stick and leaf pouch of burned rice husks. My family prepared a natural tooth powder from burned rice husks. A little crushed rock salt was added to this for flavor.

Sandhya was waiting for me at the east doorway, with a similar bundle.

"Kalii Jagadambae!" I greeted her.

"Ambae Bhagavati!" she returned, hugging me.

"Do not take too long, children; we have to reach the temple before the dawn worship concludes," reminded Aunt Preema.

After Sandhya and I bathed in the pond, we proceeded to the temple of Bhadra Kali, the benign personification of the Divine Mother. In a cloth bag I carried three husked coconuts, assorted fruits, and some camphor as offerings from the three of us. We could hear music and drums as we made our way through the palm grove.

In order to reach the central deity of our temple we had to pass through the impressive entrance, located in the main tower. This was an intricately carved granite structure that soared some hundred feet into the sky, presenting a landmark for miles around, situated as it was in the middle of rice fields and coconut groves. As we approached the tower, Aunt Preema urged us to prostrate at the threshold stone that lay across our path. We saw our neighbors coming toward us from the central sanctum. The three of us quickly greeted them and proceeded into the inner rectangle, a stone paved corridor open to the sky and encircling the main shrine. Stepping through this corridor, we came before the Supreme Presence.

Bhadra Kali was decked in a red and gold skirt; a red bodice covered Her breasts. Her eight arms were ornamented with gold bangles studded with gems that sparkled in the light of oil flames. A young priestess sat to Her side chanting mantras as she performed tantric gestures or mudras. The priestess wore a red angavastra, and her hair was tied into a knot on the left side of her head. The sound of music and drums was heavenly, and the fragrance was astral. There were numerous devotees clamoring at Mother Kali, eyes closed in divine ecstasy. Some called Her attention to them by clanging the brass bells that hung from the low stone beams. Others sang hymns in praise of Her, yet others were talking to Her in loud voices, as if She were flesh and blood. Then there were devotees who were unmindful of the clamor. They sat in silent meditation on stony ledges, the base of pillars, or on the steps, oblivious of their surroundings.

I saw tears flow down Sandhya's cheeks. I looked up at Aunt Preema's face. She stood beside me with her palms folded, lips pressed together in a faint smile. But from her eyes flowed a steady stream of tears. They washed down her dark eye makeup, dripping two dark stains upon her sari. I felt it difficult to breathe. I cast a glance at the priestess. Her eyes were closed, her left palm rested gently upon her heart, and with her right hand she weaved graceful patterns to Kali with a red hibiscus flower stuck between the middle and the ring fingers. My breath stopped involuntarily. Wave after wave of silent sobs exploded from the depths of my being. My mantra was lost to my mind. All I could mumble was "Kaliikaliikaliikalii."

▼ ▼ ▼

Aunt Preema was our mentor. This mantle naturally fell upon her because she was the preceptor of our initiation into awakening ritual. In spite of the generally rigid social structure wrought by tradition, there was an underlying informality in the actual interactions of everyday living and in the dynamics of communal life. This ease of life was a byproduct of the people's wholehearted participation in the art of loving their beloved Kali and living their religion, instead of following a central religious authority driving the community through institutionalized spirituality.

Mentorship crystallized as one, two, or three children attached themselves informally to an elder in their family, who, during the business of day-to-day life, imparted bits and pieces of experiences and advice. If the nature of a child's inquiry did not fall within the gamut of the elder's expertise, he or she would refer the child to another. When the time approached for the initiation into awakening ritual, this elder—if female—would be the preceptor for the group's initiation. Among our clan, only a woman could be a preceptor for the secret awakening ritual. But a mentor could be either a male or female. Our matriarchy recognized the superiority of the intuitive female in matters of the Spirit, especially in such a potent ritual as an awakening. What could be a better instrument than a mother's heart to gently arouse the sleeping kundalini within a child?

Sometimes children discovered prospective mentors in neighboring households, as the nature of their inquiries drove them beyond the boundaries of their own household's pool of expertise. The result was that an elder from the neighboring household would mentor such a child. Deep friendships were often forged, sometimes with profound results, as in the case of Uncle Bhadra.

Uncle Bhadra found his mentor in Kalyani, the matriarch of the House of Tandu. She was a distant cousin of our Grandmother Paru, and the daughter of Saraswati, the grand matriarch of the House of Tandu.

Uncle Bhadra approached Kalyani when he discovered an inclination to be a clay and stone sculptor. Kalyani and her husband

Sundareeshan were great sculptors and potters. They also knew the art of temple building and the occult mathematics behind it. It was during his apprenticeship under this couple that Uncle Bhadra met the other member of his group, Lavanya, the beautiful daughter of Kalyani and Sundareeshan. Later Kalyani became their preceptor during their initiation into awakening ritual. In the course of their discipleship, Uncle Bhadra and Lavanya discovered a deeper friendship in each other. Now, years later, they were betrothed. As customary in our matriarchal community, Uncle Bhadra was taken into the House of Tandu, although he maintained his links with our family on ritual occasions.

From Aunt Preema, I learned that the awakening ritual conjured different experiences for different groups. The physical settings for these rituals, too, were often different. But a common oath of secrecy bound all disciples, secrecy that sealed the intricacies of the actual ritual, the mantra transmitted from the preceptor to the disciple, the mystical experience each had, and the physical location of these spaces. Invariably these spaces were seats of power and hidden from the uninitiated. The preceptor who guided the group was in turn led by an inner feeling to these spots. Aunt Preema explained these locations as having a peculiar configuration that concentrated energy naturally, making different realities waltz in and out of one another. The disciples perceived these realities during their shifting states of awareness.

"Certain places have a special energy about them. The mystics and the odiyyas used their acute sensitivity for astral energy to discover these spots. They used these places to concentrate their own energy. And by their association with these spots they have left their astral imprints upon these spaces," she explained one evening, a month after the awakening ritual as we sat amid a massive tumble of boulders at the edge of the rice fields.

"What is an astral imprint, Mother?"

"When the sun has set and it is dark, the rock still retains warmth, doesn't it? This is the sun's imprint of warmth that extends well into the night."

"But, Aunt Preema, you don't mean the astral imprint to be the warmth of the sorcerers, do you?"

My aunt shook her head smiling, "Our senses work via a direct cause and effect relationship. For example, if you go into a room blindfolded, and if you feel warmth hitting your body on your right, you might infer that there is a fire to your right. This inference is based on a direct cause and effect relationship—there is a sensation of warmth and there is a source of warmth," she explained. "But our physical senses work only in this physical realm. Here, the physical mind grasps things by laboriously climbing the steps of cause and effect. In the astral realm, the process of cause and effect is not straightforward; it is as if the intermediate steps, or the causal links, are removed. This is especially so when the physical mind retains the memory of the astral experience. Events appear incongruous and seemingly illogical—just as you both experienced during your initiation. Every object in the physical realm has an 'astral root' so to speak," explained my aunt.

"Like the roots of a tree, Mother?" asked Sandhya, wide-eyed.

"Very much so, dear. Just as the roots of a tree are invisible to our senses, yet we trust that the roots exist, based on our knowledge of having seen them beneath trees uprooted by storms and floods. Insentient objects have astral roots, and sentient ones have astral selves. By awakening our astral self and training our physical senses to interact with the astral realm, we learn to see that every thing has an astral foundation. We peek into the astral world with our physical senses. Mystics and odiyyas, on the other hand, have the ability to manifest their awareness of their astral self in their physical surroundings by virtue of their specialized practices. That is, such a person has converted his or her physical body into energy and transferred it totally into his or her astral self."

"So by converting energies back and forth, they can exist in this realm or that!" I exclaimed.

"True. When they reemerge into the physical realm, they usually do so at these natural energy spots. This is a stable spot for them, because space-times from both realms meet here, but it could be destabilizing for ordinary people."

"Why is it dangerous for the ordinary people to be there, Mother?"

"Ordinary people have tied up most of their awareness in their physical mind. But when they chance upon these spots, the strong astral energy of these spaces dislodges their awareness, sometimes pushing it into their astral self, in which case they will 'peek' involuntarily into the astral realm. They might come back to normal awareness shaken, with tales of glorious visions. And they may experience a profound change in character, now that they know of realms other than the physical. But in other people, the energy of such spaces causes their awareness to dive deeply into their own unconscious, or into the netherworld. In either of these domains they encounter unpleasant experiences, and they rush up hastily to the physical reality with their inherent mental weaknesses made worse," my aunt elaborated.

"Is this a reason for the secrecy of these places, Aunt?"

"Yes, my dear. Proper initiation has to take place for the awakening to be stable. Otherwise, these awakenings will only be aberrant movements of awareness. A preceptor must guide the awakening properly and lend her own energy to stabilize it. Now, when odiyyas stay at these places where they emerged from the astral realm, within a short while their astral self connects with the astral root of the place, or a stone or a tree. This enhances the astral energy of that place, rather than draining it; with their increased association with that place, mystics leave an astral imprint of their energy," she detailed.

"Do we also leave astral imprints in places, Aunt?" I asked wondering if I was leaving one right then.

"Yes dear, everyone does leave one. But the power of these imprints and the emotional and psychic impact these make upon others varies with many factors. The quality of the imprints can be diminished if imprints with alien properties are superimposed upon them."

"Which is another reason why these places are protected by secrecy!" I exclaimed as I felt a piece of the puzzle fall into place.

"That's true. One can perceive these astral imprints only if one learns to use the astral senses," said my aunt.

"What are astral senses, Mother? How can we train them?"

"Astral senses begin to function when the physical mind is quieted, withdrawn from the physical senses, and the energy of the physical awareness transferred to the astral self. What happens when you exercise a muscle regularly? It develops. Similarly, the mind, like a muscle, grows stronger in a specific way, with repeated chanting of a mantra or by constant repetition of a ritual. Chant the mantra and your mind will quiet down," she explained abruptly. That was a cue that our session with Aunt Preema was over.

▼ ▼ ▼

Sandhya and I practiced our meditations together. We zealously prompted each other if one of us showed any laxity. Since I was introspective by nature, the slightest shift in my awareness tended to push me away from physical reality. Very soon, this became evident in my social interactions. Though my association with my cousins continued to be warm and friendly, I felt a tenuousness about these relationships inside me—with the exception of Sandhya of course, and ever since the initiation of awakening ritual, with Aunt Preema. The bond of friendship between us grew, and I often sought out my aunt to seek some counsel or the other.

After the experiences that the three of us had in the hills, I discovered that my image of my aunt had undergone a transformation. Unnoticed by me, the old archetype of her had crumbled and in its place a different one took form. A new and profound respect for her emerged. The woman I knew as my gentle aunt, a patient guide to my insistent queries, and the kind mother of my playmate, now revealed a more potent aspect—that of a powerful odiyatthi. With that, the concrete image of the odiyya that I entertained—shaped in my psyche through folklore, rumors, anecdotes and from other vicarious experiences—received a transfiguring blow.

In spite of the fact that a mystic consciousness permeated our community, people clung to the idea that odiyyas are beings alienated from society entities existing only as spectral forms in the hills. The very mention of their names conjured fleeting fearful shapes in the shadowy realms of our psyche. But here I was, living with one! This revelation was colossal to my prepubescent mind. In addition, my awareness was affected by recent experiences in such strange ways that with Aunt Preema, I felt that I was in the presence of a cloaked being whose true capacities she kept a secret. My mind opened up to a hitherto unfelt intensity about her presence. On an occasion I talked to Sandhya about this,

"I feel something different about Aunt Preema these days; when I approach her, I experience a twinge of fear—an unsettling feeling that something unexpected could happen."

But Sandhya's reply was shocking. "Shambu, I don't feel that she is like a mother to me any more."

"What are you talking about?" I asked. "Of course, she is your mother!" I was aghast and my outburst, defensive.

"Yes . . . yes, she is my mother. Yet she is not," she smiled, placing her arm around my shoulders. "She is closer to me than a mother could ever be to me. She is like . . . you are to me, Shambu."

"That's beautiful, Sandhya! She is your friend!"

"Yes. In many ways." Then after a pause she added, "Mother is your friend, too. She is our friend."

"Aunt Preema never inspired fear in me before. I wonder why I feel fear when I approach her these days?"

"Good question. I guess it has something to do with the initiation experiences," she conjectured.

"Do you feel fear in her presence, Sandhya?"

"No, I don't," she laughed. "But I may guess why you have fear," she gave me a coy look.

"What is that supposed to mean?" I asked apprehensively.

"Do you remember the details of the initiation at the triangular well?" she asked.

I closed my eyes and tried to remember. The image of the cobra loomed through the fog immediately.

"Some of it. It's vague—I can't quite recollect the details, Sandhya."

"Maybe when you regain memory of those details, your fear might be removed," she replied evasively. She groaned, lightly clutching her belly.

"Are you in pain, Sandhya?"

"Hmm, not much." She replied, but noticing my continued concern, she added with a smile, "I'm okay, Shambu."

I did not pursue questioning her about Aunt Preema any further, but the discussion only inflamed my curiosity. I thought I would wait for an opportune moment to ask Aunt Preema herself. The rest of the day, I busied myself helping the elders with small chores.

Later that day, my cousin Gopalan and I carried bundles of hay into our cowshed to feed our milch cows. We met my father. He was scraping dung from the floor into a bucket. We had two cows, Lakshmi and Sita, their three calves, and two water buffaloes. They provided the household's dairy needs, including ghee for ceremonial use, a large quantity of which we offered to the temple.

"Watch out children! The floor is slippery," warned my father as we leapt over a pile of dark green dung, while carrying the bales of hay on our heads.

"Get ready to clean more dung, Uncle Bhaskaran. We are going to feed them some more hay," warned my cousin.

I could not help laughing as my father rolled his eyes in playful exasperation as he put his hand on his hip and arched his back in mock agony.

"I know, I know. You kids keep feeding them and I will be running from one behind to the other catching cow-shit," he said, dramatizing this by running back and forth behind each cow with open hands, feigning intense anxiety.

We left him laughing, but when we reached the exit, he called back, "Oh! Shambu, did you happen to see Preema? She came here a little while ago looking for you."

"No Father, guess I better go look for her," I replied.

"Does this mean I will be left feeding them hay all by myself, the rest of the afternoon?" asked Gopalan.

Before I could say yes, my father playfully thrust the dirty hoe into Gopalan's hands saying, "No, you may clean the shit and I will feed them hay!" I left them laughing.

After some searching, I came upon Aunt Preema in the middle of our vegetable and herb plot.

"Aunt Preema! There you are," I called out to her. I came upon her as she pulled weeds from the chili plants.

"Muttu-root grass," she said, poking at a little heap of green grass by her side. Each tuft of grass ended in a tiny bulbous brown root. I picked up one and scratched it. A tiny scale of brown skin peeled beneath my nail, revealing a clean white starchy base.

"It smells like camphor," I said.

"It does. Will you help me take them in?"

"Of course, Aunt Preema," I said and began gathering them into my hands.

"No! Like this," she offered me a jackfruit leaf curled into a cone with which to hold the roots.

My aunt and I took the herbs to the household well by the kitchen. Following her instructions, I laid them upon a clean granite slab by the well and drew a bucket of water. A number of crows hung out by the kitchen during the day where they foraged grains and food thrown out at the bases of the coconut palms. At my approach, they flew up to a mango tree in a huff. Meanwhile, my aunt brought out a small plank and a knife from the kitchen.

"Drop the grass into the water, Shambu. Scrub the roots really clean of all mud."

I cleaned each individual tuft of grass and its bulbous root, then handed them to her. She carefully scraped the brown outer skin and arranged the grass neatly into a bundle upon the plank. Then she cut the grass leaves from the roots. Cupping her left palm around the small bulbs, she smashed them with the end of the knife handle. This we took into the kitchen.

In the kitchen, Aunt Preema and I found Aunts Susheela and Bhanu at work, assisted by Cousin Mohini.

"How is Sandhya doing, Preema?" asked Aunt Bhanu.

"She still has cramps and a headache."

"I am boiling a pot of water for tea. Would you like to use some?" asked Aunt Susheela.

"Good, good, that's what I need, and I want some ginger too," said Aunt Preema.

"I will slice some for you. Shambu, get me a root of ginger from the basket, dear," Aunt Bhanu said, pointing to a smoke-stained cane basket by the table.

After we prepared an herbal tea, I followed Aunt Preema into the women's room, where I found Sandhya seated on a purple quilt, wrapped up in a white sari. She held her abdomen in both hands, her brows furrowed as if in pain.

"Don't talk to her now, she is in pain," advised my aunt in a whisper.

I placed the tray that I was carrying and a mug of herbal tea close to Sandhya. I felt anxious about her, but did not speak. Aunt Preema snuggled close to Sandhya and cradled her head in her arms.

"Drink this tea, sweetie, it will give you relief," she said, holding the mug to Sandhya's lips. Sandhya opened her eyes and smiled weakly at me. She cupped the mug in her palms.

"Welcome to the woman's world, Shambu," Sandhya murmured, smiling. She began sipping the tea. I did not know what to say.

"Do you want to change places with me for the day, Shambu?" Sandhya asked between sips. My aunt giggled.

"You mean, sit here?"

"No, you buffoon. I meant, be me for the day," she corrected.

"What is happening, Aunt? Why is she in pain?"

"My little one has become a woman today," she said caressing Sandhya. I felt bad that Sandhya had to endure this pain.

"I didn't know it is painful to become a woman!" I said taking her hand in mine to comfort her.

They both giggled as my aunt hugged me. Sandhya tousled my hair saying, "Oh Shambu! I have yet to teach you many things."

▼ ▼ ▼

A few days later, on Amavasya day, I found an opportunity to approach my aunt with questions about the differences between men and women, especially in the context of Sandhya's first menstruation. As usual, Sandhya and I performed our meditation together in the morning; we anticipated the special Amavasya ritual later at night. At the behest of my aunt, we sat with her in the woman's room that afternoon.

My aunt began to explain the importance of Amavasya meditation by defining Amavasya as a cyclical period of mystical opportunity that occurred every lunar month, when the solar and lunar masses aligned themselves imposing their collective energies upon Earth.

"Amavasya is the first night of the first quarter of the lunar month, when the moon is invisible. Mystically, this is the period when the sun and the moon dwell together," she explained.

"The sun and moon are sensory manifestations of subtle but vaster entities of the masculine and feminine energies that govern this system. They have proportionate representations in each of us. The pervasive incinerating energy of the sun floods us during the day. This is seen as the fiery force of ha, the life forces that course through pingala, the right channel of the astral self. The sun is the extroverted, masculine presence casting its light and energy of action upon the physical domain. Every shape is thrown into sharp relief by this light of logic. This is the domain of the physical mind, physical awareness. But, this very light is blinding!" she warned, giving us a sharp look.

"It blinds what?" I asked, bewildered.

"It obscures the realm of intuition, and pushes it into the background," she cautioned, shaking her finger at us.

"The moon, on the other hand, sheds the light of feminine, intuitive energy. This represents the dream awareness and the intuitive mind. Like the moon, this awareness waits for the sun to sleep, waits for clamor of the day to calm. Then it shines . . . softly . . . after dark. It is the light shining on the secret path. This is equated to the tha energy that courses through ida, the left channel of the astral self. Objects are not thrown into sharp relief by this light. Instead, shapes blur into each other. Nor is this domain restricted by the rules of logic. The intuitive mind is fully expressed when the physical mind sleeps."

"Aunt Preema, is the night filled with feminine energy?"

"Yes, Shambu. The night is female. When you are awake at night, the physical mind is apprehensive of the dark, because it is in an alien realm—a realm of alien awareness. Twilight is the best time to meditate, to begin quieting the physical mind. For it is during twilight that either the night transits into the day or the day into the night. It is the perfect time when the physical mind begins to wind down and the intuitive mind takes over, a brief period when these two minds can be brought to each other's awareness. Twilight is a good time to still the physical mind without putting it to sleep, and to connect with the intuitive mind. That is the secret path. The physical mind learns to lay aside its fear and to relinquish control. It gradually perceives the intuitive mind. Having done this, it merges with the intuitive mind. This is Amavasya, the merging of the masculine into the feminine, just as the energy of the sun is absorbed by the energy of the intervening moon," said my aunt.

According to my aunt, Amavasya is the conjunction of the sun and the moon; a time when the earth is shielded from solar astral energy. Mystically, it is a time when the logical mind is deprived of solar astral support and the intuitive mind becomes dominant because of the overwhelming presence of lunar astral energy. While the solar astral energy is assimilated by the moon, the masculine ha astral energy merges with the tha astral energy in the being of an initiate. At this time, initiates into mystical mysteries can easily withdraw the outflowing sensory awareness of the physical mind, and route it to reinforce the dream awareness of the intuitive mind, thus merging the male with the female.

In normal humans, the ha and the tha energies remain separate and unbalanced in their flow, causing varied "disorders of perception" from the mystical standpoint. But Amavasya is a natural, cyclical opportunity when planetary and astral forces join and prepare an environment favorable for the merging and harmonizing of the corresponding astral energies in an initiate.

"Mother, you said that the sun and moon have masculine and feminine representations in our beings. Does Earth have a similar representation?"

"Our bodies are of Earth. Earth represents the instinctive, grosser female in you and me. The feminine representation by the moon, on the other hand, is in the supernatural, intuitive, feminine energy in us. Is this aspect clear?"

"Yes," Sandhya nodded.

"The solar ha energy of pingala is life force, and the lunar tha energy of ida is consciousness and awareness. Life force is moving . . . and . . . and active and forceful as the name implies," said my aunt animatedly. "But consciousness and awareness are mere presences, subtle telltale wisps of the willow. The dream mind's awareness does not come from a logic that blunders through with force and tedium. It is an all-pervasive knowingness of being." My aunt dropped her voice to a tender whisper.

"Amavasya is the night when the masculine, joined with the feminine force, dwells in the neutral. This inner joining is often preceded by a physical joining among some odiyyas. This is why odiyya couples join. The outward joining of bodies done with devotion, in the presence of the preceptor, is a powerful technique that ushers in the inner joining of energies. But ununited, the ha and the tha energies are unbalanced and ineffective to awaken kundalini. Compare them to two rivers. By themselves, each one has limited energy. But when they come together at a confluence, their combined power is mighty enough to cleave mountains that stand in their path," she said.

What my aunt said was overwhelming. I remembered my experience during the awakening ritual. I knew that Sandhya had the same thoughts pass through her mind, because she gave me a glance.

"The male and the female have great powers that, when properly joined, can benefit each other for mutual awakening," Aunt Preema said.

My aunt said that until Amavasya, just as the sun and the moon are separate, there is a polarity within each individual, a split in the astral energy that manifests as an incomplete female and her breakaway male. Amavasya is the night of joining that entails a brief period of chaos, a chaos resulting from interpenetrating energies in the process of merging. The male energy merges with the female, ceasing all polarities, just as the sun surrenders its astral energy to the moon during their conjunction. This union makes it possible for the being to shine with the full splendor of completely expressed light of intuition. The period from Amavasya to Poornima (full moon) symbolizes the individual's gradual awakening and transcendence into the fullness of being, to shine with the light of the full moon. After absorbing the masculine energy, the feminine self shines replete. As with each night a fresh facet of the moon is brought to light, the mystics experience this awakening gradually. Thus, like the sixteen phases of the emerging moon, the mystics identify sixteen kalas or aspects of the Divine Mother emerging in them.

In the initiate, the emergence of each aspect of the Divine Female is heralded by a unique celestial harmony, which is heard as a syllable. On each night of meditation from Amavasya to Poornima, sixteen different syllables manifest as the joined, androgynous energy ascends through the central astral channel called Sushumna. On the sixteenth night, this energy is absorbed in the light of the Divine Mother. The combined sound of these sixteen syllables is heard by mystics as the mantra *Shoodashaksharii*—meaning "She Whose Form is of Sixteen Syllables." My aunt said that what the Divine Mother revealed in Her totality is experienced by the initiate as a sixteen-armed goddess (each arm representing a phase of the moon and revealing an aspect of her divinity). In this form the goddess embodies her benign and destructive functions. I asked my aunt to explain this.

"With the eight arms on Her right, the Divine Mother creates and nurtures the universe. And at the height of Her benevolence, Her uppermost arm of Her eight right arms is lifted high, palm and fingers open in divine benediction. The uppermost of Her left arms holds a scimitar with which the Divine Mother begins to dissolve the universe. And the bottommost left arm holds a severed head, symbolic of complete annihilation," she explained.

The light of the full moon is considered the light of the Divine Mother. That is why the odiyyas, mystics, and the tantriks consider full moon meditation a special spiritual treat, similar to Amavasya meditation which symbolizes awakening. While mystical experiences on an Amavasya night signal the transmutation of an initiate into an awakened mystic, mystical experiences carried through into the full moon transform this awakened one into an active mystic.

Aunt Preema expounded that a female was modeled after the Divine Mother, which endowed women with faculties symbolic of the cosmic functions of the great creatrix Herself. I was assailed with questions on my own significance as a male, in the context of this casuistry.

"Aunt Preema, could it be true, then, that the male is modeled after Iswara?"

"Male and female are the obverse and reverse of each other, depending on what is projected into sensory reality," she explained.

"Can you explain this, Mother? Male and female are obverse and reverse of what?"

"I have already explained to you that every physical object has astral roots. And a sentient body has an astral self, not a root," she said. "The astral self is androgynous, as it is grounded in a realm more subtle than our physical one. The more subtle the realm, the lesser the objects therein are fragmented by dualisms that plague our world. This is a fundamental spiritual law."

"What is a dualism, Aunt?"

"A dualism is a tension of two principles, each embodying the contrasting features of the other. But their very contrast is what causes the opposing principle to emerge as an object of perception in this realm. Therefore, what you physically perceive is the obverse of that which is hidden from your perception, the hidden being the reverse. Thus you have the obverse and the reverse, which with their antithetical qualities mutually support each other's existence," explained my aunt animatedly.

"Oh, Mother! Can't you give a simple example?" asked Sandhya in exasperation, her brows furrowed with growing irritation. I was thankful for her intervention.

"Both of you close your eyes and imagine a light . . . Tell me what you see."

"I see an oil lamp, its wick glowing with a flame," I said, beaming, my eyes screwed shut as I watched my imaginary flame.

"I see a homa fire, Mother," said Sandhya.

"All right, so both of you see a flame. Look around the flame; tell me what you see."

"Nothing, Mother, just air, I suppose."

"I see a glow around the flame, Aunt."

"Look beyond the light, what do you see?"

"Blackness—darkness, Aunt."

"I see darkness too, Mother!"

"Try and imagine sunlight surrounding both your flames."

"But my flame is at night, Aunt Preema. There is no other light then."

"Well, imagine your flame during the day, in bright sunlight . . . Tell me what you see."

"It is difficult to see the flame, Mother!"

"I cannot distinguish the flame at all, Aunt!"

"Open your eyes, both of you. Now do you realize that without darkness you cannot see the flame? When I asked you to imagine a flame, you perceived only the flame, even though the darkness was around the flame. But when I asked you to look at the darkness, the darkness appeared in your perception in the contrasting light of the flame. So the flame you perceived was the obverse of the unperceived darkness. That is the tension of dualism. Look around you, this world is a spin-off of dualism into multiplicity."

"So when we brought the flame into sunlight, the flame disappeared because there was no darkness," I said.

"By taking the flame into sunlight, you banished dualism. With dualism removed, there were no differences to perceive. The contrasting qualities in the opposing principles of light and darkness sustain each other in this realm of physical perception. If you remove one, the other disappears. What is revealed is unity."

"Where do they go, Mother?"

"Their disappearance is an act of merging into each other. They still exist, but they disappear from our field of perception. Dualism is the basis of all physical perception. If dualism is removed, we perceive unity," Aunt Preema explained. "In a male being, the female acts as the reverse. Maleness is projected into the realm of perception and acts as the obverse. In a female being, the female is the obverse with the male hidden. In most of us, our physical mind is most active in the day-to-day reality of living. Therefore, others perceiving you as male and your self-perception constantly reinforces the impression of you being male, Shambu. It is the same with you, Sandhya. Your femaleness is reinforced by perception."

At once, I was reminded of my transfigurative experiences at the awakening ritual.

"Aunt, can a male become a female and vice versa?"

"Yes, dear, when you first experience yourself as the astral self, through certain practices, you perceive the reverse of what you are in the physical realm. This is a momentary experience before your astral self reintegrates into its androgynous existence as a transsexual being in the other realm."

"Like during the initiation?" asked Sandhya, giving me a knowing glance.

"Yes, Sandhya. This must be your experience too," she answered with a questioning look. "From the neutrality of the Great Void emerged the supreme Mother Kali. She is the originator of movement and thence space-time and all subsequent dualism. Kali is the supreme obverse of the great stillness of the Void. The Great Void is the power to be, while Kali is the power to become and move. From Her emerged Shakti-Shiva, the supreme androgynous principle. We are modeled after Mother Kali, especially we women," my aunt said.

There she goes again, with her superwoman stuff! I thought.

"Women give birth to males and females. Maleness buds from a fundamental female substratum as a product of segregation from the female—a more dense derivative of the female emerging from the more subtle to the more gross planes of expression. From the grand unity of principles in the beginning of creation to the gross expression in this physical plane, there has been a gradual segregation of principles in the process of the emergence of dualism. From the subtle substratum emerged gross derivations; with more dualism, there was multiplicity. Now multiplicity becomes a substratum from which more sophisticated forms are fashioned."

"Mother, we see Mother Kali dancing upon Shiva. How would you explain this if Shiva is a product of Kali?" I was glad Sandhya asked this question.

"Just as you see pictures of Kali dancing upon the recumbent Shiva, you can also visualize Shiva dancing upon a recumbent Kali," my aunt said, laughing. "Whatever is suppressed here has to express itself somewhere else. The female is suppressed in the physical realm, but she expresses herself in the inner realms. Just as Shiva dances his Tandava upon the sublimated ogre of self-importance, so does Kali perform her dance of joy, united with her male obverse Shiva. These dances are figurative expressions of the progressive reabsorption of gross dualisms into their subtle overstrata, experiencing an ever-expanding joy of cosmic unity. The activities of the derivative forms are struck down and these forms are assimilated into the higher whole. Shiva is the supreme male derivative of the protofemale Para-Shakti or Kali.

"Maleness and femaleness stops at the astral plane. Beyond this there is unity of this dualism in its forms, with the distinction of gender retained only in the energy of transformation. Beings in the subtle realm transform their gender identities by sheer intent," she said.

According to my aunt, the female principle is supreme among dualisms. She also alluded to Shiva as a derivative of Kali. But this contradicted the mythological origins of Bhadra Kali. I remembered a story wherein Kali sprang into existence when, in a fit of anger, Shiva plucked a couple of tufts from his matted locks and threw them upon the ground. Bhadra Kali and Vira Bhadra sprang into existence from these locks. I broached my doubts to Aunt Preema in the light of this story.

"It seems, Aunt Preema, that it was Shiva who brought Kali into manifestation. In fact it appears that Kali is the crystallization of Shiva's base emotions, such as anger!" I exclaimed, vindicating the superiority of my gender.

"The ego-principle usually manages to solve its problems with the help of the logical mind. But there are times when it cannot. At such moments the ego relinquishes its control, invoking and accepting the subtle astral mind. The story of Shiva illustrates that. With his mate Sati destroyed, he was helpless. In a fit of helpless rage, he surrendered his maleness into his reverse, the female in him. His act of pulling his hair is symbolic of the surrender of the lesser ego to the higher mind. Kali emerged, along with her minion Vira Bhadra. The history of humankind is replete with instances when the higher mind has come to the rescue of men and women in crisis."

"That is a consolation, hearing that women, too, had a lesser mind, Aunt Preema," I said laughing.

"The ego principle in the female can be as gross as the ego principle in the male. But what matters is the ability of the ego to surrender its energies to the higher astral mind. The female seems to do this easier than the male. The male mind seems to entrench itself in the physical realm, thus making it difficult to let go and surrender. This is the only other reason why the male is considered a derivative of the female. Separation from parts of one's self is painful. Separation disrupts equilibrium and promotes anger. Unity promotes surrender and joy," explained my aunt.

At that moment, Radhika poked her face into the room, announcing tea. We thanked Aunt Preema as we departed. It would be several days before we were treated to another illuminating discourse from Aunt Preema.

▼ ▼ ▼

Our village supported a school, which we attended from morning till noon. Over a hundred students from all the households attended this school. Apart from the grammar, mathematics, science, and literature that we learned, boys and girls over 17 studied ayurveda, elements of astrology, and crop planting. Sandhya was in a different class because boys and girls were segregated after puberty.

One day after school Aunt Preema summoned Sandhya and me to her room. She said that it was time that we began our formal education in the scriptures.

"I have informed your teacher that you two will be studying with her," my aunt said. "This is a great privilege as she does not normally accept any students. Consider yourselves fortunate, children."

"When do we begin, Aunt Preema?" I asked brimming with enthusiasm.

"Well, tonight just after sunset is an auspicious time to introduce yourselves to your teacher and the scriptures," she said and gave us precise instructions on how to introduce ourselves and made us practice this introduction. Her explanation was that the teacher was somewhat particular about these formalities.

Just before sunset, my mother prepared a light meal for Sandhya and me. After our meal, we took a purificatory dip in the pond in preparation for our visit with our teacher. Aunt Preema sent us off, each with a cloth bundle of offerings. In addition, we carried two palm-frond torches to light our way back home.

It took us forty-five minutes to wend our way to the teacher's residence. The bundle that I carried reeked of alcohol. Within the bundle, I felt the shape of a bottle, inside which some liquid sloshed, with my movements.

"It's toddy, I am sure," said Sandhya when I sniffed at the bundle.

"You can smell it!" I was amazed, as I picked up the odor only then.

"Smell my bundle and you might vomit," commented Sandhya with a tinge of disgust while she thrust it under my nose. I pulled back my head in haste as the distinct smell of putrefied flesh hit my nostrils.

Normally Sandhya and I would skip and run to any place whenever we were sent out on errands. But tonight we felt weighed down by Aunt Preema's instructions on the precise formality with which we were expected to greet our new teacher, plus the personality of the teacher was an unknown and intimidating factor, considering the "offerings" we carried to her.

Aghori Narayani was a mystic who lived in a barn-sized shed in a secluded grove behind our village temple and close to the colony of the vallichappads. It was almost dark when we walked up the wide, broken brick steps that led to her huge plank door. At that precise moment a loud raspy voice issued from behind the massive door, startling us.

"Walk around the mandala. It took me hours to draw it!"

We hastly sidestepped a large mandala of elaborate design drawn upon the hard mud at the entrance. Sandhya cast a glance at me with a slight smirk. Gingerly we pushed the massive door open. Contrary to my fears, a pleasant mixture of fragrances from flowers, incense, and wood smoke assailed our nostrils.

"Come in, come right in. Here, over here," said the aghori, grinning, and waved us to a space beside her. She was a large woman who looked to be in her early 50s, and she sat upon a mattress of sorts, made from neatly bundled piles of hay covered with a broad buffalo skin. She had her hair in an untidy heap upon the crown of her head, held in place by a wooden comb with a broad handle that looked like a ladle. As I scrutinized her, I could not help feel a rising sense of loathsomeness. She had on a white dhoti, which she tied at her waist like a man, while her large pendulous breasts draped over her belly, like two enormous brown jackfruits.

Before her, a log fire blazed in a ritual fire-pit that was built into the floor of the shed. A crude wooden tripod supported a human skull, in the hollow of which she had stuffed what looked like rice pudding. A buffalo skull lay beside this tripod of human skull. I was so engrossed with the bizarre details of the environment that I was startled when Sandhya ribbed me with her elbow.

"Namastae Shree Maha Mayaee!" we intoned as we prostrated before her.

"Namastae Chinmayae Jagadeeswarii Mahaeeswarii," the aghori replied, and to our consternation, she fell at our feet.

"Ha! Ha! Ha!" she cackled. "Caught you by surprise, didn't I? Let's wave arati at the Divine Mother. Come."

"Mother Aghori," I called tremulously, "we have these for you." Sandhya and I extended the bundles toward her.

"Ah! Preema knows me like her own sister. May the Great Shakti bless her!" She took the bundles from us and dropped them onto her buffalo skin and hay mattress.

Red cotton drapes hung down the entire surface area of the walls. But the wall at the far end of the room, facing the door, was black, and upon it was a two-dimensional relief of Kali. She was about twelve feet tall. Even with a cursory look, I knew that this was no work of art. Kali's face and body were misshapen. Nine kuttuvilakkus were arrayed in a semicircle at Kali's feet.

"I carved that woman myself," said the aghori, watching me stare at Kali. "Isn't she gorgeous?" she asked almost in a whisper, as a mother would refer to her daughter.

"Eh . . . the face . . ." I began but Sandhya pinched my rump and cut me off in a hurry saying, "She is so beautiful!"

"Hmm!" said the aghori, beaming.

Our lessons began with chanting Kali's thousand and eight ascriptions. Over the days and weeks that followed we studied Sanskrit and the scriptures. The aghori made us memorize the Amarakosham, a classic Sanskrit thesaurus in verse.

Aghori Narayani never used any modern instruments of learning, such as books or chalk-boards, to conduct her lessons. Sometimes we sat by the fire-pit, around a large wooden tray of fine river sand. The aghori wrote the scriptures upon this sand with her index finger, straight from memory. She exhorted us to memorize verses from the scriptures, as well as aphorisms describing rules of grammar.

Each evening, we spent two hours with the aghori memorizing scriptural verses and studying grammar. Apart from these formal studies, she supplemented our education with insights from her personal mystical experiences. She was grave at times, but never stern; in fact, most of the time she was slightly mischievous. Before long Sandhya and I began to like her.

It became common for our household to see us blazing our way home after dark with our brightly-lit torches. My father taught me how to select dry coconut leaves and weave them into torches, so I kept Sandhya and myself supplied with these. Aunt Preema would always wait for us to return home before she partook of her supper.

# CHAPTER FIVE

## *Forces from Beyond*

By the end of our fourth year with Aghori Narayani, our relationship with her could be described as cozy, friendly, and less formal. But intermixed with these feelings were disgust and fear. We found her loathsome because of her total disregard of things considered by society as sacred, clean, and hygienic. This was especially evident in the things that she ate and drank, which smelled foul and looked nothing like what we knew as food. She cooked her food in the sacred fire pit and ate out of a human skull.

Initially, our studies with her were in the late evenings. The aghori taught us chants and rituals; often she put us to work around the barn. Our fear had stemmed from certain inexplicable incidents that both Sandhya and I encountered over the first few years of our association. Aghori Narayani had begun to push us into the strange realm of the odiyyas.

On several occasions we noticed a pack of five large dogs with the nondescript, short, reddish-brown fur that characterized mongrels in front of the aghori's barn. One evening, while we were yet a few hundred feet from the barn, the dogs saw us approach. They stopped whatever they were doing and began to yelp. Then a large female dog from among them slipped into the barn through the door. The rest trotted away behind the barn and disappeared into the bush country beyond.

When we entered the barn, we saw the aghori seated as usual in front of her fire. She appeared to be in trance. Her bloodshot eyes were fixed unblinkingly at the flames. Sandhya hastily stifled a greeting. The dog was nowhere to be seen. But I had been so sure I saw the dog enter the barn. From the look on Sandhya's face, I knew that she was equally perplexed. Throughout that session the aghori was strangely serious. We set our minds on finishing our studies with her to get home quickly.

We would have sought Aunt Preema's counsel, but she was off on a trip with some of her female companions to collect herbs. Therefore the mystery remained unsolved for several days. I remembered two other occasions in the past when my aunt had made these trips with her friends. Aunt Preema was somewhat of a nonconformist: she never explained where she went or what she did during these forays into the hills. Nor did any of the matriarchs question her. Even though our matriarchy upheld great power for women of our clan, women on the lower rungs of the power structure were usually subservient to those above them. Aunt Gauri was the only one who voiced her opposition. My impression was Aunt Gauri felt my aunt's outlandish ways somehow infringed upon Gauri's own future role as the matriarch.

A few days later, on Aunt Preema's return, Sandhya and I described the incident and asked for an explanation.

"If you both saw the dog disappear, then the dog did disappear. Why would that need an explanation?" my aunt asked.

"How can something disappear just like that? There is no other exit from the barn," I argued.

"If you saw the dog disappear, then the dog disappeared," repeated my aunt with a blank look on her face. Sandhya and I felt that she was hiding something from us.

"Please, Mother, tell us what is happening," implored Sandhya.

"The aghori is strange, Aunt. She is unpredictable," I added.

"We are afraid to study with her," Sandhya said.

"The aghori has her ways. There is no need to fear. No harm will come to you from her, I assure you," Aunt Preema said. My aunt who was usually sweet and explained everything with patience was now taciturn. This increased our fears.

"Mystical experiences cannot be explained. Explain it and you may shatter the experience. Explanations are demanded by the physical mind. How can this lesser mind explain the experiences of the higher mind? Tell me," asked my aunt. Then after a pause she added, "Enjoy your experiences. Have patience with the aghori. She has her ways."

One evening a few days later, the aghori gave us some chants to memorize and walked out of the barn, saying that she would be back after some errands. After a few scores of repetitions, I decided to probe around the inside of the barn, while still saying the chants. Sandhya was by my side instantly. The mystery of the dog's disappearance was uppermost in our minds.

Red drapes hung from the walls on the long sides of the room. We gingerly lifted the bottom of these drapes and inspected the walls for exits, but we saw only the brick wall. There were no holes or passages through which even a mouse could pass, let alone a large dog. The back wall held the imposing two-dimensional image of Kali; Her eyes glowered down upon us. The wall here was bare for all to see. I returned to my seat.

A slight movement from the far wall attracted my attention and immediately Sandhya gripped my shoulder with a guttural whimper. Seated on the floor near Kali's feet was the large female dog. She gazed at us with strange luminous eyes. I shivered with fright. At that very moment, the barn door flew open behind us and the aghori burst in bringing a gust of cold night air.

"Ah! My children, you are praying to Kali! Good . . . Good."

I thought that I detected a glint of mischief in her eyes. When we turned around, the female dog was nowhere in sight, as if a trap door had opened beneath and it had fallen through.

"Mother Aghori, there was a dog in here!" I exclaimed, pointing at that spot.

"Dog? I see neither dog nor cat," she replied.

"But, it was there, I saw it, too," confirmed Sandhya.

The aghori squinted and cocked her head at the spot and pronounced, "Either my eyes are growing old and my sight is getting dimmer, or you two are seeing things." Then she looked about her as if searching something. Her eyes fell upon a dark brown, hollow gourd that hung suspended from the rafter midway to the floor. At the sight of it, a knowing smile played about her lips as she began a slow nod of her head.

"Did you drink some of this?" she asked taking the gourd down and popping the cork of its mouth.

A stench hit our nostrils. I heard Sandhya grunt her breath out in a desperate attempt to keep the smell off. The stench was indescribable; the foulest of foul smells that I have smelled.

"You must have sipped this. Have you?" she asked us as she came toward us with the gourd.

"No, we didn't—and we don't want to," said Sandhya emphatically, taking a step backward.

The aghori stopped in her tracks and stood with her mouth ajar.

"Hey! Who said I was going to give this to you?" she remarked defensively, at once clutching the gourd to her bare bosom. I could not help notice the fact that the gourd looked like a third pendulous breast on her chest. I began to smile at her comical seriousness contrasted by Sandhya's open display of disgust. The aghori caught me eyeing the gourd between her dusky breasts. Her eyes widened and a grin broke out on her face.

"Shambu, you have an eye for aesthetics," she declared and began to jiggle her breasts along with the gourd. That blew off the lid of respect that clamped down my mirth, and I burst into a belly laugh. Soon the three of us were beside ourselves with glee. The aghori took several swigs from the gourd.

"Really, it's not that bad, you know. The effects are wonderful," the aghori said holding the gourd out at arm's length.

I was getting curious about the "wonderful effects."

"I'd like to try a little," I surprised myself with this request. I noticed a subtle expression of disbelief on Sandhya's face.

"Here, this is good for now," the aghori said as she poured about ten or fifteen drops of the dark greenish-brown liquid into a small coconut shell and handed it to me. I held my breath as I swallowed it. The liquid tasted astringent and bitter. Within a few moments I felt a mild burning travel all the way down my gullet into my stomach. Pleasant warmth and a strange buzz—that was more of a sensation than a sound—spread out of my belly and reached every part of my body.

While these curious sensations engaged my attention, a part of me watched Sandhya receive a similar portion of the liquid from the same coconut shell.

▼ ▼ ▼

I must have lost track of events, for I could not remember when we began running, or what else transpired between the time we took our swigs of the liquid and the time we began running. But, here I was, trotting at a comfortable speed through the bushes.

Momentarily, I checked to see if Sandhya was with me, and sure she was, trotting alongside on my right. Often, we parted for short periods of time as bushes and boulders intervened. At times our clothes touched as the terrain permitted us to run shoulder to shoulder. Ahead of me was the aghori, and I was amazed that a woman of her age and hulk could lead us with such ease, especially in this terrain. She ran in a peculiar fashion, her head bobbing ahead of her as she stooped forward.

Something about the terrain puzzled me. It was almost dark, but I could see everything with great acuity. My head was close to the ground, and sometimes the foliage whipped by my face. Then, incredible smells wafted past.

I played with my new discovery for a while. The aghori, for example, had a strong smell, that swept over me with the shifting wind as she ranged ahead. I kept track of Sandhya's familiar smell as we weaved in and out of mutual proximity.

Then I saw something peculiar about Sandhya; she ran on all fours. After watching this for a while, I realized that I did the same. It was incredible! Curiously, I did not feel my limbs as they stretched and crossed each other with every gallop. The sense of power was astounding. I was master of the terrain. Some strong scents indicated that there were others in the vicinity.

Instantly, the aghori slowed down, giving out a high pitched yelp. Several answering yelps and whines came from the bushes on either side. Soon five dogs emerged from the bushes and trotted along with us—the same dogs that visited the barn! The large female dog snuggled close to the aghori and they ran shoulder to shoulder. After trotting for several more minutes we slowed down to a fast walk.

Presently, we arrived at a little brook. The large female dog led us to it and after a drink we sat upon the grass. Sandhya sat close to me and I felt the slick moistness of her sweat as her arm rubbed against mine. Darkness had fallen all around us and a fading trace of twilight smeared over the land. I observed the dogs that now lay on the grass panting. I watched the female closely. This was the closest we ever came to these dogs.

"This is the dog we saw back at your place. This is the one," whispered Sandhya to the aghori. At that moment the female rolled over onto its feet and came to us.

"Meet Odiyatthi Nedunga, my sister disciple. She is a good dog," the aghori said and roared with laughter. Sandhya and I did not laugh—we were quite disconcerted.

The aghori sensed our confusion and explained, "Odiyatthi Nedunga has chosen this form to interact with the human world. As you can see, in this form her interaction with humans is very limited. No humans can really mingle with her. Ha! Ha! All she does is come to the fringes of our village and meet me at my place," she said, cackling.

At that point the female dog came close to us and put Sandhya and me through an extensive sniffing. Aghori Narayani was beside herself with glee at our discomfort. Having satisfied herself, the female dog went back to her pack.

"Now, these four are Nedunga's longtime disciples. This one here is Kora. He is her oldest disciple," explained the aghori. At the mention of his name, the dog thumped his curly tail, throwing up pieces of sticks and dry leaves in the process. Kora had a burly look, as if he had been in many street fights.

"That one over there is Rangan," she said pointing to a dog with a dark brown tip on his tail. "That is Chunda," she pointed to the one lying furthest from us. Pointing out to the one closest to us, she said, "And this is Pandi."

The dog named Kora sat up and uttered a low belly growl. In an instant, the rest of them were upon their feet and took up the rumbling growl. For some reason I did not feel any aggression in their display. It was as if they expected others. Their growls turned to muted barks. I felt a slight tremor in my belly. For a few moments I thought that I was having the shakes; then I realized that I was growling from the belly, too.

"They are here," whispered the aghori.

"Who are here?" asked Sandhya anxiously.

"You will see. They are coming."

We looked around, peering into bushes and spaces between boulders. Then Sandhya produced a deep-throated growl. I was puzzled. A peculiar force surged through my body. A savage energy rippled under my skin. Soon I let out a belly growl.

"Calm down, there is no need for such agitation," the aghori exhorted. But the power was unnerving and exhilarating. The only way I knew to soothe it was to allow it to manifest its savage energy. The aghori felt our state of mind, for she said, "They who come from the forest are wild. Your awareness senses the wildness of their energy. Digest your power and it will emerge refined."

"How?" I asked.

The aghori gave me a sharp look. Then a smile flickered in the corners of her mouth.

"Jump, jump like this," she said, hopping on all fours like a deer. It felt foolish, but I hopped beside the aghori.

"Ease it back. Ease it back," she urged.

A sudden placidity came over me. I began to feel at ease.

"It is fear of their unearthly energy that prompts this surge of power in you. You sense an otherworldly energy," said the aghori.

The next instant the dogs began a low moan, which developed into a canine symphony of sorts. They all fell silent abruptly. The ground trembled beneath us. A mysterious rumble filled the air. Then there was stillness, utter quietude. The dogs stood rock steady, almost rigid. I was terrified seeing the hair on the dogs go stiff, giving them an enlarged appearance.

They appeared from the bushes, probably scores of them. At first I thought they were jackals. But on careful scrutiny, I found them to be large canines with dark stripes. They sat there glowering at us, with not a movement or sound.

"Who . . . who are they?" I asked when I found my voice.

"Children, look at them well," the aghori said loudly. "You now have your first glimpse of the woodland odiyyas. These are truly wild (non-humans). Their practices in the course of centuries have helped them accumulate vast amounts of power."

"Centuries!" I heard Sandhya exclaim under her breath.

"Not here on earth. They appear from a dimension adjoining ours," said the aghori.

"Is that how they have been disconnected from humanity?" I asked with a tremor in my voice.

"These have never been part of humanity in the first place. Watch them. Now," ordered the aghori.

"These are beings from the boundary. Beings from the boundary," repeated the aghori.

Her last words grabbed my attention. They took me back a few years when Aunt Preema said these same words to Sandhya and me, during our ritual of the initiation of awakening. Aunt Preema said the same about the ravens. As my mind drifted along these thoughts, the aghori's voice intruded, "Watch their eyes, children. Now, be ready!"

At that moment, the eyes of those striped creatures grew as large as saucers, with a bright yellow-green luminescence. The next instant I felt lifted as if by a strong puff of wind.

I felt someone shaking me vigorously. I opened my bleary eyes and caught Sandhya in the act of waking me up. It was very dark, except for one oil lamp that cast a faint orange glow all around. I raised myself up on my elbow, only to collapse back to the floor. At length, I mustered the strength to sit up. Fatigue claimed my muscles. Sandhya and I were in the aghori's barn.

"How long was I asleep? I had this fantastic dream . . ." I began, but Sandhya interrupted me, saying, "Yes, you ran with me, the aghori, and the dogs . . ."

"How do you know my dream?" I exclaimed in amazement.

"It is no dream, Shambu. If it is a dream, then I dreamt it, too."

I was overwhelmed. I looked around—we were in the barn all right. I looked up at the gourd and saw it suspended as usual from the rafters.

"Where is the aghori?"

"She is not here. I woke up only moments before you did, Shambu."

"I think we should go home now, Sandhya."

"Yes, I guess it's very late. We should tell Mother about this. What do you think, Shambu?"

"Of course, we should. Only Aunt Preema can explain as to what is happening to us," I agreed.

We lit our torch and headed home as fast as we could walk. We dared not run for fear of extinguishing the flaming torch. Aunt Preema was waiting for us. She greeted us at the entrance saying, "My . . . my! You are in an awful hurry to get home! Are the hyenas after you, or what?"

"Mother, how did you know about the hyenas?"

"I know Aghori Narayani like I know the lines on my palm. We will discuss this tomorrow. Now you should have your meals and get some sleep." Aunt Preema replied.

I slept lightly, with my mind busily processing all the images from our extraordinary experience. The numerous times that I lay awake, I was subject to impressions of green grass, other foliage, and stones, all fleeting past close by my face.

I woke up fatigued. I felt drained. Sandhya felt the same. Somehow we sat through our early morning session of chanting, with drowsiness claiming our minds frequently. Aunt Preema prepared a rice and vegetable broth for breakfast and served it to us. Then, in an unprecedented act, she bid us snooze for awhile.

It was noon when Aunt Preema woke us up for our midday meals. The two to three hours of deep slumber left me somewhat refreshed. After our meals, my aunt led us away from our home, toward a secluded spot under the shade of the coconut grove by the edge of the paddy fields.

"Power, as I have mentioned several times, is the basis of all transformations," Aunt Preema began without any preamble. She used the Sanskrit word Shakti for power. "Among all classes of beings, the odiyyas have gathered it in abundance and are most dexterous in its use."

"Do you mean that the odiyyas are more powerful than the divine beings of the higher realms?" Asked Sandhya.

"Dexterity is often more useful than raw power," answered my aunt. "The divine beings of the subtle realms are less dexterous, but they may have more power by virtue of the fact that they have subtle bodies to contain and channel cosmic astral energy. The more subtle the realm, the more vast the consciousness of the being who dwells there. Such expanded consciousness commands great power."

"Mother, the demons command great power, too. But they don't have expanded consciousness."

"True. Remember that with beings from higher realms, power is directly proportionate to their compassion and welfare for the beings in the lower worlds. But for beings such as the demons from the under world, power is proportionate to their greed and selfishness."

"Why are the odiyyas more dexterous than even the divine beings? That sounds like a contradiction to me when we know that the divine beings originate from a higher realm than that from which the odiyyas do," I asked.

"Power has to be channeled through the body-mind in order for it to be effective. This body-mind complex is unique to each realm, as it is the instrument through which the spirit projects this power. The divine beings are less dexterous in projecting power in this material plane because it is not habitual for them to interact physically with this realm. To interact physically with this plane, they have to acquire body-minds that are physical," explained my aunt.

"What prevents them from acquiring a suitable body-mind? Logically, beings from a higher realm should easily be able to accomplish this," commented Sandhya.

"Indeed, it appears to be so. But in truth, all classes of beings are bound by the inertia of the level of knowledge that determines their makeup, which distinguishes them from other beings. For example, we know that a mirage appears in the summer like a sheet of water along a stretch of road in the distance and is only the product of the heat haze. This is a knowledge-based conditioning that beings are encased in, material knowledge, as in this example.

"Consider this case; people assume that plants and trees are unintelligent compared to humans, therefore they are deemed incommunicable. This assumption introduces a mindset that prevents them from interacting with plants and trees. But the odiyya knows that plants and trees respond to human feelings and intuition, a level of awareness higher than intellect or reason-based communication and awareness. Therefore the odiyya has access to a vast consciousness unavailable to normal people."

"You mean plants can speak to us?" I asked.

My aunt looked at me for several moments thoughtfully. Then she said, "Yes, when you are ready to hear their voice. Normal people, who are higher in the scale of consciousness than plants and trees, prevent themselves from descending to the consciousness of the plant kingdom. Among the plant world, awareness is linked collectively in a loose fashion where cosmic awareness flows unhindered by ego barriers. The odiyyas consider this a great opportunity and immerse themselves in this awareness, while normal people limit their awareness within the barriers imposed by their material knowledge and their egos. Am I clear?" she asked. We nodded.

"Beings of higher realms are bound by limitations imposed by knowledge based body-mind, as opposed to a mindset."

"What do you mean, Mother? What is a mindset versus a body-mind?"

"A mindset is consciousness limited by partial knowledge, which is based on insubstantial and erroneous perceptions and conclusions. Partial knowledge puts up enormous barriers sustained by beliefs stemming from this knowledge. This is a mindset. As opposed to this, the simpleton has an open mind as he or she is in awe of everything.

"A well-learned materialist argues that the stone image in our temple is just a stone image, a lifeless piece of sculpture. But a simpleton believes that the image is possessed by divine power. Here, the materialist has a mindset fashioned by his limiting knowledge that precludes his mind from higher awareness. The simpleton is less informed, so his or her mind is less conditioned, thus opening the mind to higher awareness."

"So the simpleton has less of a mindset compared to a learned materialist," I said.

"Correct. A body-mind is just that, a body-mind. Now, a mindset can be considered to be a body-mind within a body-mind. Ideas compact into an impenetrable kernel of tough self-importance and create this mindset. Imprisoned in their own little world of ideas, these tough materialists barricade themselves from higher consciousness. They are like the proverbial frog in the well," she said.

"Belief-based conditioning prevents certain classes of beings from exercising their power. Belief without reason or intuition limits lesser minds in almost all classes of beings.

"The divine beings who inhabit higher realms are constrained by their knowledge. To acquire a human psyche they have to set aside their higher knowingness and limit themselves to the baggage of limitations that are inherent in being human, just as the material mind is unable to escape the limiting clutches of reason and descend to the level of the simpleton. The divine beings have to set aside their divine body-minds and take on a human frame to experience this realm.

"The odiyyas on the other hand, are thoroughly deconditioned—well, almost—yet retain their position within the material realm. This gives them the unique advantage of being able to ascend into the higher realms by affecting appropriate transformations to their body-minds. They are equally adept in descending into the lower realms, besides being able to transform shapes, as in assuming different animal forms. This dexterity is their strength. All this comes from constant deconditioning and incessant accumulation of power."

Continuous spells of cool breeze assuaged us in the heavy shade of the palm trees, even though the heat in the open fields was sizzling, causing the images of trees and leaves to continually break up just above ground level. Men in white raiment appeared to be dismembered in the shimmering heat as they moved among the ripening rice.

"I congratulate you both in acquiring some power, meager though it is," my aunt surprised us with this compliment. "It takes time, practice, and repeated familiarity with this power just to know that you have it, let alone manipulate it skillfully. The physical mind constructs many mundane explanations for this sublime experience. Be aware!"

"Was that what happened last night, Mother? Did we use our power?"

"Aghori Narayani controlled your power for you. You had just enough power to transform your body-mind partially into another life-form. As with any discipline, constant gathering of power and frequent exercises in shape transformation are required to master this talent."

"Aunt Preema, we both saw the large female dog within the barn for a few moments; then it disappeared. How could it appear and disappear?"

"Odiyyas can transform their mind-bodies into pure astral energy. Spatial and temporal barriers cannot confine them. They can range freely, unencumbered and not limited by conditions. Their one intent is freedom, and their only work is to gather power to fulfill this."

"What is power, Aunt? How do we know that we are gathering power?"

"Power is the use of life-energy in desired ways. Minute amounts of life-energy are used to perform the acts of daily living that define the life of a normal person. Life-energy powers countless interconnected mechanisms driving the human body in its movement through space-time. Similarly, countless motives, powered by astral energy, manifest the personality in a human being.

"In most humans, these motives sustain and entrench themselves by the continued appropriation of astral energy from the being within, and life-energy from food absorbed from without.

"To a large measure, the biological mechanisms that activate the body are driven to sustain their psychological cohabitants that define the personality. Thus, these motives tend to drain the being of its life-

energy. This interconnected web of motives and biological mechanisms appear like a behemoth without beginning or end."

My aunt paused and grabbed a decayed leaf from the sand. She
held it up to the light, revealing hundreds of tiny veins in a network
that defined the shape of the leaf.

"Look at this skeleton of a leaf. You cannot mark the beginning
or the end to this web of channels, can you? You just see them
branch out or drain into these larger channels," she said.

A strong breeze frisked the palm-leaf canopy. A dead palm frond
detached itself and, sliding down the trunk with a loud rasp, fell to
the ground.

"A human being is like this," she said, shaking the leaf at us. "It
is coexistence and interconnectedness of thousands of astral and biological channels, psychic motives, and biological mechanisms, all
meshed to form the body-mind."

Then, poking my chest with her finger, she said, "You are the result of power being manipulated by all these mechanisms that define
you. But this power itself is drained in the process." She paused.

"Consider this leaf again," she said. "If a drop of water is all the
power this leaf had for this moment, then, can you see how thin this
drop could be drawn by the time it is pulled through all the veins in
this network?

"When the limited power of a normal person is drawn through
the extensive meshes of a person's body-mind, he or she just exists
driven by a million motives. People drain more power reacting to
others, or to their environment. A person is left with no power for
transformation or proactive change. Such a person is powerless.

"But when a person halts the process of draining power through
such reactions, then he or she begins to gather power. Existence of
gathered power is evident when a person is able to effect changes in
habits, lifestyles, and character.

"When a person is able to project this power into the surroundings to manifest certain life goals, then this power becomes concrete.

"A person becomes power itself when he or she is able to transcend limitations impressed by gravity and space-time. Such a person has an undefined body-mind as an odiyya, a siddha or an
aghori." My aunt used the Sanskrit word *avyakta kayin* for undefined body-mind.

"Why did we have this experience, Mother?"

"Your experience last night was partly the ripening of your own
efforts at gathering power, and partly the grace of the odiyyas," my
aunt explained. "Aghori Narayani and her cohorts, who appeared as a

pack of dogs, initially aided you both to direct your power into changing your forms. The aghori knew that both of you have accumulated enough power for such an experience. It was she who summoned her cohort, Odiyatthi Nedunga, to activate your astral or dream awareness. It is power that enables us to activate this awareness in physical reality. The appearance of Odiyatthi Nedunga in the room as a dog helped couple your power to your dream awareness."

"Why didn't the aghori help us herself? Is Odiyatthi Nedunga more powerful than Aghori Narayani?" I asked, wondering why the aghori had to summon her cohort. My aunt gazed at me in silence for a few moments, then she spoke slowly.

"There are only three ways a neophyte can be led to such an experience. In the first category, the neophyte has gathered sufficient power to briefly dismantle his or her conditioning and initiate an experience within the protective envelope of the teacher's power.

"In the second category, the neophyte has only enough power to sustain a brief experience, but the teacher takes the responsibility to briefly dismantle the student's logical awareness for the duration of the experience.

"In the third category, the teacher floods the neophyte with her power and forces an experience because the student has not enough power for either of these tasks.

"The first is the best method because the student undergoes the experience under his or her own power, while the teacher uses her greater power to protect the student and to provide guidance into and out of the experience.

"The teacher's power, however benign, is foreign to the body-mind of the student. The least this is infused into the student the better, for the body-mind of the student can become dependent on the teacher's energy for spiritual growth.

"The third method is the least desirable, as the teacher blasts the logical mind away and carries the student through a turbulent stream of experience. Only the strongest devotion to the teacher can bring the student back to normality." My aunt paused as she gazed into the distance while my mind was busy categorizing myself within this above scheme.

"At all times the teacher is extremely careful and avoids any unnecessary infusion of her power into the student," she continued. "The teacher will use any trick that she can safely use to dismantle the student's logical mind for the purpose of conferring an experience."

Hearing this, Sandhya interjected in excitement, "I think that Aghori Narayani gave us some intoxicant from the gourd. Drinking that was the last thing I remember before I began to run through the woods."

"The drink was a ferment, all right. But I can assure you that it did not produce the experience. Besides, if this experience was hallucinogenic, how could both of you have an experience that corroborates in every detail and respect?" countered my aunt. "The aghori summoned her cohort to manifest in the room, thus unseating your logical mind. Then she skillfully manipulated your own energy vested in your assumptions about her, the pack of dogs, and the contents of her room, to loosen your stored power and couple it with your dream awareness.

"How, Aunt?"

"For example, she had noticed your assumptions about the properties of the contents of the gourd. Giving you the drink reinforced the coupling of power to your dream awareness, thus making it manifest in physical reality. Your assumptions about the properties of the drink did the trick, and not any actual hallucinogenic property that you considered it to have. There was no need for the use of any substances.

"Adepts can manipulate simple situations with great force so that the student is benefited and the teacher saves her power. They are always alert and on the lookout for such opportunities," she expounded.

Even though Aunt Preema corroborated the actuality of the experience to us, it seemed incredible to me. Thinking about the experience, I was amazed to note the uninterrupted continuation of the usual atmospheric changes induced by the passage of time and the setting of the sun, from one state of mind into the other. This suggested that the experience happened in real time and space. I felt that it was the mistake of processing this experience in retrospect with my logical awareness that gave rise to this incredulity.

"Indeed, when you think about it now, it defies explanation," commented my aunt, as if my incredulity was writ upon my face. "This is because your power is so trifling, unlike the power of the odiyyas that flows uninterruptedly day and night, constantly feeding their astral awareness.

"Do they not have a logical mind then, Mother?"

"When they can manipulate everything—including themselves—where is the need for such a burdensome division as a logical mind separate from their astral mind?" countered Aunt Preema.

"Why did we have the experience of being dogs? Why not some other animal or bird?"

"Shambu, odiyyas are almost totally unconditioned, as I explained earlier. Although with their power they can assume any form, they are consistent in assuming only one when dealing with normal people. This allows the logical awareness of normal people to transact sanely with the odiyyas. Logical awareness can deal only with stable forms. This is because it categorizes things in memory for future reference. If outside objects shift shape frequently, then inner references won't match, and the minds of normal people will be thrown into confusion.

"The aghori and her cohorts had been preparing you both for this experience for some time. Your own power was not enough to safely sustain and complete your experience last night. The aghori and her cohorts had to bolster you somewhat. Since they assumed dogs' form themselves, they chose the same for you. However, in order to return to the barn, you two rode the power of the woodland odiyyas. This change in power prevented you from getting accustomed to the power of the aghori and her cohorts."

"Mother, what would have happened if we had not gotten the help of the woodland odiyyas to complete the experience safely?"

"Then you would have had a long walk back to the barn," she said, laughing. "To experience the supernatural, the logical awareness has to be unhinged and the dream awareness has to be coupled to power. And then proper application of power is required every step of the way. Many things can go wrong during this process. An untrained and unprotected logical awareness can easily fall into the crack between space-times and will remain unhinged or become lost. Also there are predators who can consume your power if you are not protected.

"Predators like what, Mother?"

"Raiders of awareness. This is a subject that will lead us away from our current topic. I may explain that some other time.

"Logical awareness is the storehouse of references, limits, and conditions pertaining to you and this world. It holds the essence of your physical identity. Though limited, it contains everything you need to transact with this physical world. Dream awareness, however, is unlimited in its scope. But you are not yet trained in using dream awareness through your physical senses," concluded my aunt.

Time passed swiftly; we were so wrapped in the dissection of our experience that it was almost tea time. The sun slipped to the west, tinting the ripe paddy golden yellow. Nevertheless, the heat was still formidable. The men had begun to head to the cool shade of the grove for a brief respite; their approach signaled an end to our discussion. Aunt Preema did not meet with us again for several days.

# CHAPTER SIX

# *The Book of Aghora*

By the close of the summer of my 14th year, the men were busy retiling our homestead's extensive roof and effecting minor repairs to the wood rafters. Unseated tiles were repositioned and broken tiles were replaced. Bitumen, garnered from abandoned drums belonging to the Public Works Department, was mixed with fine sand and used to reseal the roofing joints. The monsoons would be heavy and the rains torrential—any holes in the roof would prove disastrous.

Since we boys were more nimble-footed and lighter than the older men, the task of inspecting the roof fell upon some of us. I clambered up the awning and crawled upon the tiles directly above the family shrine. It was past lunch and the shrine was closed. Creeping forward and gingerly distributing my weight along the rafters, I carefully inspected the tiles for fractures.

Some of the tiles were black with dried moss and lichen, and had been on the house for several years. I pulled one loose that was too old to be left on the roof. As I lifted it up by a corner, the entire tile crumbled like an old biscuit and parts of it fell through the hole into the loft below. A moment later, I heard a series of thuds as the pieces hit wood. My heart skipped a beat and I fervently prayed that the heavy fragments would not pierce the wooden floor of the loft and crash onto the centuries-old images in the shrine below.

I cast a covert look at my cousins. Busy as they were poring over the tiles themselves, none seemed to notice. With great care, I lifted five adjacent tiles, and with ample sunlight pouring into the loft, saw the broken fragments scattered on the wooden floor. The cross wood that had held the tile cracked inward as it spanned the sturdier rafters. I pulled the pieces out and laid them on the roof.

Judging the wooden floor to be only about five or six feet below, I eased my legs through the hole. Clinging to the rafters, I entered feet first into the loft. I slid down into the loft, and hanging by my hands, dropped softly on to the wooden floor.

The square shaft of light that hit the floor lit the rest of the loft in a dim glow. Cobwebs hung like tiny fishing nets, their strands black with soot and dust trapped over time. The light illumined a trap door cut into the wooden floor opening into the shrine. A cloud of dust bellowed up into the sunlight as tiny scintillating points.

As my eyes adjusted to the gloom, I found the rest of the tile pieces that lay shattered on the wood. A large brass pot in the corner caught my eye. What riveted my attention to it was its unusual shape. It was conical and approximately three feet tall. A brownish-yellow skin was stretched tight like a drum over its mouth, held in place by a slender copper wire. I brought the pot into the shaft of light and took the skin cover off.

A bundle wrapped in rose-red silk rested at the bottom of this pot. This I manipulated out of the pot. It was fairly large, about eighteen inches long by nine or ten inches thick, with a tight knot in the middle where the silk edges were tied together. Clearing a spot on the wooden floor by blowing the dust off, I placed the bundle upon it and undid the knots.

A second rose-red silk cloth bound the bundle, one corner of which had a long silk thread sewed into it that kept this cloth wrap in place. I undid this and laid open the second wrapping. Sheaves of rectangular skin in three distinct bundles lay within. A faint, foul smell emanated from the bundles, a smell like that from a dead rat or perhaps from that of a snake's newly sloughed skin. Each bundle had a rectangular cap-wood and a bottom-wood that held it together. Two leather thongs penetrated each bundle an inch from each end and these wound around the bundles describing neat rhombuses. The ends of each thong were tied to bits of what looked like shriveled, human fingers. I was revulsed to see an intact nail at the end of each finger.

When I undid the bundles, I saw brownish yellow leather pages resembling smoked latex sheets. They were extraordinarily supple and felt buttery to the touch. The words *Aghora Rahasya* were etched upon the leather.

Repackaging the bundles carefully, I inserted them into the pot and pushed the pot back into its place in the corner.

The manuscript would have to wait for another time. Having collected the pieces of the broken tile, I tied them into a bundle using one end of my turban. Tying the other end to my right ankle, I leapt up and hauled myself out by the rafters, through the hole in the roof. Once on the roof, I hauled up the tile pieces.

I was busy making repairs to the thatched roof and the walls of the cowshed for the next several days, but my curiosity about the contents of the manuscript worked on my mind. By the end of the week, I had gathered enough courage to venture into the loft again. I waited till mid-afternoon when all activities in the shrine ceased and the doors were closed. The family shrine was six feet by twelve; the trap door to the loft was by the entrance. With the aid of a short stool I was able to push open the wooden flap and haul myself into the loft. It was very dark within, but I moved a roof tile ever so slightly to let in sunlight. I knew that I was trespassing and even Aunt Preema would disapprove of my presence here if she found out.

I quickly undid the cover of the pot and removed the manuscript from its silken wrappers. Pithy Sanskrit aphorisms were followed by explanations. There were descriptions of techniques for mind control and the perception of different realms. The aphorisms also contained powerful statements on the true purpose of life, the evanescence of this existence, and the need to focus one's energies—especially in a person's youth—in the pursuit of the knowledge of the Self.

As I read the manuscript, I was overcome by a deep feeling to abandon all material comforts, to seek my true self. The manuscript claimed that at the end of one's life, old age would ravage memory and bring to naught all material learning, expertise, and accomplishments. One would carry nothing but one's state of mind through the doors of death.

It took me several secret forays into the loft to read and understand the contents of the manuscript. The opportunity to be alone in a large household such as mine was rare, and it was only over a period of several weeks that I completed my reading.

The Aghora Rahasya presented doctrines in support of a cosmic philosophy, the convoluted arguments of which eluded my adolescent mind. I was only able to understand the ideas presented in this doctrine with sufficient clarity after repeated incursions into the manuscript during the following months and years. But at that time I was almost 15, and was on the brink of an intense mystical quest. Much of the doctrine in the manuscript proved invaluable and complimented the teachings of my Aunt and the Aghori. By then, I also gained sufficient experience to realize why the manuscript was kept hidden—actually, forbidden.

Aghora Rahasya described the descent of consciousness and cosmic astral energy from the great void, followed by the emergence of space-time. While consciousness manifested in human beings as the

Self, the cosmic astral energy became the mind. The human body was fashioned from space-time so that the Self could interact with it. In its transaction with the body, the Self fragments into a collection of desires, fears, emotions, impulses, and drives (expressed and submerged)—a constant stream which generates the great flux called the personality. Feeding and sustaining these varied structures of the personality is the mind. The mind is thus an ocean of food, a living environment that nourishes the personality. It is an ocean of astral energy surrounding the personality.

A moment-to-moment awareness of the contents of this stream of thoughts helps us exercise great control over the personality. In time, we can even dismantle the personality, releasing astral energy tied down as so many modifications. Once this is accomplished, we can experience the Self. Releasing this astral energy is the fuel necessary to propel the being to freedom, claimed the manuscript.

People normally identify themselves with thoughts and memories. To them, this is selfhood—real being. So stopping thoughts and eliminating the personality is to invite death itself. Aghora Rahasya, however, described thinking and memory as signs of an active personality and not the being itself. The personality sustains itself by engorging upon astral energy. It mutates under the impact of experiences and with memories that are altered with time. But the being behind the personality is beyond change, unruffled by phenomena.

By consciously focusing awareness it is possible to slow down thought processes, enabling us to exercise control over the personality's consumption of astral energy. The gradual slowing down of conscious thought processes allows us to embrace each moment. This process arrests the fragmentation of astral energy that is dispersed in order to sustain the voracious appetites of the numerous drives, motives, various thought-drifts and thought-forms, a coherent ensemble of which is the personality. This brings to a halt the stream of thoughts that define the personality (or sankalpa dhara as Aghora Rahasya called it). The result is pure, undifferentiated awareness without modification. In time, we learn to sustain this pure awareness by feeding it astral energy bound within thought-drifts, helping to further whittle away the personality.

When the fuel of active thought is consumed, awareness now draws energy from thought kernels, compacted desires that pepper the vast mental firmament. This, in the long run, helps release the astral energy tied up in these kernels, which bound the being within changing physical forms and locked it into cyclic transmigrations. Reversing the flow of astral energy, or "making the river run back to its source," as the manuscript said, was the course to freedom.

According to the manuscript, this newly released energy of awareness has to be harnessed immediately and put to positive work. Otherwise, like water, it would flow downhill to reinforce other habits, motives, and drives or awaken latent ones. The sudden and powerful manifestations of these erstwhile slumbering habits could overpower the naked being, weakened as it is with a fragmenting personality, dragging it irrevocably into the dark and murky terrain of the deep unconscious.

Positive work was described as any mental engagement that is uplifting to the self. Altruism, for example, connoted an act that is undoubtedly beneficial to someone. The manuscript enjoined readers to ponder well before committing an act of altruism. True altruism, in addition to being beneficial to the other, would not be detrimental to self. It would not generate an expectation of something in return, nor would it bring in an aftertaste of remorse and disillusionment. Thus, according to the manuscript, altruism is a calculated and premeditated selfless act. Act and be gone from the scene before reward or disillusion claims one.

Releasing awareness is cathartic, as it will unhinge the mind from memory. It is a critical period, especially when one succeeds in releasing awareness from thought kernels by oneself—without a teacher—a period when the aspirant will experience shifting states of mind with phases of lucidity alternating with a chaotic mind. The aspirant works intimately with his or her body-mind so much so that it is difficult to keep a portion of one's memory from being affected by the mystical process, where he or she can keep a logical record of all actions taken and the changes that have occurred. The manuscript warned that a metamorphic mind is not the most indelible of one's spiritual records. It advised that an aspirant should maintain a daily record of thoughts, the foods eaten, other sensory input allowed, and so on. During periods of lucidity, one should immediately write down these mystic experiences. These records would be good to have if one strayed into deep waters and a need arose to backtrack.

Prolonged release of awareness from thought kernels and the subsequent, frequent impact of exotic phenomena would warp the mind and the senses. One's memory becomes unreliable as mystic experiences begin to infiltrate dreams and extend into waking consciousness. It becomes imperative, for the sake of cognitive clarity and sanity, to keep a daily record of what happened and why.

After this initial period of chaos, a new and stable mind will take form. Then experiences will become coherent and the aspirant will experience constancy in the details of the environment that pervades during these supersensory experiences.

This old family manuscript explained that the awareness released from thought kernels is pure mental energy without thought contaminants or modifications. Instead of using this energy to explore the Self, one can also route this energy to enhance any physical or sub-mystical faculty, such as an art or an occupation in mundane life. In fact, in the early days of one's explorations, this tendency—to let this energy flow into lower layers of the psyche to reinforce one's mental and physical abilities—would be strong, the manuscript warned.

This tendency of awareness to flow downhill becomes fatal in people who have investments in subhuman consciousness, as it would activate and empower their most gross aspects—a process that might eventually cost even the community dearly. Odiyya Narayanan Namboodiri seemed to have had a glimpse of the shape of things to come for him and he struggled to warn himself.

The Aghora Rahasya further explained that awareness is intimately linked to time. When awareness is altered, an altered sense of time ensues. Eventually, a person experiences the Self in its totality by transferring awareness from numerous disparate desires and drives to the present moment. During this process, the breath slows down and there occurs a state of deep and involved meditation on being in the present. In the beginning, the mystic aims to achieve awareness of thought itself, to sustain uninterrupted volition on a single thought unit or content by the selective occlusion of every other thought. This is the gist of the doctrine of awareness expounded in the manuscript.

The manuscript prescribed a few exercises to aid us in this process. I prepared myself meticulously and plunged into the intricacies of these techniques wholeheartedly. Privacy was ordained. To help to maintain this, the manuscript suggested midnight as the best time for practice. This posed a problem. I had to elude my family members to keep awake at midnight, and it was impossible to carry out strange practices without their knowledge in my home. After school hours I explored different areas in and around the house. I scrutinized and discarded various locations that I thought were too close to home, for none had the required isolation. I finally decided the local cremation ground was isolated enough for my practices.

I had a healthy fear of ghosts, fanned by the enormous number of ghost stories we exchanged at home. This belief was reinforced by the stories from such exalted sources as our grandfathers. I visited the necropolis by day to familiarize myself with the place and to gradually ease out my ingrained fear.

The cemetery was adjacent to a Shiva temple. The land to the back of this temple was uninhabited and extended over a considerable area. For several hundred years, the villagers have been using a portion of this territory to cremate their dead and the pilgrims who died in our village during the annual Night of Kali festival. Portions of ashes, in little copper pots, were interred into this hallowed ground of Shiva. Beautiful stonework marked each burial mound, over which enormous carved granite cobras shielded black shivalingas.

A *shivalinga* is typically a piece of black granite, usually in the shape of an elongated oval or sometimes a short column (which is a stylization of the oval). It is ornamented with three short, horizontal ash marks that lie parallel to one another and in contact with each other. Cutting through the center of these three marks is a single vertical eye.

From Aunt Preema I learned that the shivalinga represents the great Cosmic Astral Self. *Linga* means "subtle" and *linga sharira* meant "subtle body." Our own astral bodies are microcosmic representations of this great macrocosmic Self. The astral body is free of the sexual dualism that characterizes physical bodies. The three ash marks represent this freedom from sexual dualism, among other things, as the ashes are of the physical body.

Aunt Preema said that the shivalinga's oval shape is the closest to amorphism, showing a tendency to nondualism, and the only way to physically represent a nearly shapeless existence. Oval is the mother of all shapes from which the astral self could shape at will; physical shapes are ascriptions of dualisms that qualify objects of physical perception.

The snake curving over the shivalinga represents the feminine energy that transforms—as in the periodic molting of the snake. Only the cobra has an expandable hood, hinting at the expanding of awareness with the destruction of the physical body and the transformation of energies. The vertical eye in the center of the linga is the eye of total awareness, of integrated senses. With these profound implications, a shivalinga was a perfect capstone over the ashes of the dead that lay in these grounds.

Verses from the Atharvana Veda, the Garuda Purana, or the Markendeya Purana were inscribed in embellished calligraphy upon the bases of these stones. Some signs of worship were evident as I saw stone oil lamps with half-burned wicks in them.

A faint foot track led from the back of the temple through this burial ground and disappeared amid the stones. To the west, the copse hemmed in the cemetery as if fighting for reacquisition of the piece of ground that it ceded to the dead. A wooden fence at the perimeter kept the thicket at bay. Buffeted by the wind, a wicket sagging on its rusty hinges kept up an eerie baritone.

I looked around with some hesitation. Cautiously, I followed the foot path as it wound its way among the stones. I passed by several termite mounds adorned with flowers. The place oozed an awe-inspiring silence.

I walked up to the cemetery's perimeter. The space beyond the cemetery abounded with vegetation. I did not venture into that green impasse, but stood there to ponder. What was I getting myself into? I felt my enthusiasm drain at the sight of this forbidding barrier.

I had heard that the crumbling ruins of an abandoned temple and an adjacent pond were the only man-made disruptions that punctured the otherwise wild and tangled proliferation of natural vegetation that lay before me. This jungle gave way to the sea about ten miles toward the west. Bizarre tales associated with this temple found surreptitious circulation among the people. No sane person ventured into its gloomy depths during the day, let alone at night.

The cemetery at one end, and the temple ruins on the other, was enough to deter human intrusion and preserved the intrinsic tranquillity and isolation that the place exuded. Without human interference, this space became a natural habitat supporting a finely balanced ecosystem of different species of birds, rodents, reptiles, insects, ferns and other plants.

Exhausted both physically and mentally from wrestling with my indecision, I retreated, but vowed to return when I could summon the courage to enter these woods and search for the temple ruins. Days passed before I mustered enough energy and courage to venture beyond the cemetery. Then one morning, two weeks after my initial visit to the cemetery, I ventured beyond.

The fence along the western edge of the cemetery was broken in places where peepul, mango, breadfruit, tamarind, neem, and banyan trees burst in. Their spreading branches and leaning boles competed for light and air as they stretched into the space above the burial ground.

I gazed at the wall of green that bordered the boneyard. The forest seemed impenetrable. There was no sign of a break, or even a hint of man-made intrusion into this burgeoning impasse. It was almost mid-morning and the heat was building up. Probing about, I pushed and shoved at the undergrowth, wary of slumbering reptiles. At last I found an opening and decided to enter here. I cast a furtive look at the recumbent caretaker. He was stretched out as usual upon his favorite tombstone. His right arm convulsed, startling a striped lizard nearby. It bobbed its head askance at his somnolent antics. Reassured, I plunged into the forest.

For an hour, I crashed and crawled, inching my way through the thicket. At one point I blundered into a thornfield. Impeding spikes staked their claim upon me from all sides. Desperation reigned in the place of adventure, and spasms of pain shot through my lower back. I decided to rest, and eased myself down through the tangle. Beads of sweat broke out all over as stifling heat enveloped me. As the sweat rolled down my body, I winced from the searing sting of a thousand lacerations. I sat there for a while.

A swath of cool breeze stirred the canopy. I settled back against the very thorns that restrained me and stretched my limbs with profound relief. But, hardly had my head hit the ground when I smelled putrescent flesh. And to compound my tribulations, a buzzing, iridescent fly sought out my nose. I swiped at it frantically, but was thwarted by the thorns that restrained my flailing arms. Enough was enough, I thought, and I rose up from that fetid spot. After what seemed to be an interminable tearing and rendering, I broke loose and once again plunged forward, free at last from the clutches of the thornfield. I entered the forest again. The cool shade of the trees and the undergrowth was a welcome contrast.

I had stopped paying attention to my surroundings, as my entire focus had been to get out of the thorns. So it was with great relief, though exhausted, that I found myself forcing my way through ferns and much greener vegetation. I was amazed that I did not see a single creature of the many that were supposed to inhabit these parts. But on closer analysis, I realized that they would have been acutely aware of me, rather than me of them, what with the tremendous racket I created in my passage. I continued to work my way through the forest.

All of a sudden I whipped past the last of the foliage, the momentum of my careening body throwing me upon ground paved with stone. I scrambled up bewildered by the abrupt transition from the rustling thicket into the open. The silence was profound and the sounds of the jungle penetrated but very little. Startled, I stood there as if suspended in time. I shaded my eyes and squinted from the sudden increase in light.

Rectangular pieces of dressed granite sandwiched tufts of grass upon the ground. About fifty yards away stood a crumbled wall, and through the gaps I saw the remnants of a granite colonnade of grandiose design. The whole structure looked like a giant's jaw with broken denture. This must be the ruins of the temple that I have heard about. Beyond the columns, I could discern a second wall. The sanctum itself, perhaps, I thought.

I crept closer and surveyed the ruins with a mixture of awe and trepidation, as well as with a puzzling feeling of being thrown back into the past. Dislodged blocks of beautifully carved granite extruded out from the masonry as roots from encroaching trees made their slow and insidious intrusion into the walls. Numerous clumps of ferns and creepers had staked their claim upon the remaining walls and columns that retained their architectural integrity. These moss-covered walls stood the passage of centuries of time.

Breaking out from the edge of the glade, I stepped cautiously among the columns. This was sacred territory; I felt that my presence here was unwarranted and therefore sacrilegious. I gingerly stalked along the colonnade. The crossbeams of two of the columns had fallen. Adjacent to the last column was a pond of more than 500 feet in diameter, the sandy slopes of which had scattered patches of grass. Clumps of bamboo rose like mangroves from one corner. As I gazed upon the quietly rustling leaves, I became aware of a poignant feeling in my heart. It was as if each sensation were in slow motion—a fleeting whisper of familiarity pervaded this place like a wistful dream. Fragments of memory flitted by, filling me with longing and a strange anxiety.

My eyes wandered down the thick, sleek bamboo stems to the sandy slopes. A fractured section of a heavy crossbeam lay partially buried in the pond. The water was dark green and covered with dead leaves and weeds. Humming dragonflies hovered and skimmed over its still expanse. Once in a while the snout of a frog poked through the floating debris; the clear water beneath would gleam momentarily across the puncture before the flotsam closed in again.

I stepped closer to the edge of the pond and squatted upon its rim. Disturbed by my heavy tread, a tiny avalanche of fine sand streamed down the slope and tumbled into the water, rippling the mossy expanse with hidden waves.

The north face of the temple had an entrance, but the door was missing. I peeked through the ancient doorway into the sanctum. A strong musty smell pervaded the room. The stone floor inside the sanctum was strewn with dry leaves and bat droppings. Large clumps of grass appeared as bursts of brilliant green between the granite floor slabs. A piece of obsidian, carved into an ornate cube with an extended waterspout, occupied the center of the ten by ten room—the pedestal that once supported a deity. It must have been pillaged a long time ago, I thought.

The atmosphere was lonesome and smelled of a hoary past, and I could sense the presence of an unseen power imminent in this place. A deep veneration filled my heart. Then I became aware of a curious fact: dry moss, bat droppings, and dry leaves littered every surface in the sanctum, except the obsidian cube. A vague feeling clutched my heart—something nagged in my mind. My thought processes became slushy and confused. It was irksome not to be able to put these vague thoughts and feelings into lucid words and images. As my mind rambled chaotically, I became aware of images rising from within, and they melded with sensations from outside. My mental moorings slipped, and I lost clarity of perception—everything seemed nonsensical and incongruous. I heard the sound of a conch blown outside, and it annoyed me. I paused, distracted from the ritual offering of red hibiscus to the goddess who sat before me. I was in another time. I got disconnected from the last invocation I chanted.

"Do not pay any attention to that," she chimed in her childlike voice, "do continue with your chants, they are melodious," she said, encouraging me with a smile.

Amazingly, the rest of the chants came clear to me. A part of my mind even began to process invocations yet to be chanted. The instant I became aware of this, I realized that I was dreaming. But in spite of this realization I kept on dreaming. It was as if I had split awareness that flitted between two realities. The logical awareness that realized I was dreaming became inquisitive and began to look around urgently, to memorize as many details of my dream environment as possible. I was in a granite room, approximately ten by ten feet in size, and brightly lit by numerous oil lamps. The walls were black with grime and soot, but glistened with condensation.

The moment I reasoned this out, my awareness returned to the dream. I cast a flower onto the goddess' lap and saw it tumble down. The goddess was decked with row after row of red hibiscus garlands. They began at her neckline and extended down to her waist. A gold-embroidered red silk cloth was wrapped around her waist and flung diagonally across her left breast and over the shoulder, enhancing her fair skin. She had a disproportionately elongated head, with large, amber eyes. A ravishing crown of black hair fell past her hips.

I looked around and saw that there were others with me seated before the goddess in a semicircle. I was amazed that I had been unaware of their presence. The stone floor before us was cluttered with various items of worship. Vessels of water with floating leaves and flowers, small containers of sandalwood paste, minute conch shells balanced upon miniature metal tripods, round trays of fruit, flowers, and coconut, and a tray with a heap of saffron crowded the space before us.

As we picked up the last of the flowers, the incantation slowed down. Then the ceremony began with each one of us waving a multi-tiered wick lamp. The sanctum echoed with the peals of bells and the rumble of conches. Then the goddess stood up and gave us a dazzling smile. She looked at me, and lifted up her right palm in benediction. A strobe of pearly light flashed out of her palm. . . .

The intense light seared my eyes—I lifted my arms involuntarily to shade them. When I opened my eyes, it was midday and the sun was overhead. Scorching rays beat upon my face through the roofless sanctum. I was lying on the floor beside the obsidian cube. An incredible combination of sandalwood, jasmine, and basil permeated the atmosphere. As I smelled the perfume, I began recollecting the details of the dream experience. With the perfume still in the air, I wondered if the dream itself were real. Perhaps it was a memory from a past life. Experiences from the present merged with those from ancient past. I propped myself up on my elbows and thought longingly of the bewitching face of the lovely goddess.

The raucous cawing of a raven shook me out of my reverie; a moment later a large raven flopped down upon the wall. It hopped closer along the top of the exposed wall, tilted its head and blinked at me with one eye. The bird clucked as if in query, then hopped around, its back to me. Apparently, its curiosity was satisfied; the raven wiped his powerful beak on the wall and flew off.

As I sat there, it dawned on me that this was the perfect place for my practices. I looked at the obsidian cube and ran my palm over its smooth top. There was surely a presence in this ancient room. I began to entertain the idea that some mysterious force or entity had led me to this spot. This place had a powerful etheric vibration, and I felt energized. I remembered Aunt Preema talking about special places of power imbued with astral imprints of greatly evolved beings—places where people could enhance ordinary awareness. It struck me that this sanctum could be such a power spot where space-times intermingled. Could it be that I was moving in and out of two realms? Did I wander into a conclave of invisible, divine beings?

With the sun moving west, I decided it was time to go home. I felt a deep veneration for the place, and I prostrated before the stone. I prayed that my intrusion be forgiven, that I came here inspired to seek the Great Unknown. With that I walked backward as was customary in sacred presences. As I stepped out onto the cobblestone colonnade, I wiped some dust from the threshold stone and reverently applied it to my forehead.

I reached the edge of the forest, at the very spot where I made my entry, and took a last look at the inspiring grounds. Then once again I plunged into the undergrowth. My return to the cemetery was uninteresting and tedious, but I had better luck with the thornfield. I learned to take the line of least resistance through the thorns. With great relief I returned to the cemetery. As I walked past the familiar tombstone, I looked for the caretaker. He was nowhere in sight. I approached the east entrance to the Shiva temple just in time to hear the priest chant the concluding verses of the great Rudram, a Yajur vedic hymn to Shiva the Supreme Being. I could not help feel that this was an auspicious sign; it reinforced my gut feeling that what I experienced at the temple ruins was real.

I walked up the granite steps, and prostrated before Shiva. The inner shrine was a small room, lit mildly by a few oil lamps. The sanctum had a well inside it, and I watched the old priest haul a small brass pitcher of water from it. While pouring the water over the shivalingam, he chanted:

| | |
|---|---|
| *Triambakam Yajamahee,* | We worship you three-eyed Rudra, |
| *Sugandhim Pushti Vardhanam;* | Of heavenly effervesence And who bestows divine prosperity; |
| *Urvarukam Iva Bandhanath,* | As a ripe gooseberry breaks free, |
| *Mrutyoor Mukshiya;* | Release us from the bonds of death! |
| *Mamrutath.* | But not from immortality. |

At the conclusion of this verse, he greeted me with a nod. He stepped out of the sanctum and approached the threshold with a small conch shell in his hand. The priest, who was in his 80s, wore his white hair tied into a knot above his right ear. He offered me ritually purified water from the conch. I collected some of this in my right palm and sipped a few drops, and the remaining I sprinkled upon the crown of my head.

"Name?" he asked.

"Shambhasadashivan," I replied.

"Birth star?" he queried.

"Rohini, and three-and-a-half into ascension," I answered.

He nodded his head with a smile and stepped back into the sanctum, where he performed a short ritual. I could hear my name and birth star being uttered along with the other mantras. He returned with some bilva leaves and sacred ash.

"*Ayushman bhavatu,*" he blessed me, "May you live long," and gave me the sacred offerings.

I left the sacred precincts of the Shiva temple deep in thought. My mind was caught in the imagery of the dreamlike experience at the temple ruins. A faint voice from within me kept whispering that the goddess was none other than Ambika, the Great Goddess.

▼ ▼ ▼

My experience at the temple confounded me for several days. I was euphoric for weeks. Contrary to my usual habit, I decided not to confide this to Sandhya nor consult Aunt Preema. I was afraid that Aunt Preema would scold me for entering the loft and breaking into the secret manuscript, and forbid me to visit the temple ruins again.

The face of the goddess haunted my mind. She became a strong focus for my spiritual ideals. It was as if a different mind took over during the experience and continued its hold for days. As time passed, I debated on the significance of the phenomenon. It was not entirely clear whether the event was real or just a dream. I began to sink into a state of doubt, considering the whole incident as a peculiar effect that the ghostly surroundings had upon my young religious mind. A more rational mind surfaced now.

After that first trip, I became curious about visiting the ruins at night, but was unable to leave home without being discovered. So I spent time there during the day. On several nights, I lay on the sandy slopes of the family pond. Lying on my back, I would pick out a bright star and gaze at it for a considerable time, tracking its slow motion overhead. This practice helped me still my thoughts, and eventually I was able to focus my mind away from everything. The constant internal chatter lessened. During this period, I felt light and unencumbered, and my awareness was like that of an animal that oozed out of me to mingle with the darkness that seemed material, a silky texture that enveloped every shape outside. I became a mass of awareness that watched in silence.

▼ ▼ ▼

The philosophy propounded in the manuscript fascinated me. The manuscript reinforced the principle of thought suspension, of moving beyond the personality and discovering one's identity in the Self. Anyone practicing these principles would gain mastery over life—to be like an odiyya.

I periodically experimented with thought suspension. But to my dismay, I found myself drift away in fantasies without my least awareness, and would nab myself doing this far downstream. The more I used my will to force my mind into submissive silence, the more strongly it rebelled. But all the same, I was excited with the prospect of training my mind, to be like the odiyyas or the mystics known for their fantastic feats of mind control—to be able to float free into the infinite and timeless vastness that lay beyond.

To remain without thought for the whole day was well nigh impossible. After much musing, it occurred to me to tackle the problem by analyzing the thinking process itself. I first sought to discover what caused thought or thinking.

It was written in the Aghora Rahasya that if one analyzed each thought it would contain an essence, an underlying phenomenon from which a thought, or a chain of thoughts, manifests. Repeated reinforcement of this essence over one or more lifetimes produces a thought kernel. A thought kernel could have an incredible amount of life-energy stored in it. Although thought kernels are preexistent, they are powerless by themselves to manifest as thoughts. The manuscript mentioned that they were specialized energies compacted by time, unable to self-activate without some outside awareness. At birth they float dormant in the firmament of human mind, waiting for awareness from the growing personality to ignite them into action.

I visualized these thought kernels coming into existence by layering the original thought essence with desires and emotions, reinforced with memory and such. The Aghora Rahasya had described the mind as an ocean of energy, an ocean of fuel that kindles thought kernels. Mental energy is a specialized derivative of an even more fundamental energy called *prana* or cosmic life force. Each thought kernel, when awakened, is like a vortex into whose center mental energies drain like stars that spiral into galaxies to feed their voracious appetite. The mental firmament is as dotted with thought kernels as the universe is filled with galaxies. Fantasies are the psychological activation of thought kernels into vortices, and a thought vortex is experienced as a fantasy. A person's attention, when seized by a fantasy or reverie, can consume awareness rapidly. These are like the enormous gravitational forces that draw nebulous cosmic substances into the maw of a galaxy.

Aghora Rahasya described attention as the action by which awareness is drawn into a fantasy. Awareness is the conduit through which thought kernels suctioned mental energy. Herein lay the secret to thought control. Ignite a thought kernel and withdraw awareness from it. This prevents it from growing into a thought vortex. Now instead of drawing in energy, a thought kernel burns, releasing awareness. This awareness released from thought kernels can be routed to strengthen attention. Without awareness to siphon mental energies into a "thought vortex," the vortex collapses. If such a collapse could be sustained, the thought kernel itself would be snuffed out.

Thought kernels, when activated, could sustain a slow burn-out, expending the enormous energy compacted within, and at the same time replenishing themselves with energies from conducive memories that lay in the surrounding mental field. Memories, unlike thought kernels, are comparatively recent agglutinations of "mental matter." They, too, can draw awareness to themselves through the same process of attention. For memories to awaken into active thought, they need to contain a threshold of energy. Otherwise they would float dormant in mental space-time until memories with similar energies chanced upon them. Then, like newborn stars, they ignite to active thought.

Both dormant and activated memories are favorite fodder for thought vortices. Groups of thought kernels ignite into vortices at different times in a person's life. The collective effect of these determines the nature of the personality and defines trends and changes in the personality of the being. I surmised that mysterious factors drove this complex metaphysical mechanism, thus defining the life of an individual. I realized that thought kernels tried their best to defy extinction, seeding the mental firmament for rebirth, thus perpetuating transmigration. This was exciting!

Aghora Rahasya described a seat of sublime cognizance, a region in the mental firmament devoid of memories, desires, or thought kernels. Only pure, undifferentiated awareness filled this region, occupying it as a vast and seamless entity. From this domain of sublime cognizance, undifferentiated awareness communicated with the region peppered with thought kernels through free awareness. Thus the higher voice constantly streamed into the region of the personality. The message of sublime cognizance is simple; it presents a divine alternative to every thought, desire, and action that is detrimental to freedom. It says, "Unite all thoughts into one awareness and be free! Fragment awareness into thoughts and you will be bound!" The amount of free awareness available to a person determined the clarity of this message. But most people could neither hear nor act upon this divine counsel. Normal humans have only a trace of free awareness available, as the bulk of this is tied up in innumerable thought kernels. What free awareness is left helplessly rushes in to feed other kernels activated into thought vortices.

Energies that would otherwise be drained to sustain a thought vortex, as the energies also compacted in them, could be channeled to strengthen free awareness. In order to break the grip of a vortex upon awareness an expenditure of some initial energy was required. But where could a lay person lay hands on some free awareness? According to Aghora Rahasya, a fantasy in progress is an easy source of awareness; interrupting the fantasy provides an instant source of free awareness.

Initially one had to will this quanta of energy in storage and label it suitably for future use. From the manuscript, I learned that labeling energy was a simple process. Any small ritual will help stamp a label into place. Aghora Rahasya recommended that one light a small wood fire in isolation, sit before this fire, and speak aloud one's intent to label some awareness by interrupting a fantasy. After this, the person must wait for a fantasy to spring into existence.

Labeling awareness specialized its function—in this case, to be the energy of vigilance that would alert the person of a fantasy in process, disrupt it, and divert the freed awareness to strengthen communication with sublime cognizance. The energies gained from dismantling a thought vortex could now be used to replenish this vigilant awareness and fortify communication with sublime cognizance. It requires special skills to dissipate the awakened energies without harm to the personality. But once this process is established and nurtured, the person's life will be guided by the wisdom of sublime cognizance. Thought vortices will work themselves to extinction, and the waxing influence of sublime cognizance in the realm of the mundane mind will prevent any future kernel formation.

The manuscript laid great emphasis on the conservation of sexual energy, and the gradual and total sublimation of sexual urges, sensations, and cravings. It spoke of a great power resident in a person, wrapped up within the cocoon of sexuality. Sexuality, as a drive to preserve the species, was the first and major claimant of this power in the physical realm. Surrounding this is a firmament of drives and desires of varying importance and claims to this power. Like gradually expanding doughnuts, these lay above and below this central power. Enveloping all these is the microcosmic vault of the Great Cause or the Self. Immediate to this Great Cause is a primordial essence that permeates all, and from this essence comes the plethora of physical drives and desires. Next to this is the region of sublime cognizance. The power within the cocoon of sexuality transforms primordial essence into potent awareness that fuels desires and thought vortices. It is the central power that activates life. The Great Cause is the last claimant to this power.

The area of activity of this power determines the identity of the person. Since the power courses strongly in physical desire, most people identify themselves with the body. By gradually preparing alternative routes to divert these desires, a person can absorb them into the Great Cause. Thus, the prime directive of the manuscript was to invest this central power into the Great Cause, thus restoring the identity of the person from the body to the Great Cause.

I set aside a regular time to practice thought suspension. After I came home from school in the evenings, I had over an hour to do as I pleased. The boys and girls from the neighborhood would gather in the vast spaces that surround the Kali temple to play. This was a good time to make my way to the deserted temple for my practices.

▼ ▼ ▼

During one of my excursions to the abandoned temple I fell into an extensive dissection of the anatomy of mind and thought as propounded in Aghora Rahasya. I arrived at the temple early with some floral offerings which I placed on the obsidian cube. In my heart I knew that this stone once supported the icon of a goddess. I felt a deep veneration and kinship for this place and had a strong feeling that I was watched over by a mighty and benign Being. Then I walked outside and sat upon the flat top of an ornate stone that was the foundation of a fallen pillar. Sitting amid the fallen pillars of the temple I wondered whether thought was essential for existence. Without thought, would the personality cease to be? The process of thinking seemed intimately linked to the process of being human, though I had a strong suspicion that thinking may not be essential to life or biological existence. Living beings more primordial than mammals live with no indication of any thought processes. But to be a human being, to hold the personality together, I felt thought might be necessary. Lack of thinking was akin to death of the personality. I pondered this over and over. It came to me that at the time of birth an infant's mind has thought kernels and free awareness. Environmental stimuli awaken some thought kernels and form new thoughts, just like wind whips water in a still pond into a wave. This process could be considered a primary thought. This primary thought has a stirring or churning effect upon a region of the mind, which leads to the disturbance of thought kernels. The process of attention causes areas to gravitate to one another and join together, or "clump," like a wave that compresses regions of the mind, bringing into close contact memories and thought kernels to form a "clumpy mind."

In this clumpy mind, the aggregated areas are cognitively active. Sense stimulus from outside helps link the awareness with preexisting thought kernels. This awareness, in the process of giving attention to the sense stimuli, links one or more thought kernels to the sense stimuli, thus activating the kernel and producing a primary thought. This thought initiates the manufacture of a chain of thoughts and activates memories and thought kernels, thereby generating a vortex.

Caught up in this paradigm on the origin of a thought, I continued to explore it. The chains of linked thoughts furiously feed upon awareness, with the process of attention helping maintain a basic structure of acceptable logic. Before long, these thought chains create a full-blown fantasy that streams out of control.

I noticed that I used plenty of nervous energy indulging in fantasies, thus substantiating the manuscript's claim of energy expenditure during this process. To further prove that the energy expended was that of awareness, I tried to focus my awareness upon a mental image of an icon. To my dismay I found that I could not hold the image steadily in my mental focus. Furthermore, the image was instantly swept aside by other trivia, without me being aware of this for several seconds. But on occasions when I snuffed out the fantasy at the level of the primary thought, I could focus my awareness upon any mental icon with startling clarity and for lengths of time. At the end of every successful exercise, I returned to normal awareness with an energetic sense, an acute perception, and intense vitality that lasted for a day or two.

I sat so the ruins were behind me, and I faced the placid waters of the pond. As I sat upon the foundation stone, the resolve to regulate thought came to me with amazing clarity. I must eliminate these fantasies to start with, and begin saving as much energy as possible. To do this, I must somehow shut off sense stimuli. The task ahead was daunting to say the least.

At this point in my experimentation, logic was my only ally. I began an analysis of the types of stimuli on the basis of their effect upon the mind. Again, using the thought kernels as a background on which reactions to outside stimuli were registered, I saw a pattern emerge. Some sense stimuli stirred up specific thought kernels. I also discovered that some thought kernels were compact storehouses of emotional energy, waiting to be ignited into a chain of emotions. Others were intellectual. But the activators of both these came strongly from the social environment. A seemingly impossible solution sprang into my mind—erase the social environment, itself, for the duration of my endeavor in thought suspension. The isolation of the temple grounds provided the perfect environment for my experiments. I rose from my seat and stretched. I walked down the slope and waded a few feet into the pond. Sloshing cold water upon my face invigorated me. Then, entering the sanctum, I brushed clean a small area near one of the walls with some tufts of dried grass. Here I sat, partially facing the obsidian cube. Evening light spangled the wall in front of me. The manuscript had emphasized that a steady posture was important to keep the body from interfering with the mind's efforts. I closed my eyes, but sounds from outside usurped my conscious awareness—reptiles squirming through dry leaves, birds singing.

Soon a curious thing happened. A witness-like state descended upon me and I noticed that my breathing became a long drawn-out conscious event. Immediately my thought processes became slow, alternating between spates of thought and complete vacuity. I could observe and hear these thoughts as they rose and fell back into the mental substrata, like arcs of plasma on the sun.

Very soon my thoughts became logically dissociated; bits and pieces of disconnected thought fragments followed. Then thought ceased to be words. Instead, colorful images sprang up, sustained themselves in the mental field, disintegrated into fragments and disappeared.

Here, I became acquainted with a fascinating process—some of the images were objects or people. As these took shape and presented themselves, I felt the rising of a subtle urge to sustain them, to initiate trains of words and pictures. Presently, I felt another desire to smother the first urge, and to continue with the mind quieting process. Soon I was subject to an intermittent sensation of flying over effulgent waves that threw up luminous froth and spray, brushing my face and torso. Then, there was nothing—no words, no thoughts or images—but a sensation of deep contentment, peace, and satiety.

▼ ▼ ▼

I opened my eyes to darkness and the sound of the wind rustling through the trees—a sudden onslaught of sense stimuli upon a quiescent mind. A large chunk of time was unaccountably lost; I thought I was there for only five or six minutes. I glanced at the obsidian cube a few feet in front of me. It was a mass of blackness, its outlines smeared into the surrounding darkness, a telltale presence in the gathering gloom. I prostrated in its direction and prayed for guidance from the Being that once adorned it.

Stepping out of the sanctum, I discovered that there was just enough light left to negotiate my way back to the village. The afterglow in the west was a pale vermilion, and marching in from the east was an army of deep cerulean darkness. I stepped aside instinctively as a bat zoomed toward my face with incredible swiftness. It chased a hapless insect with astonishing agility. Large fruit-eating bats flapped about high in the trees, and occasionally I caught glimpses of a squadron of bats flying very high, heading inland.

I headed back to the village with a great sense of urgency. I would be missed at the evening worship ceremonies. I weaved and bullied through the now-familiar terrain, emerging out of the confines of the cemetery. By now darkness had enveloped the land and I half-trotted, half-walked with a feeling of unease, for I had to face the elders at home and present a plausible explanation for my absence.

The granite tower of the temple was aglow with a thousand oil lamps. It was a heavenly sight. There was something ethereal about temples; I always felt a powerful upsurge of ecstasy, a feeling of sublime elation in their presence. And this evening, in the gathering darkness, the distant glow of the combined light of all the lamps from the temple had an indescribable effect upon my being. A feeling of divine power, a feeling that I could ascend the pinnacle of spiritual heights, empowered my being from deep within.

I began to run at a fast gallop, my eyes set upon the shimmering lamps of the tower. I leapt over small boulders and ran nimble-footed along the thin mud ridges that bordered the rice fields. I felt the sensory acumen of a lithe animal. The lights appeared larger, and two from among the thousands bobbed free and approached me. I sensed a boulder dead ahead. With my eyes still fixed upon the bobbing fires, my body instinctively leapt.

"Stop! Who is that?" a voice hailed.

"It's me, Shambu."

Two men approached me with palm frond torches. "It is Shambu," the man echoed, "We found him!" He called back into the darkness behind him. I discerned other bobbing fires some distance away.

"Oh! You found him? Okay. We will call the others back," a woman's voice sailed back from the distance. It sounded like Aunt Bhanu.

"Shambu, where have you been?" It was Uncle Bala.

"Yes, where were you? We missed you at the worship," Uncle Mukunda chimed in after Uncle Bala.

"I walked along the fields earlier, and then I decided to sit down on one of the rocks over there and meditate," I replied, pointing to a cluster of boulders in the distance. "I did not realize that it was late until I opened my eyes," I said half truthfully.

"Well, your mother and Gauri have the whole household out looking for you," said Uncle Bala with a note of exasperation.

At the entrance to my house, I saw Sandhya waiting with a small brass pitcher of water. It was important to wash one's hands, feet, and face before entering the house, especially during dawn and evening twilight. At these times, worship ceremonies would be in progress in homes. I looked up at her as she stood upon the threshold. There was a look of anxiety upon her face in spite of her beautiful smile. She stooped slightly close to me as she poured the water onto my hands and feet.

"Everything is all right, don't worry. I told Aunt Gauri that you told me you would be spending some time meditating," she whispered into my ear. I gazed at her eyes, partly hidden behind the lovely locks that tumbled down her cheeks. Something about her voice made me anxious.

"I was really meditating."

"I know," she said smiling. "There is no problem, they were just worried."

That was great relief to know; I nodded my thanks to her and entered the corridor that led to the quadrangle. The big brass kuttuvilakku cast a shimmering light in the passageway. I bowed to it reverentially as I passed by. I walked through the courtyard, stopping by the tulasi altar and touching the tulasi leaves in reverence, I continued toward the central shrine.

The matriarchs had gathered, along with the grandfathers, most of my cousins, and my uncles. As I nudged my way between my cousins Sunita and Raghu, anxious faces questioned me, while they continued to mouth the chants. Floral offerings were being made to the image of Kali in the center, to a little image of Shiva to one side, and to a bundle of scriptures packed in embroidered silk.

My mother and Chandra, the third matriarch, began to chant the final vedic chants to Kali. They each waved a brass platter containing a five-tiered lamp with several little oil flames. Presently Aunt Susheela and Aunt Sukanya came in announcing, "Devi Prasadam! Make way!" They brought large brass platters of food and sweets as offerings to the deities. When the evening worship was over, Aunt Gauri approached me.

"Next time check with me before you plan going on one of your excursions," she said sternly. I was infuriated and wanted to ask why, but had the good sense not to.

▼ ▼ ▼

Late after dinner I prepared to sleep in the courtyard. I lay awake through the wee hours of the night, in the pale light of the setting moon. Members of the household slept around the central tulasi altar. The stars paraded past overhead like tiny points of twinkling lights that flared and dimmed. They moved slowly, and the fluidity of their passage was soothing. I drifted in and out of consciousness and the stars tumbled in with me. I became aware of a rocking movement; a gentle chant accompanied the movement. As the chants grew louder, I saw a bobbing row of lights. The flickering lights appeared large as they came near. Young men and women, clad in white, walked along the forest path with large butter lamps in their hands. I followed this procession. They moved slowly, the people walking in step to the chant of the mantras. Then exquisite music drifted to us above the gentle murmur of chants. The group broke into a clearing, and before us was a beautiful temple.

The doors to the sanctum were open; inside, the shrine was brightly lit. I saw enthroned a beautiful goddess dressed in red and gold. As the group entered the temple, I approached closer to this goddess, who gazed at me. To my great amazement and delight, I recognized her to be the goddess I had dreamed at the ruins. A heavenly feeling overcame me. She beckoned me to her. At that instant, the rest of the group began waving their lamps, and the chanting grew louder.

I woke up to see the ladies of my household going around the tulasi shrine, chanting their early morning prayers. I sat up in bewilderment. Then I remembered that it was my turn to help water the plants that day. I rolled my sheets quickly and dashed to my room.

CHAPTER SEVEN

# *Predators of the Womb*

 It was the month of January, in the year
1966. The festival of Maikumbham had be-
gun. During this period householders in our
community undertook an austerity called
Surya Narayana Vratam, invoking the deity
identified with the sun. On certain days families performed a ritual called Surya Narayana
Puja. People welcomed the end of winter's
darkness and the ascension of light. Cere-
monies heralded the beginning of this festival on the 14th of January
and concluded on the 14th of February. During this period people
gave special reverence to serpents, and to cobras in particular.

Ant hills were numerous in our village, and cobras sheltered in
empty ones. The people worshipped these ant hills, especially the
women, offering eggs and milk to the cobras. I was curious about the
connection between the celebration of light and worship of cobras.
There were only two people I would turn to in times of doubt—
Aunt Preema or Aghori Narayani. Because of her unpredictability, the
aghori was my last choice.

During this season Sandhya and I did our morning prayers earlier
than normal, after which I assisted my cousins with farmwork. Before
starting my work that January morning, I went in search of Aunt
Preema. I found her squatting behind our cow Lakshmi, who stood
with her hind legs spread. The cow shed was dimly lit, as the sun had
begun to rise early, marking the beginning of spring. I approached
my aunt, cautiously skipping over piles of wet dung.

"Sshhurrr! Sshhiirr!" I heard the stream of milk strike the brass
bucket as Aunt Preema squeezed the teats. I paid my respects and sat
by her. Sindhu, her calf, suckled at the teats that were free. I tried to
hold him back.

"Let him suckle, Shambu. I am done," said my aunt.

"If there is time, Aunt Preema, I have a question."

"Why don't we meet after dinner tonight, Shambu?" she said
hefting the milk bucket and hurrying toward the exit.

"All right, Aunt Preema," I said, watching her depart hurriedly. Standing there, I wondered whether I sensed an edge of irritability in her voice. Moments later, I brushed aside my concerns, thinking that I was overreacting. After my morning chores at home, I left for school.

I did not see my aunt the whole day. Later that evening, Sandhya and I went to the aghori for our evening lessons. The aghori was serious the entire evening. She taught us to draw a mandala to Bhagalamukhi and helped us learn the chants that went with this worship.

"Chant this mantra till I get back. Sit here and chant. Don't fool around," she ordered, and left the barn. We both stayed put and chanted inwardly. I threw in all my awareness and focused my mind on the invocation. After a while, I experienced a thrill. As I listened to my mental chanting, I felt power coupling upon power with each repetition. We chanted for over an hour.

We did not hear the aghori enter the barn. She had to clap her hands to draw our attention. I opened my eyes, but remained quiet with a tremendous exhilaration. Sandhya's gaze was fixed upon the fire. I knew she was far away, still riding the waves of bliss.

"You two don't come here tomorrow night. Practice this chant together tomorrow, in secret. I will see you day after tomorrow evening. Be here before sunset. Now, get going," she ordered.

"Thank you, Mother Aghori!" We touched her feet. Sandhya and I could not speak; the euphoria was strong, though it wore thin by the time we got home. Just before we entered our homestead, Sandhya stopped and pulled me into her arms in a tight embrace.

"We are a unique team, you and I, Shambu."

"Thank you!" I said, smiling. "But what is it, Sandhya?"

"What do you mean, what? We were both flying together!"

"Really? I just felt this thrill while I chanted. Mother Kali! What focus I had! But I did not feel I was flying, Sandhya."

"Oh! Shambu! Yes, we were," Sandhya asserted. In a conspiratorial tone she added, "You know what? I think we are both becoming odiyyas. What do you think?"

"Don't even think about it. Don't say it, Sandhya. If we speak about it, we may lose it," I said, alarmed. Inwardly, Sandhya had inadvertently tweaked my imagination. I was thrilled.

"The aghori was stranger than normal tonight, wasn't she?"

"Yes, Shambu. That worries me. We are to chant this mantra together in secret tomorrow! Where should we sit?"

"I don't know," I said. But even as I spoke, I remembered the temple ruins. I dismissed the idea, thinking of the extensive thorn fields Sandhya would have to get through. Then I thought of the rice fields. "Maybe in the middle of the rice fields," I said.

"The rice fields? It's too open!"

"But there are those big boulders. We can sit behind them, after sunset."

"Hmm, all right!" she muttered.

Aunt Preema waited for us. That night, while we three dined, Sandhya and I told her of the aghori's instruction.

"Aghori Narayani does not want us to go to her tomorrow, Mother."

"Instead, she wants us to chant this mantra together in secret, Aunt."

My aunt said nothing. We looked at her for some sign, but she ate quietly. I remembered that Aunt Preema had agreed to discuss the festival of Maikumbham tonight, but I felt uneasy asking her. We ate in silence for a minute and then Sandhya asked, "Mother, why would the aghori want us at her place before sunset the day after tomorrow?"

"So that she may teach you something new," answered my aunt in a curt voice.

"She taught us to draw Bhagalamukhi mandala and to chant the mantra tonight, Mother. We had a strange experience of flying," she said. "The aghori scares us, Mother."

My aunt replied, "Just as a knife can be used for a harmless purpose or to do a violent deed, knowledge can be used by the selfless and by the selfish. I have introduced you two to the Light—the use of knowledge to create and nurture. The aghori will give you a taste of the Dark." She filled her banana leaf with rice and curry, and poured vegetable soup into her bowl.

"Dark like what, Aunt?"

"Dark like chaos on the Night of Dissolution," she answered curtly. She used the word *pralaya*.

"That sounds bad to me, Mother."

"Why should the aghori teach us bad things, Aunt?"

"Good and bad are words of the ignorant. My darlings will not use them."

"Won't this draw us away from Kali, our Divine Mother?" I asked.

My aunt remained silent as she drained the last dregs of vegetable soup from her bowl. Then, setting her bowl on the floor, she said, "Go to sleep."

She got up with her banana leaf and bowl and left the room. Sandhya looked at me silently. Later, Sandhya and I spent some time together in the courtyard.

"Sandhya, I'm scared."

"I am, too, Shambu. Did you see how she talked to us tonight?"

"I know! I haven't seen her so preoccupied before."

"Preoccupied! I thought she was irritable. That scares me more than the aghori," she said.

"She seemed aloof. She is bothered by something, Sandhya."

"Let's sit and pray for a while," she suggested.

"By the tulasi shrine?"

"Sure."

We sat by the tulasi shrine in the center of the courtyard and chanted together. Members of our household gathered to gossip, while others spread their mats on the sand to sleep.

My mind wandered as I mumbled the mantra. I went over some possible situations. The aghori may transform us into dogs again, or she may give us some drink and introduce us to some wild odiyyas from the deeper jungle. She may put us face to face with some preetas. I felt a nudge from Sandhya.

"You aren't chanting. Your mind is wandering!"

I fell to chanting immediately. Then Sandhya stopped chanting.

"What were you thinking?" she asked.

"I was just wondering what is in store for us with the aghori the day after tomorrow."

"Are you afraid that Mother will stop teaching us and let the aghori take over?"

"Oh Kali! I didn't think about that possibility. That would be terrible."

That worried me. I had developed a deep attachment for my aunt; the thought of her abandoning me was frightening. Sandhya's face loomed close to mine. I felt her hand on my shoulders.

"You love my mother a lot, don't you?" she asked smiling, pulling my face close to hers. I sat silent. I was worried.

"My mother loves you very much."

I snapped out of my fears. "I know she does, Sandhya."

"Yes, but do you know that she thinks you are her unborn child?"

"Sandhya! What are you saying? How can you say I am unborn? I am right here!" I said, pulling her cheeks.

"I know that. She thinks that it is like you are born to her. I don't know how to say it."

"Did Aunt Preema say anything to you about this?" I asked.

Sandhya fell silent. Then giving me a shy glance she said, "Well once I told her that I am fond of you. She said that is because of ties from past life—samskaras. Then she said that she loves you very much, too. 'Shambu is my son,' were her exact words."

"When did she say this?"

"Oh. Actually, a few times in the past when Mother and I were together."

"Aunt Preema is my spiritual mother. I spend more time with her than with my mother and father. She is my mother and she is my friend," I remarked.

We sat silent for a while. The courtyard rumbled with the din of chatter.

"I think I will get some sleep," she said.

"Jai Jagad Ambae!"

"Jai Jagad Ambae!" Sandhya said, giving me a peck on my cheek.

I brought my mat and sheets from my room and spread them near the east side of the tulasi shrine. I lay awake for a long while, listening to the household settle around me. One by one the oil lamps were blown out. I saw somebody go into the family shrine and replenish the oil reserve in the nitya deepam. Sleep was hard to come by; I watched the stars parade past. After midnight I finally fell asleep.

Around 2 or 3 A.M., I woke up abruptly. I heard a shuffle. As I raised myself upon my elbows, I caught sight of two women departing in haste by the main door, a third woman escorting them with a lamp. She then put the lamp out and hurried to her quarters. None around me stirred. I wondered who left. Again I lay awake for a while before falling asleep.

▼ ▼ ▼

The next day, I spent most of the morning at school. Sandhya and I attended different classes. After puberty, boys and girls went to different buildings in the same school, but all learned the same subjects. That afternoon, I walked home from school feeling thirsty. Entering the courtyard, I made my way to the kitchen to quench my thirst with jeera water. My aunts boiled well water with some cumin and ginger and cooled it for the household to drink.

As I crossed the courtyard, I heard loud voices coming from the women's room. It sounded like an argument was in progress. I wondered what was going on. Even though it piqued my curiosity, I decided to assuage my thirst before investigating.

Jeera water was stored in a large clay pot in the darkest corner of the kitchen. The porous clay helped evaporate the water, thus keeping it cool. A large section of the back yard was visible through the kitchen window. As I quenched my thirst, I watched my cousin Hari split dried coconut fronds on an old piece of lumber. I whistled to Hari. He turned around, shaded his eyes with the ax and peered at the kitchen window. It became obvious that he couldn't see me, so I thrust my hand out the window and waved at him.

"Yes?" he asked, and stared at the window a few seconds. Then a grin split his face. He dropped the ax and walked to the window.

"Shambu, what's up?" he asked. He eyed the brass mug in my hand and said, "I'll have some, too."

"Come around to the back door, Hari. I'll open it for you."

"I just got back from school," I said, as Hari gulped the rest of the jeera water from my vessel. "What is going on, Hari? What's all that shouting coming from the women's room?"

"Oh! You didn't hear? Rati miscarried."

"Rati who?"

"From the House of Magha," he said, and I searched my memory of this girl Rati. "The good-looking one," he said with a sly grin.

"Chinna's daughter!"

"Yes." Then, he added in a whisper, "There was no fetus!"

"What?"

"Honest! In the name of Kali!" he swore.

"What could happen to the fetus?" I pondered aloud.

"Brother, it's gone! It's true. Rati's mother was one among the three midwives; they were with her all the time in their women's room."

"What came out, then? Rati had a big pregnant belly!"

"I know, a big shiny belly. They say just a bag of blood and water. They think that the odiyyas took the baby."

Hari's words were like a punch in my belly. "There is no such person as an evil odiyya!" I exclaimed, remembering all the teachings of Aunt Preema and Aghori Narayani.

"That is the opinion of the elders of the House of Magha, Shambu. All right, if this is not true, then how else could this have happened?"

"Kali protect us!" I cried, signing protection around me. Hari did the same. The atmosphere suddenly felt gloomy, in spite of the bright sun outside.

"I'm not sure about this explanation, Hari. I want to ask Aunt Preema about this." I whipped around and headed out of the kitchen.

"Wait!" Hari said snagging my arm. "You will not like this. Aunt Gauri thinks that Aunt Preema is somehow involved," he whispered hurriedly.

"What foolish talk is this!"

"I just want you to know. You are close to her. I just wanted you to know, brother. That is the argument that's going on," Hari said, indicating the women's room.

"I've got to go look for Aunt Preema," I said and dashed out into the hallway.

I remembered Aunt Preema's cryptic advice to us to prepare for our lessons with the aghori tomorrow. I wondered about the women who left our home last night. These somehow seemed ominously connected. I would have loved to have a talk with Sandhya first, but she was not home from school yet. I walked toward the women's room. The voices became distinct; Aunt Gauri's voice rose above the rest. I heard her mention Aunt Preema. Then followed a return volley of protests. Whatever it was that Aunt Gauri said triggered a furious response. I stopped in my tracks by the low wall opposite the room. Two things were clear: Aunt Preema was not in the room with the rest and she was blamed for something, just as Hari said. My heart pounded with agitation. I wanted so much to go in there myself and listen to their argument. But I was past the age when boys were welcome there.

"After all, she is a confirmed infant killer!" I heard Aunt Gauri shout.

"That's enough, Gauri. You behave without self-respect," I heard Aunt Bhanu scold Aunt Gauri.

"How dare you speak about our own kin in such terms? You are crossing the line here, Gauri," I heard my mother shout. I was troubled and felt insecure. Conflicts among elders were infrequent in our household. Administrative power flowed from the eldest matriarch, who settled disagreements by invoking the Divine Mother. These angry words were unsettling. Where was Aunt Preema? If Aunt Gauri was moving against her, then I must warn her. I must at least meet with Sandhya before she gets home. Together we may locate my aunt. I had barely taken a few steps toward the exit when the door to the women's room opened. Aunt Bhanu emerged along with my mother. I rushed to my mother.

"Did you see Aunt Preema, Mother?" I asked. But before she could answer, Aunt Bhanu said, "We don't know where she is, son. And I hope she stays away for a day or two, for her own safety," she added.

"Aren't we jumping to conclusions too soon here, Bhanu?" my mother asked.

"To what conclusions?" I asked.

"Hey! I did not make these accusations, Leela. It is our beloved Gauri who thinks she knows it all," said Aunt Bhanu ignoring my question.

"What is it Mother?" My heart pounded as I asked.

"Gauri thinks that your Aunt Preema is behind poor Rati's miscarriage," said my mother. I was shocked to silence for a few moments.

"That is not true! Not true! Not Aunt Preema," I shouted.

"Hard to believe it, isn't it?" said Aunt Gauri, stepping out of the women's room. "She is an infant killer, killed her own child. Did you know that? But nobody believes it," she added as she retreated to the backyard.

"Kali! Kali! Enough of this! You will destroy our household, Gauri, with your irresponsible words," exclaimed Aunt Bhanu.

Aunt Preema went through two pregnancies. Sandhya was her first child. I had heard that a year later she was pregnant again. But after only a few weeks, she lost this child to stillbirth. Aunt Preema herself never spoke about this, and I did not ask owing to the sadness this would evoke in her.

"Aunt Preema is not a bad sorceress. I will not believe this," I muttered. But even as I said this, I was appalled by a trace of doubt that pushed its way through the thick wall of faith, like the spreading smudge of moisture from a leak in a water tank. My agitation must have been apparent, for my mother said,

"Don't you worry, dear. This is just Gauri's imagination. Our Gauri is ever-ready with an exciting explanation even if it crucifies one of her own sisters."

"Where is Aunt Preema, Mother?"

"I don't know, dear. You know her. She goes off and does things on her own, collecting herbs and such. At any rate, she doesn't have to answer to Gauri."

"Who else is accusing Aunt Preema? Is Magha household suspicious of her, too?"

"Dear Kali, no. I hope not," answered Aunt Bhanu. "But who can say for sure. With Gauri's loose tongue anything is possible." I was taken aback by her vehemence.

"How did Aunt Gauri come up with this fantastic accusation? She seems to constantly undermine Aunt Preema."

"Your Aunt Preema is a prodigy. She is a radical among us, Shambu."

"Mother! You think she is an outlaw of sorts?"

"Dear no! Your mother only means that Preema takes interest in knowing and expanding her experiences in so many fields that it takes her beyond the boundaries of our tradition," said Aunt Bhanu.

"Rather, boundaries we are told to believe in!" commented my mother, giving a knowing look at Aunt Bhanu.

"Preema's sense of independence and confidence in herself threatens Gauri. It is as if Preema's world infringes on Gauri's role as future matriarch," explained Aunt Bhanu.

I heard the men come home from their work in the fields.

"Well, we'd better get the tea boiling."

"That is what I am thinking, too, Leela." With that they both walked toward the kitchen.

I went to my room to pick up a fresh dhoti and headed to the pond. Sandhya would be home soon and I must be ready to do our chants together somewhere in the fields.

Floating and swimming in the pond, I fell into deep thought. Aunt Bhanu's and my mother's explanation was enlightening. But it put a kink in the armor of wholesomeness with which I had cloaked my perception of my household, like a loose string in a tightly woven fabric.

I watched helplessly as my mind wandered into the implications driven from Aunt Gauri's accusations. How on earth could a fetus disappear after so many months of gestation? Then, Aunt Preema—of all people—to be implicated was inconceivable. As thought tumbled after thought, the seeds of doubt that germinated in my mind appalled me. I had considered the fact that Aunt Gauri was an outspoken antagonist of Aunt Preema, so her charges were at this point mere allegations, since there was no physical proof to substantiate her claims. I must warn my aunt.

A loud splash broke my thoughts. A second later, a tender coconut bud bobbed beside me.

"Are you dreaming?" a voice sailed down from the rim of the pond.

"What?" I tumbled in the water onto my belly. On the sandbank was Sandhya in a pretty red dress.

"It seemed like you were dreaming. Hey, I'm ready if you are!" Sandhya said and she took aim at me with another coconut bud.

"I'm coming. I'll be up there in a moment." I waded close to the rock slab where my fresh dhoti waited.

"Don't look!" I warned, climbing out of the water.

"I am not," she assured me, laying her hands over her eyes. But I saw her peek through a hole between her fingers.

"Did anyone say anything to you, Sandhya?"

"Like what?"

"You didn't run into Aunt Gauri. Did you?"

"No, I didn't. Why?"

"Come down here, quick."

She gathered her dress up and sprinted down the sand.

"Where is Aunt Preema?"

"Isn't she home?" she countered.

"Listen, Rati from the House of Magha miscarried. But there was no fetus. Only the bag of water."

"How come?"

"Sandhya, Aunt Gauri accuses Aunt Preema. There was an argument this afternoon. We must warn Aunt Preema."

"She blames my mother! Bitch! She has the nerve to fault my mother?" Her voice quivered in distress and anger.

"Losing control won't help. We have to warn Aunt Preema," I said, grabbing her arm.

"Where is my mother, Shambu? In what way could my mother be a threat?"

"She accuses her of dark sorcery."

"That's incredible!"

"Luckily, everyone else opposed Aunt Gauri, Sandhya."

"Were you there, Shambu?"

When I told her all that happened, her anger turned to fear for her mother's safety. Despite the profound respect the villagers had for odiyyas, they showed an irrational fear toward anyone that they suspected as a dark odiyya. And they had no way of recognizing a good odiyya.

"I think that our first line of action should be to inform Aunt Preema," I said.

"I agree. It's strange that mother is not home," she muttered. "Where should we look for her?"

"Let's begin with the main temple."

"No, it is not her day to worship there," she countered.

"What about the vallichappad colony?"

"That we can try. But I don't feel sure." Then after some thought, she said, "I think we should first check with my father."

"You are right! Let's go." I pulled her up the slope.

"Wait!" Sandhya cried, pulling me to a stop. "What did Aunt Gauri say?"

"Aunt Gauri did not provide any evidence at all. She just accused Aunt Preema of being an infant killer. She claimed that Aunt Preema had killed her second child by aborting it before full term. That was the only incident she harped on."

"My dead brother!" Exclaimed Sandhya. "He was stillborn. My mother didn't kill him. Everybody knows that!"

"Of course, we know that is the truth," I assured her, pulling her into my arms. "Sandhya, we should go now."

▼ ▼ ▼

We entered Aunt Preema's and Uncle Raghavan's room. It was dark within, but a figure hastily straightened up at our approach. Aunt Gauri walked out in haste, embarrassed.

"Find whatever you were looking for, Aunt Gauri?" I asked in a loud voice.

She stared at me with anger and discomfort. Without warning Sandhya stepped across Aunt Gauri's path.

"Just what were you looking for in my parents' room?"

"Not your concern, child," she said, attempting to evade Sandhya.

"I make it my concern, now," replied Sandhya, firmly matching her move. Aunt Gauri stopped in her tracks,

"Move aside, child," she ordered Sandhya.

"Sandhya, it is okay," I whispered. But Sandhya stood firm. Her body trembled slightly and her eyes flashed in anger.

"If you insist, I came in to look for any clue as to where your mother could have gone. Do you know where she is, child?"

"First of all, don't 'child' me," said Sandhya. "Secondly, it is not the first time my mother has been gone on a few days' trip."

"That's exactly my point. All this time I did not question her disappearances. But today, her absence coincides with the strange miscarriage by Rati. I wonder if there is any connection," she asked in a mocking tone. I bristled when I heard this. Stepping ahead of Sandhya I said,

"First of all, I don't know who gave you the authority to question Aunt Preema's or any other elder's whereabouts. You are not the matriarch yet. Next, I fail to see the connection you struggle to contrive between my aunt's absence from home and Rati's mishap." I heard Sandhya chuckle behind me.

"Behave, young man. Only Preema can bring up children as misbehaved as you two," Aunt Gauri snapped as she moved into the hall.

"Who is misbehaving? Ooh! Watch out!" cried Uncle Raghavan as Aunt Gauri slammed into him, falling into his arms.

"Oh! Kali! Forgive me, Raghavan," muttered a disconcerted Aunt Gauri as she quickly extricated herself from my uncle's arms and rushed out. Uncle Raghavan made a face at us as if he enjoyed her inadvertent embrace. Sandhya burst into a gale of laughter.

"Wow! Now then, after that brief, but sweet hug. What? Were you two caught misbehaving in this room again?" he said with a sly look toward us. "How many times should I tell you both to lock the door when you two are at it?" he said with mock seriousness.

"Father, stop fooling. Mother is in trouble."

"We just caught Aunt Gauri snooping about Aunt Preema's things," I said.

"Shambu, if she violates our privacy, she is only creating trouble for herself," he said. He looked about the room inspecting Aunt Preema's things.

"Gauri was bent on finding something. I don't know what. Look, she has gone through Preema's herbs and potions in a hurry," he remarked as he rearranged the scattered leaf packets and tiny clay vials. Sandhya helped him. Then he turned around.

"Gauri is blaming Preema for Rati's miscarriage. I know that." He sighed, shaking his head. Sandhya held him close.

"In all these years of my life with her, I have only known her to help others. I know Preema's heart. I have seen her nourish even a dying ant. I am used to her ways now," he smiled, "But when we got married, I couldn't understand why she put up such a racket whenever I killed even a few ants I found crawling in the room. 'Don't kill them dear; just drop some nectar outside the room. Then place an ant from this colony near the drops and wait,' she would tell me."

"That is what she does even now, Uncle," I said. Uncle Raghavan was silent.

"How can anyone blame her?" he muttered. "I will take care of this. You both get going."

I stood up. Sandhya sat by her father, still clinging to him.

"Nothing will happen to your mother as long as my heart is beating," he assured Sandhya.

"Come, Sandhya," I tugged on her arm. Tea was being served outside. I felt a silent oppression, a peculiar self-consciousness, as if our own people were spying upon us. We both gulped down our tea.

My mother came by asking how we fared. Then she whispered to me, "If anybody can take care of herself, that is your Aunt Preema. Don't worry. Your aunt is no stranger to Gauri's little games. Besides, your father and I will not be mere spectators if anything should happen."

Sandhya grabbed my mother's hand saying, "Aunt Leela, thank you so much."

"Aren't you two going to the aghori's tonight? I know Preema is not here. That doesn't mean that you can skip your classes," my mother said.

"The aghori canceled tonight's classes, aunt." Sandhya said.

"Really!"

"Yes, mother. We were told to practice our lessons together this evening."

"Then get going—or I will tell your aunt that you didn't."

"We are going, Aunt Leela," Sandhya assured, and hugged her.

▼ ▼ ▼

I carried a box of matches and a palm frond torch; Sandhya took a grass mat for us to sit on. We walked toward a cluster of boulders that sat like an island in the middle of ripening paddy.

"Aunt Gauri doesn't know who she is up against," I said.

"I feel helpless, Shambu."

"There is no reason to feel that way, Sandhya. You can count on me, my mother and father, Brother Padman, and Sister Kartiyayini. I am sure Aunt Ananda and Aunt Bhanu are also with us."

Sandhya just sighed as we walked.

"What if Aunt Gauri spread this allegation in the House of Magha? Won't it spread throughout the village? Then what would we do, Shambu?"

"Sandhya, if Aunt Gauri or anybody in our household does that, then they will only undermine the unity of our house. It may split our household. That, I think, is the last thing on the mind of Aunt Gauri, who is hungry for power. She will not jeopardize her future by invoking the special council of village elders, who would then look for a replacement for our dear Aunt Gauri as the next matriarch."

"The special council! That has never been invoked in years. At least, I don't remember it."

"Right, the last one was sixty or seventy years ago, I think, when both the elders of the House of Puthura became vallichappads and the next oldest daughter was a little more than a child," I said.

"To invoke the special council in this situation will be a blotch on the name of our house. The kurukkals may even perform the Astamangalya Vidya to seek the future of our household!" said Sandhya.

"That's it, Sandhya! If this allegation cannot be proved, then this is what they will do—perform the Astamangalya Vidya to seek the truth," I said, alarmed.

"That should clear my mother beyond dispute."

"But could the kurukkals be biased toward Aunt Gauri? After all, she is the next matriarch," I muttered.

"Ridiculous!" Sandhya exclaimed. "It is impossible for a kurukkal to be biased."

A bright orange sun set in the horizon behind a plume of coconut palm fronds. We climbed the boulders and spread the grass mat on a shallow saddle among the rocks. Facing the setting sun, we focused our minds upon the mantra. Even though darkness fell about us, the rocks radiated warmth. Little by little, my awareness detached itself from my senses. Soon my consciousness gathered into a powerful stream and poured itself upon the beauteous, divine Being of my Supreme Goddess. There were frequent moments when my emotions surged high. At times, I cried to the Divine Mother to grant me a single Divine experience that would transform my being forever.

"Divine Mother! Bestow just one blessed experience that would awaken my divinity forever. Just one experience, Kali," I cried in my heart. I couldn't keep the tears from streaming down my cheeks. I lost my chant to racking sobs. My finely tuned breath control disintegrated in the throes of anguish that grappled my being. We meditated thus for a while.

"Shambu . . . It's late," whispered Sandhya in my right ear. Gently, she took my hands in hers. "We should head home."

# CHAPTER EIGHT

# *Sorcerers of the Underworld*

The next day, Sandhya and I chanted as much as we could. We were tense all day long, without a clue as to what lay ahead for us at the aghori's. We had not seen Aunt Preema for two days. I heard from my cousins that the Magha household was planning an exorcism ritual that night with the help of some vallichappads. They wanted to make sure that Rati was safe, though the infant was beyond help. Elders from other houses were invited and Aunt Gauri's decision to represent our house alarmed us. With unbearable misgivings, we set out toward the aghori's barn at sunset.

The barn door was slightly open. Flames flashed in the darkness within.

"Come in!" Aghori Narayani greeted us with her hoarse cry.

Sandhya pushed open the door and I stepped in close behind her. A fire blazed in the pit before the aghori, who sat cross-legged on her mattress of straw and buffalo skin. After greeting her, we prostrated before the massive relief of Kali on the wall. Smells of wood smoke, incense, and food that the aghori had prepared filled the room.

The aghori called us back to her. On the floor by the fire pit she arranged two rectangular patches of hay, side by side, like narrow sleeping mats. Each one was covered with white dhotis. I felt Sandhya's fingers clutch my hand and a familiar flutter of apprehension throbbed in my stomach. The aghori sprang up and was beside us.

"Sit down on these mats," she ordered. Sandhya and I sat on each patch of hay. As I sank down, I realized that the hay was piled thick. The aghori checked our posture. Once she was satisfied, she went back to her own seat.

"Tonight you will learn of the existence of the Bhaikari Odiyyas. This is important knowledge that will help you in your decision to either stay on your current path or travel the cosmos along another. But you should first eat. I have been busy preparing this delicacy for you two." With that, she took two polished coconut shells and slapped into them lumps of pudding from a large quantity she had in her buffalo skull.

"Eat," she said, handing them to us.

"But why would we not want to stay on this path, Mother Aghori?" I asked.

"If you know of this path only, then what choice do you have? That is, until you come across the other sometime in this life," she replied. "But if you know both paths, then your choice will be truly voluntary."

"These Bhaikaris, are they the dark odiyyas people talk about? The evil ones?" asked Sandhya.

"They are like ourselves, children of the Divine Mother expanding into the cosmos. Only their approach is different. But eat now." The aghori began to hum chants while offering rice into the fire.

We ate the pudding, which tasted like a sweet mixture of rice, jaggery, cardamom seeds, and black pepper. This situation made us uneasy. We had eaten with the aghori before in more casual surroundings, but never in the precincts of a fire ceremony. It portended some serious enterprise, I thought.

"Rinse your mouths and wash your hands. You know where to find the water pot."

The pot of water was behind the barn. A stream flowed nearby. It was already dark outside when Sandhya and I made our way around the barn. The night was warm; the sky was filled with stars; and with each step, my eyes became accustomed to the starlight. We heard the brook gurgling through the vegetation beyond. Sandhya led me to the pot that stood out against the white of the lime-coated barn wall.

After I poured water for Sandhya, I stooped low to catch the stream of water Sandhya poured out for me. I heard someone clear his throat in the darkness to our right. At once, Sandhya stopped pouring water.

"Mother Aghori, is that you?" Sandhya asked as we peered around us. A cough came from the bushes. We gazed intently at the spot.

"The dogs," whispered Sandhya.

"Where?" I asked. But even as I asked, a portion of the darkness near the bushes seemed to come alive. A pack of dogs emerged and approached the barn. We hastened back to the door. We were sure these were the aghori's cohorts.

Bursting into the barn, Sandhya announced, "Odiyatthi Nedunga is here!"

"Yes, she is," the aghori said, sweeping her hand toward the Kali image. A flash of fear convulsed my legs. Somehow the dogs managed to get in the room before us. The five dogs lay on the floor before Kali.

"We should begin," announced the aghori. "Sandhya, you lie down there, and you here." The aghori assigned the mats to us. I lay beside Sandhya, our heads toward the image of Kali and our feet by the fire. Watching the flickering light playing on the high rafters, numbness seized my mind. Instinctively, I began to chant. Moments later, I heard the dogs creep up close to our heads.

"Close your eyes," I was startled to hear a woman's voice above my head. I closed my eyes. The chant began as a hum or a murmur of sorts. I felt a vibration that began at the back of my heels and spread along the surface of my body that pressed into the hay. The room was spinning, I thought. Fingers of warmth pushed between my body and the hay, and I felt a fleeting sense of being lifted. My eyes were closed, but I could see every item in the room in my mind. It took a while to discern the image of Kali, which appeared at a peculiar angle—her head and feet were below me, and I could not correct her image. I gave up trying and focused on the fire pit. Incredible, I thought. The fire was coming up at my face from below! It generated no heat, but its flames passed through my face. Without warning, the room vanished, and I was in total darkness.

Within moments, I felt straw under my fingers. I was on the roof of the barn!

"Sandhya! Sandhya," I cried in panic.

Something grabbed at my left elbow. With fear, I sprang to my right. Instantly I was flying off the roof. As I tumbled through the night air, I bumped into something.

"Shambu, stop moving so fast," I heard Sandhya say. She clung to me like a monkey as we spun out of control toward the branches of the fruit trees. I winced an instant before the leaves whipped my face. Strangely, there was no sensation.

"Sandhya, how did this happen to us?"

"I don't know. Just help me get behind you," she cried. I could see the tree tops now as we sailed through the air. Something sizzled through me like a bolt of light.

"There, that should get you two to fly straight," I heard Aghori Narayani say. Miraculously, Sandhya and I began flying straight—I had my face down, speeding above the treetops. I could see and hear with astounding clarity. Something luminous kept appearing

above my head. I craned my neck to take a look, and at once I
flipped onto my back. A large luminous oval was above me speeding through the night, matching my velocity. I stared at it in fascination. This must be some kind of protective power thrown over us
by the aghori and her cohorts, I thought. I wondered whether
Sandhya saw it, too.

"Sandhya, can you see it?"

"See what?"

"This oval light!" I said indicating the light.

"You have been staring at me for some time, Shambu," I was
puzzled to hear Sandhya's voice come from the luminous oval.

"Is that you, Sandhya?" I asked, reaching out to touch her. But I
stopped myself for fear that any extraneous movement might fling me
away from her.

"Yes, this is me," she said. "And you look like a blob of light,
too!" I heard her giggle.

"Stop fooling and keep flying," ordered a hoarse female voice
from above and behind us.

I twisted myself around to look behind us: I saw six brilliant ovals
follow us. At the same instant, I felt myself spin away—but two arcs
of light shot around me and pulled me close. I was beneath Sandhya
again. I flew thus for a while over trees and farmland.

Without any warning, the space around us turned translucent
with a massive brilliance. I felt a crunch, as if a giant fist had slammed
into my innards. The space surrounding us shook with soundless
tremors as brilliance after brilliance pulsed through the area.

"Malasi! Malasi!" I heard a faint female voice call. I was perplexed—it was as if someone was whispering in my ear. The voice was
familiar, but the word meant nothing to me.

"Malasi!" The voice called. I sensed an acute urgency in the
voice—she needed help.

"Did you hear that, Sandhya?"

"Yes! Oh Kali! That's my mother! My mother is hurting! Shambu, we must help her now!"

"That's it. It's Aunt Preema! Mother Aghori!" I called out to the
aghori. "Sandhya, get the aghori!"

Ahead, I saw six blobs of red light in the sky. They surrounded an
oval of intense white light. Three of the red blobs plummeted and
punched through a rooftop. With stunning speed, the aghori and her
cohorts shot past overhead.

"Ajamushti! Ajamushti," a voice screamed. Even as the voice cried,
I saw a barrage of lance-shaped light shoot out from one luminous

oval into the cluster of red blobs in the sky. The luminous ovals of the aghori and her cohorts moved about so fast that I lost track of what oval was who.

"Victory to Ghora Kali! I invoke Ghora Bhairavi!" I heard another cry as their luminous ovals streaked above us at incredible speed.

Within a few minutes, we had entered a zone of intense astral energy—I sensed raw power everywhere. I could feel the burning fury of the astral combatants.

"Shambu, I sense much fear! I hope Mother is safe," I heard Sandhya's voice in my mind.

"Sandhya, how do we respond? We must find Aunt Preema!" My words were more like an intense feeling than actual speech.

"Look! Look, the odiyatthi. She chants and throws! Do you see?" Sandhya cried.

At that moment, Odiyatthi Nedunga's oval luminescence brightened a hundredfold. An arm of sorts emerged from it, flashed downward, and grabbed a tree branch. In an instant we saw the entire tree uproot from the ground near the house. It hurtled skyward at one of the red blobs that engaged the intense white oval. The red blob broke away from the other two.

"We are going in. Let's go, Shambu. That is my mother! That white light." I heard Sandhya's thoughts. For some reason, the Bhagalamukhi mantra began repeating in my awareness.

"Chant, Sandhya," I thought to her.

"I am. I can hear you in my being."

"What?" I asked.

"Don't speak. You can feel me if you stay quiet."

As we hurtled into the gap left by the red blob, I felt a ferocious power fill my being. A growl rumbled from my luminous midparts. I felt that Sandhya wanted me closer to her luminous oval. Immediately I blended into her partially as we streaked upward. We sped past Odiyatthi Nedunga, who engaged a red blob. We glimpsed them grab at leaves and twigs, transform them into shafts of energy, and hurtle these at each other.

Just as we slipped in front of the intense white luminescence, we saw the luminous oval of Kora plunge downward and through the rooftop below us.

"That's the House of Magha!" exclaimed Sandhya.

"Why is Kora going in there?" I asked. Even as I asked, I saw that a ceremony progressed in the courtyard of the House of Magha.

"The exorcism, Shambu." I heard Sandhya answer in my mind. "I think Kora has gone after the underworld odiyyas."

Without any warning, two successive pulses of energy slammed into us. I was separated from Sandhya's awareness and we began to tumble downward.

"Join, children! Join! You will not survive separated!" I felt Aunt Preema cry. But before we could pull together, we saw coursing toward us an intense energy, shaped like a peculiar trident. We tumbled, dazed and helpless with terror.

In the blink of an eye, an arc of light emerged from Aunt Preema's luminous oval. It plucked a fist-sized lump of luminous material from her midpart and cast it at the trident. Blinding light filled the space. When the light dissipated, Aunt Preema's oval was near us, pushing us into each other. Just as Aunt Preema moved away, a force hit us. I felt Sandhya begin to fade. Her life force was spewing into the astral firmament. I was alarmed and furious. Sensing another pulse of energy come at her, I willed myself between her and the bolt of power.

I felt an evil energy pummel my being. The sensation was peculiar. There was no pain seeing my life-energy drain away through a million ruptured channels—like it was happening to someone else. I was floating in cosmic darkness and I watched fascinated as a hundred thousand tiny fountains spewed soothing light from my being.

Sandhya, the aghori and her cohorts, and even the ground had disappeared from my sight. I was bewildered as I realized that this was my astral body. It must be falling apart. Then I felt a presence, someone I could not see—a being invisible even to my astral senses! Or was this presence my true Self? I was perplexed. I sensed imminent disintegration, and I wondered if it was mine. It did not matter because peace enveloped me, like a womb around a fetus. I lay suspended in darkness, quiet and insensate.

It was a sound that gathered my dispersed awareness, a sound like wind rushing through a blazing fire. Out of the darkness there appeared a multitude of swirling light. Millions of eddies of whirling light surrounded me. I permeated them—they were part of me and I of them! Is this my actual being, this universe of whirling galaxies of astral energy? How exquisite and blissful! Where will this immense energy drain into when I cease to be? Who takes my life force? A voice rang out, "Life drains from the Self into the Self. None can drain the Self." As the voice fell silent, a divine sadness expanded outward from every twirling cluster of light. Soon it pervaded my entire awareness, and I knew that this was the beginning of a massive disintegration. I tumbled gently through a sea of exquisite sadness.

A terrifying and indescribable roar filled the space, pulling my awareness away from cosmic sadness. In utter perplexity, I suddenly realized that my luminous oval was still joined to Sandhya's and we floated in the sky above the courtyard of the House of Magha. Below us, men and women in ceremonial costume danced around a young woman. Flames and smoke lifted up into the night from a miniature pyre in the backyard.

Then the roar blasted above us again, a terrifying thunder from another world. We felt that space itself was compressed and released under its resonant force. A luminous oval of tremendous size coalesced above us, blotting out the ether beyond. It was over a hundred feet in length and it radiated massive energy into the surrounding space. The three red blobs in the sky whirled into a tight ball of red luminescence. We heard a wild shriek from the coalesced red luminescence. Hearing this, three other blobs of red energy emerged from the House of Magha and sped away. The underworld odiyyas were routed. I realized with relief that the astral battle was over.

Like famished vampires, we drank in energy from the mighty luminescence. Through a million mouths all over our joined beings, we drew in sustenance. We looked up at the enormous oval. Who was this benevolent being? I heard Sandhya muse with awe and reverence. The massive form triggered a faint memory in my awareness. As it moved beyond our range, recognition cascaded within me—"Amorphous Being! Sandhya, this is the Amorphous Being!"

But Sandhya did not respond. I twisted around to look. That movement caused me to settle downward as if gliding against the sides of a steep abyss. The space around me became turbid, choking my erstwhile lucidity. A strange vibration droned with a disconcerting hum. Then I felt a sensation on my back. Where was I? Shapes appeared around me, which shifted in space with the slightest movement of my eyes. Some liquid streamed over my face and head.

"Massage some on his chest," I heard the aghori's voice.

"Life force is feeble, Malasi."

"I know, but he is young. He will gain it back. Nedunga, why do you call me that? I am Narayani in this body."

Malasi! Aunt Preema had been calling the aghori earlier! It is a strange name, I thought.

"How is she, Nedunga?"

"Same as him. Like him, she absorbed some force."

"Is Kora okay?"

"He will need some nurturing to put his body together, Narayani. Pandi and the rest have taken him into the hills."

"Nedunga, we will gather and put him back together."

"Later, Narayani."

Flickering light filled the room. Wood smoke? I smelled wood smoke and incense.

"Lay still," the aghori's face loomed over me.

"Mother Aghori, where is Sandhya?"

She placed Sandhya's hand in mine.

"How is Aunt Preema?"

"Don't worry about her. You will see her tomorrow. Rest now. I will send word to your home and tell them that you two are with me tonight."

I drifted into a deep slumber.

The aghori woke us early the next morning. I sat up on my hay mattress, but I lacked energy even to think. A fire blazed in the pit. The aghori boiled some broth in a stone pot over the fire. Sandhya lay to my left, curling up and stretching, making valiant attempts to wake up. When I leaned over and rubbed her shoulder, she began to groan. She opened her eyes and blinked as if she did not recognize me. I put my head to the floor and blinked back, teasing her fondly.

"Where are the others, Mother Aghori?" I asked, looking for Odiyatthi Nedunga and her disciples.

"They left last night. I won't allow those dogs to sleep in here. They smell!" The aghori broke out into a rumbling laughter.

"Wake up. Mother Aghori wants us up," I said, but Sandhya just grunted.

Aghori Narayani stirred the broth, dropping in a bunch of leaves that lay soaking in a pot of cold water. She glanced at Sandhya and me as she did this. I observed a glint in her eyes. She selected a particular piece of wood from a pile against the wall behind her and threw it into the fire. After a few moments, the wood burst into flames with a crack, throwing sparks half way up to the ceiling. Immediately, Sandhya got up on to her elbows and stared at the flames.

"The broth will be ready in a few minutes. You may wash up behind the barn when you are ready," the aghori announced.

"Mother Aghori . . ."

"Yes?"

"Did we really fly last night?" Even as I asked that, I saw Sandhya eye me with disbelief.

"He is a hard case, isn't he?" said the aghori with a chuckle to Sandhya. She stirred the broth a few times, pulled the ladle out, and rapped the stone pot twice.

"Depends on who and what you mean by we," the aghori remarked.

"Me, Sandhya, you, and Odiyatthi Nedunga's group!"

"Yes."

I sat up. That was incredible. "You mean I flew with my body?" I asked.

Sandhya was sitting upright now.

"No, not with your body." I felt somewhat disappointed to hear that. "With your astral body," the aghori added. She eyed me as she pushed in unburned wood with a pair of iron tongs.

"We all left our bodies in here while we flew?" Sandhya asked.

"No, we all did not. You two left your bodies in here. The rest of us took ours with us," the aghori said, laughing.

"Why didn't we take our bodies with us?" I asked.

"You couldn't. Not enough power," she said, lifting a ladle full of the broth and sipping it. "Ah! It's just about done. You both should go to the brook and wash up now."

"Yes, Mother Aghori," I said, helping Sandhya up.

Sandhya and I stepped out into the cold, predawn darkness. I clutched my upper cloth closer as the nip drew my warmth away.

"You know how early it is, Shambu?"

"Looks like an hour before sunrise, Sandhya."

Sandhya leaned against the barn wall for a few moments.

"Are you all right?"

"I feel drained!" she complained. I stood close to her.

The brook flowed about fifty feet behind the barn through vegetation that grew wild. The water was shallow here, so we walked upstream a hundred yards further into the woods where the brook curved around and the water ran deep along one edge.

It was refreshing to wade into the knee-deep water. We rinsed our mouths and washed our faces. I felt the grogginess wash away with each splash of the cold water. We let the breeze dry our skin on our way back.

Inside the barn, Aghori Narayani had lit the lamps by the Kali image against the far wall. Guided by the aghori, we prayed here for a short time.

"Drink this. Drink it all," ordered the aghori. "It will help you draw in prana and refresh you," she said, giving us both two large bamboo containers filled with the broth. It tasted astringent, like ginger. I felt full when I was not quite half done with it.

"Drink it! Drink it," said the aghori as she watched me make a face. When we finished the broth she said, "You both may step out for a while."

"Why?" asked Sandhya.

"Go on, just outside the barn. What flows in has to flow out," she said with a giggle. So we went outside and wandered among the vegetation on the further bank of the brook. There I described to Sandhya my experiences last night after intercepting the second bolt of energy that came at her. I was surprised to know that she did not have a similar experience of an immense sadness of a massive astral disintegration. The last thing Sandhya remembered was that the massive being descended upon the scene with a blood-curdling roar. When she felt life-giving energy flood into her from the being, she felt relief and then her awareness faded.

I told Sandhya that I did try to tell her the moment I recognized it as the Amorphous Being whom Ahalya Mata tried to exorcise several years ago.

"I shouted to you that this was the Amorphous Being. But when I turned around you were gone, Sandhya."

"No, I did not hear you, Shambu. I saw the aghori's barn and I saw myself floating down through the roof into my body."

"I think everything went dark at about the same time. I was falling down the walls of a chasm. I didn't experience floating into my body," I said.

"So that was the Amorphous Being!" she exclaimed. "Didn't she call herself Nishachii?"

"Yes! You remember these details, Sandhya?"

"How can I forget? I was by your side day after day as you lay with fever. Do you remember I would smuggle mango pickle and fried bitter-gourd slices to you?"

"Yes. I hid them under my pillow," we laughed as we reminisced.

"This Amorphous Being is huge, Shambu! She is gigantic! No wonder Ahalya Mata and her disciples were routed when they tried to exorcise you."

"Remember Aunt Gauri trying to hold me down?" I asked.

"Oh Kali! I remember how she fell when you threw her down!" said Sandhya, and we laughed.

"Shambu," Sandhya addressed me with a serious look, "I thought I saw Ahalya Mata down there last night!"

"In the courtyard of the House of Magha?" I asked.

"Yes."

"You know Sandhya, I felt the same. When I saw those costumed people dance around that girl, she reminded me of my own exorcism," I said. We walked in silence for a while.

"Why is the Amorphous Being helping us? I mean, she is definitely helping you, Shambu."

"I don't even know who she is, Sandhya."

After we urinated four or five times with irritating frequency, Sandhya asked, "You think that's it?"

We washed in the brook once again and entered the barn. "When do we get to go home?" I asked.

"In a few hours," replied the aghori.

"That long!" exclaimed Sandhya.

"You are still weak from last night's exertions. Nobody at home can help you."

"Aunt Preema can," I said.

"Yes, she can. But she is not home yet. I will help you."

When the sun came up, the aghori made us both wear loin cloths and rubbed us down with an herbal oil. Piling hay in two neat rows, she made two troughs in them, which she lined with jute cloth. After we lay down in the troughs, the aghori covered us from head to foot with several enormous banana leaves, layering them over one another. We lay underneath the leaves for a long time. When sunlight struck the banana leaves, it flooded us with a bright, translucent green light. It was so soothing that in a little while we both fell asleep.

When we woke up, the aghori was fanning smoke from a mixture of herbs and tree resin all over us. The banana leaves had faded to a crisp blackish-brown. They looked as if they had been burned. The aghori made us bathe in the brook. When we returned to the barn, she surprised us with a feast—rice pudding, a mixed vegetable preparation with coconut and buttermilk that was a favorite of Sandhya's, plain rice, bitter gourd slices cooked with spices, and mango pickle that was my favorite.

"Children, it's time to eat. Eat plenty because you need to replenish yourselves."

We were overwhelmed. Sandhya and I hugged the aghori, something we usually did not dare to do. Then we fell to feasting. I helped myself to several servings.

The aghori did not eat with us; she sat on her buffalo skin and watched us eat. Sandhya was not as voracious as I was, and the aghori had to coax her often. For the first time, in all these years of our kinship with the aghori, I noticed that the aghori watched us with much affection, and I felt her love for us. I wondered why she did not join us for lunch. When I asked her why she did not eat with us, she said that she was satisfied just watching us eat.

Then Sandhya asked, "Mother Aghori, how did you cook all this food? I don't see a kitchen and I don't see any cooking pots!"

"This is my kitchen and this is my pot," she replied with a wide grin, pointing to the fire pit and her buffalo skull.

"But you can't make all these dishes just with that," persisted Sandhya.

"All right, what sweet do you both want?" the aghori asked. I stopped eating.

"Pidi," said Sandhya with a smile.

"And you?"

"Coconut burfee," I said. We watched the aghori intensely as she picked up the buffalo skull and lowered it into the pit.

"Warm fresh sweets!" she declared, lifting out the skull and thrusting it under our noses. At the bottom of the skull were two pidis and two burfees. This magic left us speechless.

"Come on, take it and eat. I cooked these for you."

Sandhya picked up a pidi and immediately dropped it back, exclaiming, "It's hot!"

"Oh! Not that hot," countered the aghori, pulling out the pidi and handing it to Sandhya. But Sandhya refused to take it.

"It's not hot. Trust me."

"How can you do that? It was hot when I touched it!" Sandhya exclaimed, holding the cold pidi in her palm. I took a burfee from the skull.

"How did you do this, Mother Aghori?" I asked, savoring the most delicious burfee I had ever tasted.

"Cosmic energy," was the aghori's simple answer.

"Can we do it, too?" I asked.

"In time. You will laugh at your questions then," she said. "Finish this," she said as she extended the skull to us. We ate the remaining sweets.

The aghori bid us wash, then we sat with her by the brook and meditated. After more than an hour passed, she made us stop, telling us that we should get back inside the barn immediately. Sandhya and I were alarmed by her insistence.

"You both should be going home now. Here, mix this in water and drink it before you sleep tonight," she said scooping out some ashes from the fire pit into a small banana leaf. "Now, do not volunteer any stories to anybody. You know that, don't you?"

"Yes, Mother Aghori," we replied.

We thanked her, touched her feet, and left for home. We had walked only five minutes when we saw Uncle Raghavan coming toward us in the distance.

"Shambu, I think the aghori knew he was coming."

"Yes, that is why she sent us out in a hurry. Should we hide this packet?" I asked, indicating the banana leaf.

"Yes, yes," she said. I tucked it in a fold around my dhoti. Sandhya ran ahead and hugged her father.

"How is Mother?"

"She is home and she is fine. She sent me here to look for you two."

The three of us walked homeward, apprising each other of events. Of course, Sandhya and I did not narrate our astral experiences and the aghori producing food miraculously.

"I hope Aunt Gauri has not given her any trouble," I said.

"No, she has not. In fact, Gauri is keeping herself out of our way," he said, smiling.

"What happened?" asked Sandhya.

"The karanavar from the House of Magha came over this morning to convey their household's gratitude for helping them out in their crisis."

"Did someone from our house help them?" I asked, probing to find out how much if anything Aunt Preema told Uncle Raghavan.

"Ahalya Mata's exorcism on Rati uncovered evil spirits." At the mention of Ahalya Mata, I nudged Sandhya gently. She was right, I thought.

"They also found a number of beings helping their household. They discovered your mother's presence keeping the evil spirits at bay." He then turned to me and said, "Shambu, your Aunt Preema never ceases to amaze me. Sometimes I think that she is a mantravadini. Sandhya, you should have seen Gauri's face when the karanavar thanked your mother in particular."

"Father, I am so happy to hear this!" said Sandhya.

"Me too! I am relieved," I said.

"I always knew that my Preema could not harm anyone even in her dream. When I asked her how she helped them, she said that she sat in isolation for two days and prayed for them. Poor thing, she is so tired," said Uncle Raghavan.

"Uncle, did the vallichappads find out who the other good beings were who helped the Magha household?"

"The karanavar said that the vallichappads were about to see the faces of these other beings, but at that moment their minds were overwhelmed with the roar from a monstrous entity and they were overcome with fatigue. Only Ahalya Mata caught a glimpse of the entity, but by the time she got over her astonishment, the being had disappeared along with the rest."

"Did she say who the being was?" asked Sandhya with unconcealed curiosity.

"Your old friend Nishachii, Shambu. So peculiar," Uncle Raghavan said to me. Sandhya nudged me now.

I walked into my home with great confidence, now that Aunt Preema was vindicated. The enemy within was subdued, for the time being.

▼ ▼ ▼

Two days later, the matriarchs from the House of Magha came to our house. They brought a variety of homemade sweets as presents. It was tea time when they visited with Aunt Preema, Aunt Ananda, and a few other elders in the women's room. Sandhya was present during their visit. She told me that the matriarchs from the House of Magha thanked Aunt Preema for helping protect Rati's life. When they invited Aunt Preema and Sandhya to a lunch at their household the following week, Aunt Preema requested them to include me, telling them that I had prayed along with Sandhya for their welfare. Sandhya said that they apologized not knowing to include me in their invitation.

Aunt Gauri did not like this attention and respect given to Aunt Preema and us by the matriarchs of the House of Magha. There was nothing she could do but fester in her own jealousy; she became a laughingstock in her own home. Aunt Gauri's incredible accusations and theories about Aunt Preema's obscure activities backfired.

Aunt Preema kept to her story of prayer and fasting as the method by which she invoked protection over the Household of Magha. She did not say a word about her battle with the evil energies; she did not divulge this even to her husband. She also kept secret Sandhya's and my involvement in the skirmish. Ahalya Mata was the only outsider who could have some inkling of our involvement in this extraordinary event, only because she had recognized the Amorphous Being's identity. She could tie in the presence of this Being to me from her past encounter with this Being when she attempted to exorcise Her from me a few years ago. But Aunt Preema told us not to worry, as Ahalya Mata rarely associated with the general public. Besides, being a sorceress herself, she was wise and understood the need for secrecy in such matters.

Aunt Preema also assured us that she and the aghori would take us on a major trip into the mountains to help the odiyyas heal Kora, whose body lay preserved somewhere deep within the Ramagiri range.

# CHAPTER NINE

## *Stirring of a Primal Force*

 After eight years, Sandhya and I completed our scriptural studies with Aghori Narayani. During this period we committed to memory scores of verses from the Vedas, practiced several rituals to the aghori's satisfaction, and acquired a good grasp of Hindu metaphysics and cosmology. But unknown to others, with the exception of Aunt Preema, the aghori had also acquainted us with a deeper realm of awareness.

First, we had begun work to gather energy. The aghori said that without a good stock of energy, rituals and chants are useless. Under the aghori's guidance, we practiced gathering energy in seclusion, usually in the jungle behind the barn. Often these practices were simple exercises of fixing the image of special yantras in our minds and chanting appropriate mantras. Aunt Preema and Aghori Narayani taught us special rituals to gather astral energy, and under their supervision we learned to manipulate it. Sandhya and I always ventured into these experiences together, and our minds and awareness bonded in many inconceivable ways. Then one night, the aghori decided that she had taught us enough.

"It is time to move on, my dears," she announced. "Seek your freedom at all costs. In the end that's what matters."

"Are we not to visit you again?" asked Sandhya, with a slight pang in her voice.

"When you chant the name of Kali, this aghori will be with you. Be assured," she said. "You both have had a taste of the 'other.' When you practice more and are able to immerse yourself in the 'other,' you will realize the foolishness of wanting to visit this limited body," she added, laughing. "Preema will continue to teach you. Go, now." With that, the aghori led us to the door.

▼ ▼ ▼

Our apprenticeship with the aghori created a very special bond between Sandhya and me. I was on the brink of manhood, and the elders recruited me to perform the duties of the men. Sandhya was similarly pulled into the work that befell the females. Functionally, this drew us apart, but it also engendered in us a mutual anxiety to get done with the tasks so we could be together.

Occasionally, I sat with the elders chanting the Vedas during informal ceremonies called avadhanams. At these times, I joined men from various households who gathered in the evenings under any one of the enormous banyan trees that dotted the temple grounds. Sitting in a loose circle, one of us would begin a verse from the Yajur Veda and the person beside him would chant the next verse and so on; thus a whole canto would be chanted. Since the men had no active part in the everyday temple and household rituals, they found this a unique way to preserve their knowledge of the scriptures and the rituals. On most days, I assisted my father and my uncles with work in the rice fields. Thus, along with my cousins, I kept myself busy tending the growing rice, fruit trees, vegetable plots, and maintaining the structures of our homestead.

During the past few years there had been a slight turnover in the members of our household. Uncle Bhadra married Lavanya and the couple moved into Lavanya's household, the House of Tandu. Cousin Radhika, the eldest daughter of Aunt Gauri, married Sudhakaran, from the House of Nalamba, and the couple had an 18-month-old girl. This was Roshini, my first niece. When Radhika was pregnant with Roshini, Aunt Preema prepared a charm for her. This was a black silk cord that Aunt Preema put through a special ritual. Radhika wore it around her belly.

I remember Roshini's naming ceremony, which started on her tenth day, and was celebrated for three days. The atmosphere tingled with great happiness, and Grandma Paru was in seventh heaven. Roshini would be the eldest one in her generation, and in the years to follow would be appointed as the eldest matriarch of our household. Vallichappad Agnimitra cast her horoscope, and Roshini's life events were portended in a bundle of palmyra leaves. With Roshini's arrival, Aunt Gauri had become a grandmother.

Cousin Padmini, the eldest daughter of Aunt Tara and Uncle Mukunda, married Raghu from the House of Vembala. Padmini gave birth to a baby boy named Balaraman, who was now 8 months old. During each of these pregnancies, I observed the intense care with which Aunt Preema and the other women of our home treated the pregnant mothers. Charms were prepared, ritual protections were often renewed, and one or the other elder women always accompanied the pregnant women in their daily excursions outside the house, and never were they allowed outside after dark. The fear of a dark odiyya lurking in the neighborhood was deep. I, too, was recruited to look out for these elusive, nefarious ones. I joined some of my uncles in constructing extensions to our homestead to accommodate the new couples.

In consultation with Kalyani Amma and her husband Sundareeshan from the House of Tandu, we decided that an extension adjoining the southwest corner would be in harmony with the lifelines of the house. Vastu Purusha Mandala, the spiritual science of homestead layout, determined these lines.

I was 17 years old and Sandhya was 18½. I was poignantly aware that we were poised on the threshold of somber adulthood. At this juncture, I became conscious of a strong and growing attraction for Sandhya. This attraction, powered by limbic undercurrents, sometimes welled up to the surface. Like insurgents they appeared out of the backwoods of my mind, commandeered my faculties for short periods, and vanished.

To compound my problems, I grew up amid orthodox Hindu surroundings, and the elders viewed adolescent turmoil as uncurtailed expressions of decadence. Their directions to contain these hormonal upheavals were very rigid, and brooked no complacence. But any adolescent conditioned to contain these desires in the orthodox way was forced to face an even more powerful and unrelenting energy from within.

This created a dichotomy between pleasurable abandonment and an aftermath of guilt. In the ongoing inner battle for supremacy, the fortunes of war frequently crossed camps. Adolescents were subject to a plethora of emotions—guilt, stigma, and shame, versus cunning, delinquency, and turpitude. I was no exception. But the force of Eros was strong, and when it could not be fulfilled overtly, it resorted to the clandestine in darkness and isolation.

The size of our extended family and the fact that there were plenty of adolescents at any time of the year spoke volumes on the reproductive achievements of the adults who espoused celibacy for the rest of us. Rampant juvenile carnality found satiety in apparently innocuous gestures and games like hide and seek, wrestling among boys and girls, and while swimming in the pond.

One somnolent summer afternoon, Sandhya and I broke the sexual taboos. The stifling heat and the still shade from the palm trees lulled the elders into indolence, just as it lured us boys and girls to the placid bowers. The seniors were too glad to be rid of us. Ample spicy food and the soporific climate had them lying on the cool cement floors inside, while we boys and girls spilled out into the family grounds to play a game of hide and seek. Among twenty-three pieces of leaves, five were marked to be chasers. These were jumbled in a coconut shell. Those who took the marked ones became the first chasers, who closed their eyes for a count of one hundred, while the rest of us scampered to hide. Sandhya grabbed my arm and ran, pulling me to the pond where a thick cluster of bamboo grew. This bamboo grove spread into the grounds of the neighboring household, defining a natural boundary.

We wormed our way through this thicket into the neighboring grounds, but still within the grove. Our passage was difficult as old and dry bamboo stems turned into sharp spikes at ground level. Sandhya froze ahead of me as we heard the pattering of stalking footsteps on the outer perimeter. We crouched, our bodies pressed close together. Whispered voices faded in and out as the searchers inspected the grove.

Sandhya began to slowly ease herself on to me. My right foot was poised on a bamboo spike, and to ease the strain I began to settle on my haunches, with Sandhya on my lap. Presently, the sounds faded away as the chasers departed.

We huddled together for a while. I smelled jasmine from Sandhya's hair. Then, to my great consternation it began . . . a great welling of pounding energy. I could only smile stupidly as Sandhya turned her face to me, her brow perspiring and her cheeks reddened with a strange shyness. I could hear my heart thumping, and then I drew her closer to me. My arms wound around her belly as if commandeered by some invisible power. We lay there in the thicket, our lips and hands in feverish exploration.

Hours after our erotic involvement, I felt an urge to get away from everybody and meditate. My act, I felt, was tantamount to incest; I was plagued by guilt—a vexed and outraged mind cried for self-correction. My mind raged with anxiety. I wondered if I had a pathological addiction for incest. It was a paradox to me that at a time when I was driven to seek the nature of my true Self, I encountered a force so powerful as to draw me into sexual indulgence. What made it so unbearable was that Sandhya was my sister disciple.

To assuage my embattled mind, I took shelter in the abandoned temple beyond the cemetery. Initially I did not have the courage to enter the sanctum, but sat on the edge of the ancient pond and gazed down at the calm waters. Somehow, the light green, algal surface soothed my mind. Pacified by the salubrious quietness, the tumult subsided gradually. Then I felt an intense rationality overwhelm me; an acute analytical state of mind poised on the brink of my inner depths. From the isolated haven of the temple ruins, I observed my thoughts on sex. I clearly recognized the fundamentality of sex to life. It was the other face of death and the precursor to birth and growth. I was puzzled as to why the elders influenced such profound control over our emerging sexuality. Why do they look down upon our sexuality? If sexuality is unnatural, why does it manifest so powerfully in Sandhya and me? Why are we conditioned to look upon sex as a dark instinct? Should we suppress these feelings? Questions tumbled into my mind. I found that my sexual fantasies were as powerful as those periods when I cleared my mind of thoughts at this temple.

In spite of all my analysis of sexuality, this inexplicable mental capacity to vacillate from one extreme to the other nagged me. Paradoxically, my experiences of erogenous arousal began around the same time as my sincere attempts at inner growth and self-control. I wondered whether my cousins also experienced these extremes. I could not reconcile these states. Rising up from the edge of the pond, I moved into the temple. I wanted to pray. So I sat upon the granite floor inside the temple and, facing the obsidian cube, I prayed for understanding. At length, peace descended upon me in the guise of a warm, foggy blanket of sleep.

I woke up abruptly, and decided to seek Aunt Preema's counsel. It was then that I noticed the passage of time. It was almost evening. This temple had been a panacea to my turbulent mind. Mentally, I paid my respects to the unseen power I always sensed within its sanctum, and started homeward. My numerous trips through this terrain had created a faint foot track through the undergrowth, though not discernible to a casual glance. The thornfield still posed a formidable barrier, exacting its customary toll on my clothes and skin.

It was after supper that I mustered the courage to approach my aunt. But before I could pour out to her my turmoil, she pressed her finger upon my lips and whispered, "Sandhya has spoken to me, sweetheart. Come, let us go find her."

I felt my face flush hot with embarrassment. I walked in silence behind Aunt Preema as she led me to Sandhya. I was glad it was night and our faces were hidden in the darkness. My aunt felt our discomfort. For, when we were all together she said, "There are periods in everyone's life when major shifts in karma occur. The time of sexual maturity is one such. It is neither good nor bad. But how these feelings are acted out can affect the community. Our society manages it through marriage.

"Human sexuality, channeled through marriage, provides a safe outlet for awakening karmas. Therefore marriage is an evolutionary necessity for people within communities." Aunt Preema exuded an aura of deep compassion as she wrapped her arms around our waists. With Sandhya on her right and me on her left, she herded us toward the family pond.

"Marriage provides a sanctuary for the exchange of love between two," she discoursed as we approached the fringes of the pond.

A pale quarter moon cast a fleeting sheen over the pond as clouds moved in and out of its path. From our homestead behind us rose the clang and clatter of vessels and the accompanying chatter that marked the close of our communal supper.

On one hand, a great shame weighed upon my heart, but on the other I felt an exhilarating attraction for Sandhya, whose hand I felt upon my elbow. Even as my aunt counseled us, I wondered how Sandhya felt now. I hoped that she would still be a friend to me. She must still be! Why else would she touch my arm? I thought. Then my aunt turned to me saying,

"The sense of touch is the primal sense." She startled me with this statement—it was as if she sensed my body language. "Let me talk to you about touch. Touch is the principle conduit for sexual love. The tactile sense embodies within it the potentiality to express the rest of the four senses. They evolved out of the sense of touch. Of these four, three became complex, specialized, and drifted away from the sense of touch. Their specialization narrowed their capacity to experience. Thus smell, hearing, and sight became the most complex but less holistic. Moreover, these complex senses alienated themselves from the object of perception, while the more primitive senses of taste and touch experienced direct contact with the object of experience. Touch and taste provide a first-hand experience of an object, while the complex senses provide a somewhat vicarious one. For example, with sight and hearing you cannot 'feel' the object intimately as with touch and taste," she explained.

The three of us edged down the sandy banks of the pond. About halfway down, we stopped on a coconut palm trunk staked into the bank. My uncles put similar trunks on these slopes to catch the eroding sand.

"Let's sit here," motioned my aunt. "The sense of touch is a link between two realms, the outer and the inner realms," she continued. "This sense is intimately connected to sensual feelings of pleasure, as well as to sublime emotions like bliss and intuition."

"Is pleasure from sexual feeling a base emotion, Aunt?" I asked in a cracked voice. I anxiously hoped it to be a higher emotion.

"Sexual feeling, if rooted in love is a sublime emotion," explained Aunt Preema smiling. "Then it will lead to bliss and a state of expansion of the spirit. When the spirit expands, the astral bodies reach out into each other seeking astral union. The karmic sheath of both loosens allowing the dream minds to permeate each other's being."

A bullfrog croaked in the waters below, calling out to its mate. Instinctively, I picked up a small pebble. But Sandhya gripped my wrist and gently shook the pebble out of my hand.

"It is therefore no wonder that the sense of touch is the chosen conduit for the exchange of love between two spirits," continued my aunt. "Sight and hearing can at best only orchestrate the symphony of love expressed through touch," she added.

"I agree, Mother. I heard nothing and saw nothing. I felt as if my body was sizzling with light," said Sandhya with a muffled giggle.

"Yes, Aunt, that is true. Her touch consumed all my awareness!"

"Touch and feeling are inseparable. Yes, touch can consume all awareness," agreed Aunt Preema. "There is nothing like good sex to prod the divine Kundalini awake," said my aunt mirthfully, giving my back a playful slap. "Feeling is an intuitive emotion; it is comprehensive. Just as we feel through the skin, through all of our body, intuition is feeling through our astral being. Feeling is fuzzy. When we feel, we learn and know through our higher conscious mind. This transcends the limitations placed by the logic-bound physical conscious mind. The complex senses work more through the physical or logical mind."

"But beautiful melodies and chanting can draw the spirit into a state of bliss? And the sight of my beautiful Sandhya draws my mind to abstraction. . . ." I argued. Sandhya interrupted my argument by giving a resounding whack on my back with feigned disdain.

"Good, good," said Aunt Preema approvingly. "Now he is getting bold," she added with a mischievous grin.

"In this case, aren't the complex senses hitched to the higher conscious mind?" I questioned.

"Normally, hearing and sight are directly involved with conscious processes. But as I said earlier, these complex senses evolved out of the sense of touch. It would not be far-fetched to consider these senses accessing the higher conscious mind, provided the stimulus impinging upon these is sublime enough—Sandhya's body, for example," said Aunt Preema with a poke in my ribs.

"Sexual bliss is a comprehensive experience. During these moments, there is a complete transcendence from the grip of the logical senses, a time when the dream mind manifests. This is when the energy of physical awareness is absorbed to strengthen this higher mind. Here the awakening ritual is a great help and is important to a sincere devotee of the supreme goddess.

"This ritual and the subsequent practices enable a person to realize the androgyny of the astral self. Realizing this at an early age helps the devotee to manifest the correct attitude when engaged in sex in later years. It is only this experience that can provide true humility, for if you *know* that you are indeed sexless, then how can there be a sense of sexism or feminism?" my aunt elaborated.

"What is the correct attitude, Mother?"

"Utmost, worshipful humility toward each other, dear. That is the only way sex can be used to awaken the divine Kundalini. Used any other way, sex will only power the base emotions, giving the dark forces a foothold," answered my aunt.

Touching Aunt Preema's feet, I requested, "As my preceptor, I beg you to guide me." I felt a deep sense of surrender.

"Mother, I feel Shambu should know what you told me, if only to alleviate his grief," Sandhya pleaded. Aunt Preema fell silent for a while. A gentle rustle of the palm fronds filled the night. It was a silence I could not bear for long. Then Aunt Preema began.

"We have to go back to the day of the initiation of awakening ritual, eight years ago," my aunt paused, "to the meeting with the seven ravens. That was the day you two had a glimpse of your past incarnation. Much as I had suspected, it was that day I knew for sure that your lives were entwined. When the fair one embraced you, she lent you her energy that made it possible for you to glimpse your previous forms.

"You both fell out from your collective pursuit of Cosmic Awareness in your past life. It is only the undying love of your group that has caused you to incarnate in these forms," and then she added in a whisper, "and they are pursuing you."

My aunt's words were so sacred. I felt a deep, peaceful, and mystical elation that gave me goosebumps.

"Strong desire is the forger of karmas," my aunt's voice intruded into my thoughts. "But however strong these karmas might be, they must bend to an even stronger force from countless lives that you both spent seeking the divine. Thus you have come to be born into an atmosphere of Kali consciousness," my aunt explained.

"But, Aunt Preema, why are we cousins? Why not friends from different families? At least then I would not be consumed by this guilt," I lamented.

"That is a direct result of the abundant grace of your teacher, the fair one, the leader of your band. You and Sandhya are related, no doubt. But this relationship has enough distance to allow you both to specifically fulfill these karmas, yet is close enough to prevent a disastrous consummation. With a relationship as this, you both will never be able to consummate this ripening of your karmas in a marriage that could potentially draw you both farther and farther away from your group, and thus be lost to them."

I felt a deep shudder pass through Sandhya as she sat hugging me, and it triggered a wave of fear inside me. I silently prayed that we should not be lost.

"And if you go down into the nuts and bolts of this relationship, you are not as close as a brother and sister are. Your Grandma Sathya and Sandhya's Grandma Chandra are sisters. That makes Sandhya only a distant cousin to you, not even a direct cousin, much less a sister. Therefore, fulfill your karmas with great zest, and not with guilt. Your zest should be such that your karmas be completely erased," my aunt emphasized with a smile.

"Aunt Preema, what if this great zest creates more desires and thus breeds more karmas?" I asked.

"Oh dear; oh, my dear," Aunt Preema crooned as she hugged me. "Fulfill your karmas with zest, not lust," she whispered. "Zest comes from the knowledge that your actions are a product of karmas. This knowledge makes you aware of the limits of your actions. Lust comes from ignorance, a lack of awareness of the karmas that propel you into certain actions, the limits of which you are equally unaware. Lustful actions breed more karmas. Guilt is a product of bondage to social conditioning. While lust makes one grab at life with greed and selfishness, guilt promotes a depreciation of one's self-worth. Both lead to darkness."

My aunt elaborated that ethics defined through social conditioning has no bearing on a mind that remembers relationships over many lifetimes. The friend in one life may incarnate as a wife in another, or a wife in one life could become a sister in the next.

"The human mind is a continuum of experiences from birth to death, into beyond, and back to birth again. The memories of all these different relationships exist in the minds of every individual.

These memories could generate feelings that transcend the rigid ethics enforced by society. A wife in one birth could even become the mother in another.

"Normal people cannot penetrate the veils that separate memories of different lives and peek into the nature of previous relationships. Human society enforces these logically concocted ethics to maintain the integrity of the relationship sanctioned by birth. Only death has the power to alter the relationships that are otherwise incumbent on each of us from birth.

"In spite of this rigid ethical substratum that surrounds everyone, tendrils of strong feelings from previous lives may perforate these veils that shroud the past. As a result, two souls could find themselves attracted to each other, despite artificial ethical barriers that oppose this in the current life. Physical attraction and love transcend transient social ethics and sexual identities."

"Aunt Preema, desire overwhelms my mind and makes me do this. Then I feel guilty and remorseful. It is as if my mind is split."

"Your desire is the result of your karmas; like seeds they are sprouting at this ripe station of youth. Yes, the mind splits because of guilt. That is why ordinary people have split minds; they do something that they are conditioned not to do, and then feel guilty. When the mind is split, the intent is weakened," explained my aunt.

"Can desire arise without a precedent karma, Mother?"

"Yes, dear, new influences from outside can condition behavior, and if these are prolonged, they can create new desires. But when these conditions are no longer available, as in a change of environment, the behavior still remains and cravings can arise. Thus these cravings are a result of certain behavior that was a product of outside conditioning and all these within a single lifetime. Only spiritual wisdom can reveal this truth. Without right knowledge, the argument whether karma is first or desire first can be endless."

"What I meant was, are we helplessly trapped in karmas? Is there a way out, Mother?"

"That is a pithy question, dear. I have to put into place some assumptions if I must answer your question adequately.

"Desire is the precursor to everything. Desire is spontaneous to existence. It characterizes the lowest form to the highest mystic who desires freedom. It also characterizes this universe, whose desire is to Become—to unfold as this great space-time. If a desire is pursued with appropriate action, then it manifests as karmas in its journey toward fulfillment. Any desire can be fulfilled. All it needs is correct and persistent action and, of course, time.

"In order to pursue a desire, a person needs power. Free will enters the picture now. Free will is the precursor to choice, to any decision. It is the power to the decision whether to fulfill this desire or not. This is the fork in the trial of life where the fate of a desire is incessantly tested. Free will is the embryo of the great power—intent. Once the choice is made to fulfill a desire, then awareness is diverted from other areas of a being to bring this desire to fruition. Now the person is set upon fulfilling this desire. This soon becomes a drive. And this drive generates a mindset. The mindset is the next step in the germination of an intent." My aunt paused, "Is this clear so far?"

We nodded our heads vigorously.

"While free will sanctions the use of free awareness, or astral energy, to fulfill a desire, the drive enables the acquisition of the necessary knowledge and ingredients to put the desire into action. Therefore, in its simplest form, karma is action," my aunt summarized.

"I thought that karma was fate, Mother."

"The connotation that karma is this mindless cyclical force of re-action to an initial desire or action is a result of ignorance of the nuts and bolts of the karmic theory. Karma means action. An action resulting from a desire can be terminal to itself or it can sprout more desires for similar experiences. These secondary desires will grab awareness, and lie latent, like seeds. Seeds of desire are precursors to action to be. When the space-time is appropriate, these dormant karmas sprout new desires and actions. People mistake this intelligent process and call it fate. Hence the use of the terms 'predestined,' 'fated,' 'destiny' and so on. But we can clearly trace these karmas to a previous action, which in turn emerged from an initial desire and free will." She looked at both of us, asking, "Am I going on too long?"

"No, not at all. It's clear!" Sandhya and I exclaimed in unison.

"Awareness could continually be invested in the pursuit of any desire, causing cyclical incarnations in bodies and space-times suitable for their fruition. Cyclical processes have no free will involved in their operation. The energy of awareness feeds the flames of desire and action, driving them through this process."

"That was my question, are we helplessly caught in this cycle? If so, then karma is fate! How can a person get out of this?" Sandhya cut in.

"I remember your question, my dear," said my aunt smiling. "I am meandering in my explanations, aren't I? But, be patient, sweetheart.

"Free will itself can act as an inhibitor to this cyclical process—free will, which originally made the choice of pursuing this desire. Free will is a combination of pure energy—astral energy that powers the astral body, and energy of awareness that makes up the dream mind, or the astral mind. This awareness is the consciousness of pure intelligence. By intelligence, I do not mean the intellect and reasoning power that defines aspects of the physical mind. Pure intelligence is from the spirit, from the higher mind." My aunt stopped her dissertation. Pulling me by my right wrist, she asked, "Is something bothering you?"

A question nagged my mind and I was squirming in my seat. "If free will is pure intelligence, then how come it makes such stupid choices?" I asked.

My aunt laughed, "You are annoyed, aren't you?" She paused and answered me.

"There is no such thing as a stupid choice," she emphasized slowly, pulling me to her side. "A choice is a choice. The higher mind, the pure intelligence, has no such divisions as stupid or bright, good or bad. For it, everything is divinely blissful. If you desire to eat mango sauce over and over again, then that is what you do, until, of course, your stomach gets upset and you choose to quit. Just as free will can lead you into 'stupid choices,' it can also break the cycle and lead you out of it. This brings up my next point. Pain, or adverse reaction from Nature, is the most common agent that reintroduces free will into this cycle of desire and action. But this time it serves as an inhibiting force, to make a choice against the fulfillment of the desire."

"Can free will stop this cycle, Mother? If that were the case, people would have no difficulty making the right choices after the first mistake."

"Good point, dear. But that is another story. The momentum from numerous cycles of fulfilling a desire becomes a power unto itself. Elaborate psychological and physical systems are built up by this cycle, which usually prove formidable to the emerging free will that now intrudes into the cycle as an adversary."

"Aunt Preema, this pain or adverse reaction from Nature, is this a punishment?"

"No, not at all. Punishment is a human concept—a self-limiting concept perpetrated by people upon them. This universe is a sea of love, bliss, and beingness. It is a product of its own desire. It exists to enjoy, and it gives joy. By giving and taking, it maintains equilibrium. But when desire becomes cyclical, then it continues to take and does not give. At the point of extreme excess, this desire grows into a demonic voice with an enormous appetite. This upsets the rest of the support system to which this voice belongs. This support system is its immediate Nature. The only way to restore balance is to cut off supplies to this voice. Once the surrounding systems are upset, and cut off the only source of energy to this voice, then the voice begins to starve. This is the beginning of pain. Our body-mind's reaction to restore balance and settle back into equilibrium thus appears punitive.

"The truth is, we punish ourselves by letting these demonic voices take over our spiritual resources."

"Aunt, I am concerned. If free will reintroduced by pain cannot put a brake upon a runaway demon, what hope is there to get out of this quandary?"

"Now we come to the meat of our discussion," my aunt said, clapping her palms. "The hope that you asked for is all around us," she said expansively. "The grace of the Divine Mother surrounds us. It is everywhere. It is always granting us our desires. This grace is most mysterious," she said in a hushed voice. "Excessive pursuit of desires brings about imbalances and generates painful endings. When the demons of desire run away with a being's spiritual resources, that being cries out to the Divine Mother. The spirit yearns for redemption. This yearning attracts divine grace into the constitution of free will. Divine grace now backs free will that is made up of astral energy and consciousness from the higher mind. The force of this holy alliance is so great that it pulverizes any demons and assimilates their energy into the higher mind. We have discussed desire, free will, action, karma, reaction, and God's grace. Have I answered your question satisfactorily, dear?" asked my aunt, lifting Sandhya's chin with the tips of her fingers.

Sandhya nodded her head. With great affection, she held my aunt's hand to her cheek. I stretched back on the sandy slope. From the clearing of the pond, a large area of the sky was visible and I observed the various star patterns. Shooting stars streaked the heavens in fractions of a moment. While I gazed at the stars, Sandhya dug up small stones and playfully piled them on my belly.

Presently, my mind returned to processing the barrage of wisdom that my aunt imparted to us. Guilt—if only I could get rid of it. I sat up in a trice, tumbling the neat pile that Sandhya had accumulated upon my stomach.

"Is it possible to be free from guilt, Aunt Preema? To do so, it seems a person has to be beyond the clutches of environmental conditioning!"

"Yes, it is a difficult and dangerous path. Yet in the end it is worth all the trouble. The odiyyas are free from social conditioning. By not conforming to social conditioning, odiyyas have removed themselves from the clutches of guilt. This gives their actions zest and power."

"But odiyyas are spoken of with fear and misgiving. I am told that they are beings of great power. I yearn to be an odiyatthi," Sandhya mused aloud with deep feeling.

"If you are an odiyya or an odiyatthi, you don't belong to normal society. But you may live in it. Odiyyas are not conditioned by society, and cannot be cataloged within the scheme of things. Therefore they are indefinable. That is why people are wary of odiyyas.

"The people we live among are normal people—people, who most of the time actively use only their physical minds or logical awareness. The physical mind has a need to define and classify things, to give names to forms. If the physical mind cannot define something, then it tends to fear the thing or believe it doesn't exist. Fear causes a need to annihilate the thing feared, for the sake of self-preservation. But odiyyas transcend names and forms, and are beyond annihilation by normal people. When the physical mind cannot annihilate the thing it fears, then the fear changes to worship.

"People cannot be blamed for their fearful worship of the odiyyas. People want stability and order in society. By not conforming to the rules of society, and by possessing strange powers, the odiyyas seem to pose a threat to the established order. Besides, there are others who masquerade as beings above guilt."

"Who are the others, Aunt?"

"Odiyyas are one extreme end of a spectrum of people who are without guilt. They are guiltless. These are the people on the higher end of this continuum. On the lower end of this spectrum are people whose minds are ruled by demonic voices. These people do not feel guilty because they seek to overpower and possess.

"Humanity is spread along this spectrum according to the level of knowledge and awareness. Self-knowledge, divine awareness, utter humility, and unconditional love elevate the odiyyas above normal humans. Mercifulness, pity, guilt, and repentance elevate normal humans above the demonic.

"But both normal humans and the demon-possessed have fear in common. Normal humans have fear of the unknown. The demon-possessed minds have fear of annihilation. All of the three—the odiyyas, normal humans and the demon-possessed—have action in common. All of them perform actions. The demon-possessed performs actions from a basis of abysmal ignorance, self-gratification, and fear. Normal people perform actions from a sense of duty and with an expectation of some return. But the odiyya performs actions from total freedom. There is no good or bad associated with any action; action performed without any expectation or self-gratification is the key to freedom. This is also action from a true experience of freedom and total awareness."

"Aunt, a while ago you mentioned that a person has to experience the spirit's androgyny to perform sex with the right attitude. Why engage in sex at all when we desire to seek God?"

"That's a good question, Shambu. It's not enough to give up sexual acts when the mind still craves for sex. How many people can elevate their minds from sexual thoughts? Only a rare few. In order to lose all desire for sexual thoughts, words, and actions, a person has to either completely eliminate all karmas that could cause these, or have a body that is asexual.

"In the first case, when all karmas and desires are rooted out, there is nothing to sustain the body. A person becomes an odiyya who is not bound by a body. Karma defines a person's body, and without karma, a person need not have a body. Such a person can take on any form.

"In the second case, it's like being a plant or vegetable, or some similar lower form of consciousness with an asexual body. But even then, some form of sexual energy will manifest. Sexual energy cannot be rooted out. It is the manifestation of the Divine Mother. To extinguish it is to negate the Divine Mother. What is the point in negating the very divine you seek?" countered my aunt.

"How can we prevent karmas from accumulating, Mother?"

"Peace of mind comes from surrender to the Divine Mother. Perform everything with a sense of surrender to the Divine Mother. Then karmas cannot take form.

"Anybody who continues to attempt to negate sex and extinguish it, also attempts to snuff out his or her very source of existence. And soon the result will be either madness or death.

"Sexual energy is pure divine energy. If humility and love for the Divine Mother are not felt, then this energy will fuel lust. But if the heart is filled with love and a sense of surrender, then even lust will be dismantled, and its energies transformed into worship. But sexual karmas will continue to manifest. Even as they manifest, their energies will be extinguished in the flames of worship. If you are lucky enough to experience the spirit's androgyny, surrender comes faster and this process of transmutation is easier," answered my aunt. She fell silent for a while, and then her countenence sparkled, as if she processed some important thought.

"Abstinence from sexuality is not a function of morality, as far as the adepts are concerned. It is only a matter of behavior modification for the conservation of energy. The adept needs power to manifest his or her intent, and sexual energy is one of the largest caches of raw energy available. A person has to discipline his or her being before the inert karmas awaken, grabbing all the energy and mushrooming into new karmas. That is why I made sure that you both practiced spiritual disciplines and experienced some level of androgyny before this adolescence," she said. She paused for a while. My aunt pulled a dry piece of coconut leaf that lay before her with her foot. Picking it up, she brushed the sand away.

"The adept is an adept because he or she has the awareness to constantly tread the fine line that separates those who, through profane practices, let their manifesting karmas completely take over their vital energy, thus spiraling them into the abyss, and those who hammer and splinter their minds by starving and antagonizing their emerging karmas, through ill-conceived self-mortification. Adepts experience life here, where life is most fulfilling," she said running her finger along the midrib of the leaf. "On this side, experiences tend toward degradation, through dissipation of life-energy; people who live here are the squanderers," she explained slipping her finger down one slope of the leaf. "On the other extreme are those who choke out life energy and starve their personalities. These are the self-mortifiers.

"Do not oppose your karmas and do not encourage them; allow them to manifest. In time they will play out their energy and be extinguished. Then you will be free," added my aunt.

"Aunt Preema, please explain to us sexuality in the context of divine knowledge. This is so fascinating. We do not want to be lost from our paths again. Yet our karmas are such that we are led away. Your words give us peace," I beseeched.

"Human sexuality is recognized by the adepts as residing in the moola chakra. It is the lowest of the higher human chakras. This is the kunda, or the pit—you remember kundabhisheekam during the initiation ceremony?

"The moola chakra is the highest among the animal chakras. It resides at the juncture of two realms, the lower animal realm of largely preconscious mind, and the intermediate human realm of conscious mind."

"By preconscious you mean unconscious, Aunt?"

"No. Preconscious behavior is more evolved than an unconscious state. Preconscious awareness is largely patterned behavior. Instincts, with some intelligent choices, but difficult to reason with.

"To most humans, the moola chakra is the only source of power that keeps alive the contents of the unconscious, preconscious, and the physical conscious mind. Since it's placed at the junction of the lower and the intermediate worlds, it's subject to constant contention by forces from below and above. The forces from below draw you down and make you create more karmas so they are kept alive through the fruition of these karmas. These forces are called demonic."

"The people in whom these voices are strong are demon possessed!" interjected Sandhya excitedly.

"True. If the demonic voices have the upper hand, then sexuality will be tainted with lust and violence. Normal people act from the physical conscious mind. This is where most of the manifested power is. This is the world of action. It is neutral by itself.

"The odiyyas work from the superconscious mind. This is the realm of angelic voices. If the angelic voices have greater hold of the moola chakra, then sexuality will be suffused with love and worship. The realm above the physical conscious plane is increasingly permeated with love, the lower planes with greed.

"Moola chakra is the seat of the divine Kundalini. She is Raja Rajeeswari or the Divine Princess. Practitioners of spiritual disciplines can gain great advances in their upward evolution and still be pulled down by karmic residues. They are like kites that soar in the wind, but with a string attached." I felt a tug in my heart when my aunt said this.

"If the forces from the deep have greater sway over such a person, then the tendency would be to perform forceful ascetic and Tantric practices, to gain powers to be used for lustful purposes. Gradually, the load of karmas would increase. If left unchecked, this person would be completely subdued by the forces from the deep. Such people masquerade as practitioners of Tantra and as students of sorcery—they indulge in violent copulation as part of their Tantric practices and perform sorcery to strengthen their ego. They have lost their goal of freedom."

"Aunt Preema, earlier you spoke of the higher, superconscious realms as the planes of the angels. Why then is the Divine Kundalini down below, albeit in the junction between the lower and the intermediate worlds, within arm's reach, so to speak, of the demons?"

"Divine compassion, Shambu. She is the Mother of all creation. She is the last outpost in the dark. Beneath Her are the murky depths of gloom, the underworld. When the demons reach up to grab Her, it is from ignorance that they do this. Unknown to them is the nascent desire to escape the clutches of their own making. They want to reach up into the Light that She is, but are prevented from living in the higher world by their weight, the weight of desires and karmas. So they try to take the Light down into the darkness.

"Now, the mind swayed by the angels worships this great goddess with humility and surrender. There is no thought of possessing the divine, but only giving of oneself, even in the pleasure of sex."

"Why is there such a contention over sexual energy, Mother?"

"Sexual energy is the first expression of volition or free will. In human beings the moola chakra defines the beginning of free will and volition, while in lower forms, this same moola chakra is their highest chakra, on attaining which they are free from the nonvolitional realm.

"Coitus is a powerful way to activate, energize, and synchronize the entire nervous system in the physical body, and the thousands of astral channels in the astral body. Beginning with sexual foreplay, mounting sensations, and emerging feelings, mating begins between couples. As they mate, there is a body-mind melding within both. Just as this happens, a male-female melding begins in both. The expressed obverse and the repressed reverse in each person unite. This is the male and the female that is in each of us.

"When Kundalini awakens, this same synchronization of the nervous and astral-energies precedes the merging of the inner male and female into androgyny, prior to the great absorption in the Cosmic Neutrality of the Self. Therefore, the act of coitus—aside from procreation—can be used for uniting the inner male and female prior to the arousal of Kundalini. When you arouse Kundalini, you have power. Now, can you see how premature sexual arousal without adequate preparation or guidance can cause the power from sexuality to fall into the hands of demons? This is why society has such tight rules to control adolescent sexuality. Without these rules and regulations, the human collective mind would be ravaged by demons.

"Human societies approach the management of sex and love through marriage. Marriage is a concept evolved to channel the emerging power of sexuality and sexual love in ways that promote spiritual growth. It also cuts down the otherwise harmful effects of sexual love freely and permissively expressed."

"Aunt Preema, is Kundalini the same in both men and women?"

"Kundalini is female in both man and woman. In the male, her awakening is associated with the unification of the expressed maleness with the repressed female within him. Now that the male is united with the female in him, his physical conscious mind becomes androgynous, thus unifying the dualism of sexual identity, in preparation of mental ascension into the higher realms. The physical mind surrenders its energy of awareness to the subtle dream mind or the astral mind. This is how a person becomes free from the thoughts of sex, or the need for sexual actions. When the ascent is completed, he or she becomes entirely free of sexuality. Kundalini has moved away from moola chakra and there are no demons in the higher realms to grab her, but only angels who extol her.

"In the lower worlds the voices are stilled. This happens as karmas are dismantled and their energies pressed to arouse the sleeping Kundalini. With no more muck, the waters of the unconscious are now clear. Kundalini, in most cases, will descend back to the moola chakra and there are no more demons below to pull her down. Now the upward path is clear and her energies are drawn up into the angelic realm. But her light shines all the way to the 'bottom' of the erstwhile underworld, thus unifying the unconscious with the higher realms, to form a single, massive superconscious mind. Now we have a mystic, or an odiyya who has no more divisions in the mind. It is one, single, superconscious awareness.

"The awakening is actually preceded by the opening and purification of the ida, or female, lunar astral channel and the pingala or male, solar astral channel—the tha and the ha astral-energies that I taught you a long time ago," my aunt said, smiling.

"This is so fascinating, Aunt Preema!" I exclaimed.

"How does the woman transform, Mother?"

"These same events happen in a woman; but in addition to androgyny, odiyyas recognize a completed female. A woman without awakening is a fragmented female. In the completed female, the expressed female has joined with her repressed male. The ida and the pingala channels are opened and purified before this unification, and when Kundalini awakens, this completed female expresses the Goddess Kundalini. Thus an awakened woman is Goddess Kundalini Herself." My aunt paused, while a sudden breeze wafted in fragrance from night blooms.

"Sex and love expressed through marriage promote stability, and provide a safe channel for emerging sexuality. It is a great avenue to express such sublime feelings as loyalty, solidarity, and eventually, selfless love. The idea of living for someone you love, to do things out of love for your mate, are thrilling concepts that can be practiced and experienced only if your sexuality and love are pledged to each other."

"Since you describe these to be lofty feelings—this loyalty and selfless love—why wouldn't those unmarried odiyyas who practice ritual sex, marry and pledge their love to one another, Mother?"

"The purpose of sex in sorcery is to emerge into greater power, awareness, and expanded consciousness. Just as sexuality is strictly controlled in human societies, ritual sex is even more rigorously guarded and intimately guided by adept odiyyas, and the process is kept secret. If you know how to use it, sexual energy is the most potent resource, unlike methods such as mental concentration and meditation, etcetera, which are but dilute derivatives of sexual energy. But without the protection of a selfless teacher, the chances of degradation are extremely high.

"The purpose of marriage among humans is to provide a controlled environment to love and develop selflessness and loyalty to one another. But marriage has no such meaning for the odiyyas. To marry and be loyal to each other is to fall into the clutches of human institutional conditioning, which is what the odiyyas strive to get rid off. They want freedom.

"Odiyya couples are selfless to start with. Their selflessness is so supreme that they are ready to activate each other's sexual energy to mutual liberation. Just think of this—under the constant guidance of their teacher, they put themselves through rigorous practices to cleanse their psyches so that they are fitting agents to awaken their partners to freedom. All the hardship and perils involved in preparing for this ritual are undertaken only to activate the partner to freedom! Can there be a greater sacrifice, Sandhya? Compared to this, marriage and loyalty pale into insignificance. For, in marriage, the partner can only give his or her limited human love. And almost always this love is tinged with hidden needs and expectations, constantly driven by the binding mandates of society."

"I do not understand what these hardships or the perils are that the odiyya disciple faces, nor is it clear why the sexual partner has to undergo so much purification to activate the sexual energy of the other, Aunt."

"Don't confuse activating sexual energy with arousing Kundalini, my dear. Just consider the mere act of mating without any thought of awakening Kundalini. Normal people don't realize that with every sexual act they transfer impressions into each other. Karmic impressions are powerful and all they seek is an avenue to express themselves. Coitus is so consuming that while the awareness is absorbed in the act, the person is laid open to the other's impressions. These alien impressions can foster future karmic ties with each other. Normal people don't realize the extent of the tangled web that their acts weave about them.

"An aspirant of freedom has to reconcile his or her sexuality with the yearning for freedom. It is a mistake to think that the aspirant can arouse his or her own Kundalini during ritual sex. Each partner does it for the other. Just as it is rare to be in the presence of a selfless teacher, it is equally rare to be with the right partner. Without the partner's selfless devotion to purify oneself before surrendering to the other, the aspirant can drag his partner into bondage from the powerful impressions transferred during the ritual. Hence the need for the aspirant to undertake rigorous self-purification to protect the partner. To attempt to arouse Kundalini with sexual energy without eliminating these binding impressions is to plunge both partners into bondage instead of liberation.

"The sexual act is also a time when both partners are open to alien energies. During sex the karmic sheaths of both partners are loosened and the astral sheaths made vulnerable to attack. For a human body is most envied by all those beings who need to work things out. The intent of the partners in ritual sex is mutual liberation. During this ritual, it is the teacher who envelops the divine couple in her protective power, thus shielding them from alien intrusion."

My Aunt Preema was incomparably and unfathomably divine. Her lucid exposition this night removed the heaviness in my heart, which had been caused by my own ignorance. Tears streamed down my cheeks—tears of joy and admiration for my aunt, and my own good luck to have her as my preceptor. What profundity of wisdom in this woman who masqueraded as my aunt, who did the humble household chores of cooking and cleaning! My God! Who is she, really?

"Aunt Preema, who are you?" I cried. Then I lost control. I pulled her into my arms and cried, "Who are you, my dearest aunt? Please ease my mind," I pleaded, holding her.

"Easy, easy now," she tenderly stroked my back as she rocked me. I went into a fit of sobbing. There were no words spoken for some time.

"You know who I am," she spoke to me softly, cradling my chin in her right palm. "You know who I am," she repeated in a whisper. "Get close to me, Sandhya, let us pray," she said.

We prayed to Kali. Holding each other in a close embrace, our prayers lifted softly into the night sky.

"Children, it's very late; we should get some sleep."

"Thank you, Aunt Preema. Your words have put peace in my heart," I said as I touched her feet.

"Thank you, Shambu. Your inner turmoil has resulted in this new awareness in me," and Sandhya touched my feet.

"We shall get together sometime tomorrow," my aunt said.

# CHAPTER TEN

# The Joining Ritual

The next day began with our morning temple worship, but for most of the midmorning and until late in the afternoon I was busy with my male cousins, bringing down ripe coconuts. Our family collective owned a large coconut grove that extended all around our homestead. Our uncles had passed on the more arduous of tasks, such as climbing these forty- and fifty-foot palms, to us who were lithe, agile, and full of youthful energy. A few of these elders directed the operations from below. We harvested coconuts every month; it took the fifteen of us two to three days to climb the 175 coconut trees, cut down the ripe nuts, dead fronds along with some of the green fronds, and then husk several nuts for daily worship and cooking purposes. We brought down an average of twelve to fifteen coconuts per tree. Our household bartered coconuts for essential foods and goods, and even for skilled labor. The rest we sold to the local oil mill for cash.

By late afternoon we broke up for the day, having accomplished a little less than half the work. Aunt Sukanya, Susheela, and Tara brought a cauldron of piping hot tea to the veranda facing the back of the house. In hot weather, or during hard labor, it was customary for the men to wear only their white cotton dhotis, with their upper cloth tied into a turban around their heads. Keeping the upper body bare helped alleviate the heat, and the turban caught dripping sweat from the brow.After tea, the girl cousins passed us fresh dhotis and shirts. These we took to the family pond, where we bathed, changed into fresh clothes, and went to the house.

A good bath after a day of hard labor always left me feeling refreshed and exhilarated. I found Sandhya waiting for me in the room that I shared with Chandra and Gopalan. She was in the midst of sorting out my few clean dhotis and shirts she had washed, starched, and pressed. A pleasant fragrance of jasmine wafted from her hair; she had a string of these flowers woven about the crown of her head.

"Mother is waiting for us. Let's get going," she urged. We met Aunt Preema outside the threshold of the north entrance. She stood there conversing with Grandma Sathya, a bulging cloth bag slung over her left shoulder. An even bulkier bundle was on the ground, leaning against her right thigh. At our approach, Grandma Sathya turned to the base of the closest palm and spat out a squirt of red pan that she chewed incessantly. Turning to me, she asked, "Did we have a good count today, Shambu?"

"Yes Ammuma, we counted 950 coconuts and we have climbed only 72 trees," I answered. She thought for a few moments as if straining to compute.

"Good, good," she nodded, smiling. "If we keep it up, we may exceed our goals this month," she remarked happily. Then, turning to Aunt Preema, she commented, "We may be able to save enough to retile the kitchen roof."

"Yes, it concerns me, too. We counted five broken tiles and two rafters eaten by termites," added my aunt.

My grandmother then focused her attention upon Sandhya. Smiling at her, she looked her up and down. Then looking at me and breaking out a toothless grin, she asked my aunt, "How are the lessons coming?" But before Aunt Preema could answer, our grandmother winked at us and said, "You get going, Preema, before the sun goes down." With that, she spat a second stream of red pan at the base of the palm and stepped across the threshold into the house.

She hesitated for a moment at the threshold and looked back once, then disappeared into the gloom of the house. I was nonplussed. But my aunt tugged at my arm saying, "Didn't you hear her? We've got to get going! Shambu, fetch two torches, we might need them on our way back," she bid me.

"But Mother, what was that all about?" asked Sandhya frowning as she hinted at my now-departed grandmother, with a tilt of her head. I knew that Sandhya, too, was troubled over Grandma Sathya's parting wink. I hurried back with two palm frond torches, for I did not want to miss out on the conversation.

"Mother, does she know?" I heard Sandhya ask anxiously as I hastened within earshot.

As we walked toward the rice fields, my aunt put her arms around us, looked at us in turn and said, "Your grandmother is my preceptor. Don't you remember me telling you that a long time ago?"

"What your grandmother doesn't know, I don't know. There is nothing to worry about. Her knowledge is of her own knowing," my aunt said.

After walking through the fields for half an hour, we reached a tumble of boulders. I leaned the heavy bundle and the two torches against a boulder. Close by, some of the boulders formed a nice, private nook; soon, the three of us had our backs against a warm rock. The ripened fields of paddy waved and rustled in the breeze, golden brown in every direction. The Ramagiri range in the east caught the purplish, rosy light of the setting sun. Sounds floated in from the temple grounds. We could see the granite temple tower rise above the coconut palms that fringed the fields a mile or two away to the northeast. We sat still a few minutes.

"Last night we discussed the mystical relationship between human sexuality, karma, and divine energy Kundalini. Tonight I will guide you through a mystical ceremony—a special ritual that only odiyyas do," she whispered. "Do you have any questions?"

"Mother, from last night's discussion, I have this impression that rituals among odiyya couples are more liberating than marriage."

"Yes they are. But let me reiterate firmly; only among odiyyas is this practice successful. Four rare elements are required for its success. Among these, correct attitude, appropriate karmas and power qualify the odiyya couple. Without these, this ritual will only be a degenerate practice. This mystical ritual is arcane only because these elements are so rare."

"What is the fourth element, Aunt?"

"The presence of an adept."

"Is my assumption correct that to odiyyas marriage is bondage, but to normal people it is spiritually liberating?" I asked.

"Good. Good. You captured an entire picture with your statement."

"How is that, Mother?"

"See, if normal people embrace indiscriminate sex without commitment to one mate, it increases self-centeredness."

"But it gives them sexual liberation!" Sandhya said.

"Sexual liberation at the cost spiritual degradation! But through marriage and sincere commitment to one mate, normal people attain a limited version of the three elements (correct attitude, correct channeling of appropriate karmas, and limited power). Therefore marriage is spiritual liberation to normal people. Marriage is also a symbol that helps condition a couple to live together in society. It also assists society to integrate two people as a couple in their psyche."

"What do you mean by symbols, Aunt?"

"Symbol is just a mental tag. It is a method of creating a new set of references in the mind for significant changes in the social environment. Symbols mark the beginning of new mind patterns in response to outside change."

"What are symbols made of, Mother?"

"Pure mental energy. Mental energy is partly life energy and partly prana, or astral energy. Mental energy, like sexual energy, replenishes itself through prana. The normal human mind is littered with innumerable, interconnected symbols. If the energies in all these knots and networks of the mind are released, you have plenty of pure astral energy," explained my aunt.

"But it is not possible to release even one knot, Mother. Living normal lives only strengthens each knot!" complained Sandhya.

"You are right. These knots are strong. However, it is possible to release all the knots in the presence of a stronger mind.

"A stronger mind!" I asked.

"Like an adept's. And with some discipline, all knots can be loosened and their energy released in due time," my aunt assured us. "But it takes time. In the end, it is worth the effort. It releases you from humanness and makes you divine. To be an odiyya or odiyatthi need not necessarily mean that you have to leave your home in search of a fantasy. This journey begins with small, persistent steps."

"We wish to begin our learning. What should we do to become odiyyas?" Sandhya asked earnestly.

"You both have already begun this work, a long time ago. Odiyyas know that humans are never in direct contact with the world they transact with. Humans deal with the world through its representation in their minds," Aunt Preema said. "We hold a representation of the world in our minds," she repeated, bunching the fingers of her right hand and shaking them against her head. "Whenever we wish to contact any part or objects of the outside world, we approach it only through the specific representation of the object within our minds. These representations are the symbols that result from our categorization of the phenomena outside. These symbols we keep with us.

"Every interaction with the objects outside leaves a mark upon their representations in our minds. Now, to complicate this picture, we even have labels or symbols that typify our reactions to the changes that happen to these symbols of the outside world. The logical assumptions and emotional reactions generated by our interaction with these symbols are invoked at times without conscious awareness. These symbols, emotional tags, and labels direct our day-to-day lives. When a group of these symbols predominate on certain days, we sum them up as *moods*. When a few of them are stable over the course of a year, we call them *personalities*. All in all, a vast amount of energy is locked up in all these definitions of ourselves and of the world outside."

I thought about the thought kernels mentioned in Aghora Rahasya. "Release all these locked awarenesses and we will be free," I said.

"Yes, but as I am about to explain to you, it's not at all easy to do so. All these value systems, symbols of objects and symbols of reactions and so on, exist as various hierarchies. The flow of free awareness through these hierarchies defines the activities of living. Some areas of these hierarchies are very stable, while others are in flux. The more stable areas stem from the values we acquire as a culture of people. The areas under flux pertain to the individuals that we are who act and react to the environment—the blooming of specific karma that defines periods of our lives. When karma suffers extinction, the value systems, symbols, etcetera, that pertain to it are also dismantled, hence the flux in these areas. The workings of the stable and flexible hierarchies determine and direct changes, growth, or stability in life. They define us as individuals, both to ourselves as well as to others with whom we transact. Without a balance in the constancy of the permanent parts, and the flux that occurs in the appropriate individual aspects, a human becomes unstable." My aunt paused. I looked in the distance and saw the sun set. In the northeast, the thousand lamps of the temple tower were being lit. Sandhya sat relaxed, with her legs crossed. I watched her as the breeze played with the curly locks waving about her forehead.

"For spiritual freedom, a person needs to break away from this mechanical working of symbols, values, and labels into which awareness is fragmented and driven through life. But you two are already doing a lot toward this freedom, even in this very life, not to speak of work done in past lives. Liquidating these knots releases the energy of awareness bound in them. Collecting this awareness and rerouting it into your Self is the key to this freedom. When all these labels and tags are removed, the world of phenomena will not impose its perception on you anymore," she explained.

"What then do we perceive, Mother?"

"You will experience pure energy. You will perceive layers of reality at will. Nothing happens overnight. Remember that you are still in the midst of human society. But by frequently pouring your joyous emotion onto the Divine Mother's form, your interpretation of the world begins to change. Day by day, your perception of the world will be colored by Kali's form. Before long, all the inner labels, symbols, and emotional tags will be tinted by this love for the Divine Mother. Then no conflicts can arise in the mind from interacting with the world. Every experience will then be a worship of Kali. An odiyya must hold a neutral stance with the world, or precious awareness will be lost in wasteful interactions.

"Perception and awareness are not the same. Perception is the apprehension and definition of the dimensions of an event or an object in space-time, with enough parameters to lodge it in the mind as a symbol, so that these same parameters can be retrieved at a later time as a specific memory. Awareness, on the other hand, is the emotional and subjective response to this event, object, or memory of it, which is now created as an emotional or subjective tag. So perception creates a logical symbol in the mind while awareness creates an affective tag. This definition of awareness is for a normal person, whose awareness is tied in with mental cogitation."

"Can awareness exist by itself, Mother?"

"Perception is not a necessary adjunct for the functioning of awareness. But awareness is necessary for perception. For example, subconscious awareness is not always active through the agency of perception. In an unconscious condition, when awareness is withdrawn from the inner symbols, perception ceases. Sensory stimulus may still impinge upon the various sense receptors of the unconscious body, but the person does not perceive, nor respond, and neither will he or she remember any external events of that time.

"In the physical conscious state, awareness is hitched to sense perception and conscious mentation. But, awareness can operate at different levels. Awareness exists at all times and is imperishable. It may shift its operational center from the physical body and move into the subtle sheaths, into the astral self, for example."

"Aunt Preema, how would you define the mind of an odiyya? What is an odiyya's awareness like?"

"Ah! That is a paradoxical question," said my aunt with a smile. She fell silent for a while as she gazed at the dazzling temple tower, lit by a thousand lamps, with silhouettes of the coconut palms gracing its girth as it rose ethereally into the blue-black sky.

"The odiyya is mindless," my aunt said, startling us both. She then added, "mindless of the dualisms of the world. Therefore an odiyya's awareness is full and perfect. This is the perfection of unity, a unity that has evolved from resolving all conflicts imposed upon the mind by society."

Sandhya asked, "When there are different types of people in society, there are bound to be different views, and conflict will naturally arise. How then can conflict be erased totally from a person's mind, Mother?"

"That is very true, dear. But if all conflicts can be erased, the mind itself is erased. Conflict is the structure of the conscious mind. It is like the game of ball boys play. There are two groups, one group opposes the other. While the first group strives to kick the ball into the opposing group's goal, the latter attempts to block the first group's effort. This opposition results in an exciting game. Conflict defines the normal mind.

"People in society impose order upon one another under various guises, to ensure that the law of righteousness, as each person understands it, is upheld. It is like a mutual policing. Now, since each person has a different mental capacity to understand this law of righteousness, this law gets misinterpreted to various extents, the collective of which is respected as the ethics of society.

"The minds of normal people are filled with karmas that drive the actions of each individual. Karmas do not obey the law of righteousness as interpreted by normal people. They only obey the law of cause and effect, which dictates that what people constantly desire will come to fruition. Therefore you may have a person driven by a specific karma to perform an action that may go counter to the mandates of society. The elders teach that doing such and such is wrong, and part of your mind believes it. But in another part of the same mind, you have karmas that drive you to do it. Now you have a polarity, a split in the mind; all the mandates drummed into your head are in one part, and the karmas that need to be worked out are in the other." My aunt stopped for a moment.

"This is exactly my mind that you have described, Aunt Preema. Now there is conflict in the mind. I can see that," I admitted with amazement at my aunt's lucidity. "But, Aunt Preema, aren't these mandates of society good for us? Aren't they true? " I asked.

"Yes, yes, they are good for the stability of social structure. They help to keep people whose minds are filled with karmas under control. But these structures are not good for those who have minds with very few karmas. But then, normal people do not have the keenness of awareness needed to assess who is at what stage in their evolution. They clamp down their collective interpretations of the law of righteousness on one and all.

"When a person starts shedding his or her karma, and begins to lighten the load, that person becomes spiritually sensitive. Such a mind is in the process of transformation, and is vulnerable. The very mandates of society, voiced as the law of righteousness, now become a constricting straightjacket to this person.

"When your uncles plant vegetable seeds in the soil, they cover the top soil with jute cloth to provide an ideal environment for the seeds to sprout. But, once they sprout, this covering is removed. Otherwise it would constrict the growing shoots and distort them. Similarly, the interpretation of the law of righteousness provides a moral and ethical protection to people whose minds are full of karmas, controlling the force of these emerging karmas along manageable channels.

"To discharge all karmas, without gaining more, requires the practice of humility, selflessness, and constant forgiveness. That means that wrong has to be met with neutral goodness, the practice of which starts to disorganize the fragmented mind of a normal person. If unprotected, others will abuse a person practicing self-control, humility, and returning kindness on receipt of harshness. That is why serious spiritual aspirants need the right environment to thrive.

"There are many who evolve under the sole guidance of an inner longing, their lives perhaps peppered here and there with the association of someone or another who is evolved a little more. Normal people cannot understand the upward ascent of these individuals, as they appear out of the norm, and they pull these individuals down, like crabs in a fisherman's basket pull down any fellow crab who attempts to escape by climbing up the sides of the basket.

"Now, to answer your second question, whether these interpretations of the law of righteousness are true, let me say this: the law of righteousness is the law of cause and effect. They are one and the same. The law of righteousness is the supreme Truth. The law is beyond interpretation or speculation. This is the great Cosmic Self. When normal people try to interpret this Supreme Existence, it's like a growing chick viewing the inside of an egg. When the chick breaks free of the shell, it gets a wonderful surprise in the expansive freedom that lies all around. Similarly, interpretations of the Cosmic Self are like little points of view, but as the mind empties of all preconceptions, conditions, and karmas, the person attains a Cosmic View. Interpretations can never be the Truth. But they are necessary in order to belong to the common herd, and progress at that rate," concluded my aunt.

"What does the law of righteousness state, Mother?"

"To put it in a nutshell, what is desired will be achieved," answered my aunt cryptically.

"You said that the law of righteousness is the supreme Truth and beyond interpretation. Aunt Preema, are you saying that this Truth is mere desire?" I was puzzled.

"Desire is the root of all existence and beingness. From the odiyya who desires to be in perpetual freedom and is appropriately bodiless or many bodied, to the normal human who desires things more down to earth, all classes of beings hold themselves together to experience the fulfillment of their own desires.

"Desires and the experience of the fulfillment of these desires constantly shape and reshape all beings. Even though, sometimes, the material body perishes before the fulfillment of a desire, the essence of beingness is preserved along with the desires and carried over into another lifetime. Desire is like the cause for a specific existence, and the fruition of desires is like the effects. In between is change of one form into another, with Shakti being throughout. In the instance of the Truth, the supreme desire is for supreme awareness that includes the awareness of all things sentient and insentient. That desire brought forth the Supreme Mother who manifested all these multiplicities. Therefore, our existence is, in essence, the desire of the Supreme Being for supreme awareness. Thus the argument that we are all divine in essence.

"What is beyond the Supreme Mother?" my aunt asked, looking at each of us. "The Supreme Incomprehensible. It is only another label for That which no one knows anything about," she added, smiling. My stomach rumbled, and Sandhya doubled over with laughter. But Aunt Preema came to my rescue saying, "Well, that reminds us it is time for supper." My aunt pulled out packets of food from her bag and gave us a bundle each. I fell upon mine with great intensity, for I was famished from all the tree climbing I had done earlier in the day.

"Mother, you said that to be an odiyatthi, a person has to go beyond conditioning. Aren't there special rules or laws that odiyyas impose upon their disciples for their proper unfoldment? In which case, is this not another type of conditioning?" asked Sandhya.

"An odiyya adept will never condition the minds of his or her disciples with such vulgarisms as laws and rules. Odiyyas never condition the mind, period," my aunt said with subtle emphasis. "All that matters is intent and ritual," she added. "In the first place, an odiyya adept will only seek out those who seek the adept, because those who seek an odiyya adept will have a strong intent, an intent that is the same from many lifetimes. Since the disciple has the right intent to begin with, there is no reason for the adept to recondition the novice's mind in any other way, through laws and rules," she explained.

"Aunt Preema, I have some difficulty with this concept. It seems to go against all that is logical. I frequently hear from various elders, and I have even read in the interpretation of some scriptures, that the first thing an aspirant does in spiritual practice is to control the mind. If the mind runs here and there, it has to be brought back to the point of focus. Negative thoughts are the cause for the vacillation of the mind. These thoughts have to be curbed. Stimulus that comes into the mind through the senses feeds these thoughts, so a person should deprive the mind of all such sensory fuel. I'm sorry; I do not mean to oppose you, Aunt, but I have difficulty accepting your words," I lamented.

"Oooh! Shambu, what have the elders and the interpretations of the scriptures done to your mind?" asked my aunt, sighing. She paused for a while, staring at the waving paddy. Then she crept closer to me and said, "To begin with, let me assure you that what the elders say and what the scriptures enjoin are correct. They say, 'You should think like this. Do not think like that. You should do this and not that. This is good. This is bad. That is evil. That is sin,' and so on and so forth. All this is correct and made to order for most people in society.

"Many ascetic, monastic traditions, and the vallichappads who guide society in spiritual matters, also follow these moral prescriptions. And the scriptures that are the product of their exertions, enjoin these. It is good for them all—all those who use their intellect, ascetics and jnana yogis, followers of the yoga of knowledge. Even the vallichappads who are devotees of the Divine Mother follow these traditional methods to some extent. These are powerful methods no doubt, and they are good for the evolving masses. But these rational philosophies only negate the manifested Divine Mother, through forceful, intellectual assertion, and suppression of thought, and so on. In a way, these disciplines tend to banish all that is feminine from those who practice them. Such philosophies imprison the heart and banish feelings. Using only logical discrimination, the proponents of these philosophies contrive to keep the mind steady, and in the end seek to merge their awareness with the Supreme Incomprehensible.

"The outcome of the interpretations of these philosophies on the uninitiated masses are sexual hypocrisy, and a lot of misunderstanding. When they punish their minds and repress their karmas, they only violate themselves. Such minds are perfect fodder for the demonic.

"According to these austere philosophies, the mind is a wayward villain, and the sensory world is a voluptuous enticer. A mind filled with karma is the greatest impediment to spiritual progress. So it has to be forced into submission, preventing further unfoldment of karmas.

"But that outlook is wrong! Are there two minds inside everyone —a good mind that could be used to control the bad mind? Is the person who controls his or her mind somehow different from the mind itself? No, there is only one mind, and all these philosophies only help create an artificial split in the mind. If that happens, then one part of the mind becomes the controller and punisher, and the other part becomes the villain or victim. The controlling half calls itself good and labels the victimized half of the mind as sinful.

"If the distractible mind is by nature bad, then why would we incarnate in this physical body with the mind hitched to the senses from birth? Believe me, the Divine Mother did not create this sensual mind, hitch it to the senses, create a universe of sensory objects, and then withhold sensory enjoyment from us. It is like placing food before us and not allowing us to eat." My aunt paused for a while, then continued.

"The mind is like a bridge between what you are and the greater freedom beyond, just as it is a bridge between sensory objects and you. It's like a ladder that leads out of the pit of sensory phenomena. Only a fool would call it an obstacle and destroy it. And once it is destroyed, the person will truly be in a deep pit. Strict control of the mind is not necessary. Only constant practice of ritual and intent is required. The mind is energy; it should be treated with love. If it gets tired, then it rests. When it is ready to practice again, it begins.

"Just as desire for sensory phenomena creates karmas that enable a person to experience the phenomena, so also desire for divine love, and desire for awareness of the Divine, can create karmas in the same mind that will eventually allow a person to experience the Divine. This is all that is required.

"Truth is everything—animate and inanimate. All philosophies that claim to represent this Truth in its entirety are mistaken. Desire is the only path, desire the only force, desire the ultimate shaper of destiny. Desire for divine love happens when you can accept loving responsibility for all your karmas, which are the results of previous desires. Then you accept the whole of your mind. Desire for divine love will eventually transform all other desires into divine ones.

"If karmas force sensual desires in your mind, then let them have their way. These thoughts come only now and then. But soon after they subside, use your free will and perform tenfold actions of a divine nature. By allowing the karmas to bloom, you will release energy trapped in them, thus exhausting the karmas. By performing acts of a divine nature, you will build up karmas that will lead you to the Divine Mother.

"On the other hand, if you project revulsion toward these karmas—shut them off and negate them—you will only succeed in creating a dark shadow person out of all these desires inside yourself. Once you have given life to the shadow being, it demands to be fed. When you deprive it of its food—fulfillment of its desires—you act violently toward it. This is nothing but self-violence, and that is the very first thing these scriptures ask you not to do." Saying this, my aunt quoted an aphorism from Patanjali's Yoga Sutras.

"*Yogaha chitta vritti nirodhaha* (Yoga is the sublimation of the modification of consciousness, but not the suppression or destruction of the mind). Stillness is the nature of consciousness. Leave it alone and it will still itself. If you try to force it to stillness, you will only agitate it. *Ahimsa, sathya, asteeya, brahmacharya, aparigraha yamah:* Nonviolence is the foremost of the virtues. To be nonviolent is to love. First the elders interpret that the scripture demands suppression of desires, which is an act of self-violence; then they require you to be nonviolent, which is foremost of the *yamas* or prescriptions to achieve Ascendance. Here is hypocrisy. But you . . . you are with me. I will be your scripture and teacher, now. Do not split your mind with these cogitations. The Divine Mother loves, and this sensory world is Her beautiful body. All your desires are fragmented attempts at adoring and experiencing Her divine beauty. And all your karmas help you achieve this in little bits and pieces through the limited physical body. I have a sacred and exquisite path for you," she said with a strange quiver in her voice, and then she held me close to her.

"Aunt Preema, your words are like a flood, like a storm that blows away all my preconceptions. My mind is at peace and my heart feels pacified." I placed my forehead upon her feet, but my aunt pulled me up and hugged me again, without a word.

"Aunt Preema, aside from a strong intent, won't the disciples have other karmas when they meet the adept? Won't these karmas scatter the nascent intent of the disciples?"

"Left alone, they would; but the adept blankets the disciple with her power, like grace. The adept knows what karmas these are, and would soon provide rituals to integrate these energies to strengthen the intent. You are correct. These karmas would otherwise butt heads with the intent. By welcoming these karmas into the intent, the split mind in the disciple is unified. But to an ordinary person, all these practices appear bizarre, against cultural norms or the established way of life. Ordinary people are terrified when all categorizations of good or bad are dropped—which happens, by the way, with the unification of the mind. Hence the secrecy from the public.

"The disciple has deep faith in the adept and her ways; a faith not enforced by scriptural injunction, pecking order, authority, or law, but by the disciple's own limitless love for the adept. Faith strengthens intent, and intent strengthens faith. It is only through lifetimes of struggle and ardent search that the disciple and the teacher find each other, having been separated by currents of desire in the great stream of existence. There is no reason for pretense, rules, and mandates. There is only love. When a child is separated from her mother in the crowds and distractions of a religious festival, when they find each other, after hours of anxiety, is the mother going to admonish the child and establish rules? No. She envelops the child in her love. The adept and her disciple are enveloped in the bliss of each other's love. The remaining karmas the disciple has are minor, and easily ingested in the fires of tapas, ritual, and worship. Life, from now on, is increasingly blissful for the disciple. Even an adept keeps at her practice of rituals and gathering of intent, in the silence and the privacy of nature, and sometimes in the company of cohorts or disciples."

"What does a ritual consist of, and what do they mean, Mother, especially the chants?" asked Sandhya.

"Ritual consists of actions done with intent. Meaning is irrelevant. Intellectual understanding of the ritual and the chants is counterproductive to the fostering of faith and intent. If you analyze the meaning, then you may lose the feeling. Explain it and you will lose the experience. That is why these experiences and practices are sacred and done in secrecy. Experience requires no explanations.

"In the beginning some rituals are for integrating karmas into the intent. This produces bliss instead of guilt," said my aunt with a mischievous wink at me. "Later, there are rituals that probe and extract power from Nature. Then there are rituals that convert this power into expanded awareness and growing freedom. The awesome power of the adept sanctions everything. The intent and power of the adept is immense compared to that of the disciple, so for all intents and purposes the adept's awareness is cosmic in magnitude," she declared. Then in a soft crooning voice she spoke, "The power of the adept is like the wind that lifts the falcon up into the sky. All the falcon needs to do is close its eyes and spread its wings. If only the disciple can just stop his doubts and arguments and merge his intent in his adept . . ." My aunt's voice trailed into a whisper.

My mind reeled under the impact of Aunt Preema's words, and my heart was a strange tumult of exhilaration. I watched the quarter moon ascend gradually overhead. As I gazed at the moon, I began to feel a strong emotion for the Divine Mother well up in my bosom. Then a thought flashed into my mind like a revelation. If the adept's intent is cosmic, then she is the Divine Mother, Herself. But what is intent exactly? I asked my aunt to explain the word.

"Let me start by explaining what intent is in normal people. In normal people, there is no intent, so to speak. In them, intent exists as so many drives. Here, intent can be defined as the collective karmic consciousness or awareness that propels the individual. The totality of the awareness, splintered by various karmas that manifest in each life as desires, tendencies, habits, and so on, find a common direction in the long run. In the beginning, however, these drives and tendencies may be at loggerheads with one another, thus foiling a purposeful direction for the person.

"Karmas fashion your bodies, minds, and hearts. Karmas deploy you in suitable families and environments that are best for the unleashing of karmic energies. Therefore, in the average person, there is no overriding intent, so to speak. Their intent is inchoate at best. With some humans, it takes lifetimes of work to gain a semblance of coherence in the collective karmic awareness that exists as numerous drives. Gradually, an overarching intent emerges from these drives— an intent that herds the rest of the drives toward a purposeful direction. This herding of the drives dissolves the tangential forces of karmas. The karmas begin to dissolve and the intent is nascent.

"As the karmas dissolve, the awareness and energy released strengthens the developing intent. Then, at some point in its growth, the intent becomes so focused, it emerges with one specific goal—the goal of total freedom. Now, this can be called an odiyya's intent. An odiyya's intent is pure energy. It is not tainted by desire, nor is it fragmented by karmas. It is not propelled here and there by drives, either. All karmas have been burned in ritual. The energy that the karmas contained is released as pure awareness.

"All throughout the fashioning of intent, devotion to the Divine Mother acts as the lynchpin. It is devotion that enables the safe release of this awesome energy and its focusing into awareness of pure intent. Without devotion these energies are horrendous. As long as the consciousness of a person is fragmented by desires and drives, that person cannot comprehend the mind of an odiyya—or the lack of a mind," she said, laughing.

Aunt Preema fell silent for a while. Sandhya contorted her body into a fresh posture. Then my aunt crept close to both of us, laid her arms on our shoulders and pulling us toward her by the napes of our necks, whispered,

"Sexual intimacy can be spiritualized, and this is never more appropriate than when two people love each other. I will lead you both through the ritual. This is a sacred ritual, so drop your reserve and body consciousness. The idea is to ignite your passions with the fire of worship."

Reaching behind her, my aunt dragged her bulky bag from the base of the boulder and pulled out a large cotton spread.

"Here, help me spread this," she said.

Between the three of us, we spread the sheet in the middle of the area circumscribed by the boulders. Sandhya began extracting various items from the bag.

"Mother, where should I put this?" she asked, pulling out a large banana leaf packet.

"That is sandalwood paste, dear. Give it to Shambu. Pull the rest of the things out and place them here," she said slapping a spot near the center of the sheet.

"Before you invoke divinity into the body, you must evict body consciousness," my aunt said, peering through the darkness at each of us in turn. "I am going to complete a ritual I initiated several years ago," she paused.

"When I performed the initiation of awakening ritual, I realized how strong your affinity for each other was. Now, those affinities are maturing. It is time to sanctify these karmas, to release the energy for your spiritual upliftment. I will show you worship through lovemaking. You must let go of all sense of *I* and *mine*."

"How is that possible?" I asked nervously.

My aunt leaned close to me and slipping her right palm under my vest, she began to massage my chest.

"Remember, there is no right way or wrong way. When you made love to her, did you question the correctness of your feelings or actions?"

"But, Aunt, we are about to mix sacred Kali worship with sex!" I whined.

"The ugly shadow of guilt looms up again," she murmured. "What are your feelings for my daughter, Shambu? Describe to me what you felt when you made love."

"It was blissful. Something I never felt before. My whole being was aflame."

As I uttered the words, my heart pounded, and an impulse surged through my groin. She laughed at my embarrassment, detecting my heaving chest and pounding heart. She kissed my right eyelid affectionately.

Sandhya crawled close to me, "It's fine, Shambu," she said hugging me, "I felt the same for you."

"Your feelings for Sandhya are admirably transparent. But to an odiyya these are earthy," my aunt declared.

"We both enjoyed each other and gave to each other, Mother. How can that be earthy? Aren't you being too critical?"

"Yes, the loins took more than what the heart gave. I have told you this before. Karma has energy that, if encouraged to unfold by itself, will drive a person downhill. But, if this energy is presented in the spirit of devotion, it will help a mind vault into cosmic consciousness."

"You mean we did not surrender to each other?" I asked.

"Correct. You surrendered to your own enjoyment, your own passions. The flames of passion subdued your hearts' attempt at surrender. In your past life, you both strayed from a higher existence because of your self-centered passion for each other. Now, at this juncture in your current lifetimes, these karmas are awakening. This is the time to learn to surrender to your mate's passion. Absorb your passions into your hearts. In your hearts these will sublimate into love."

"Your proposal is fascinating. But how is that possible, Aunt?"

"Through worship, my dear. Worship flows from surrender. Only surrender can manifest worship. Acts of passion, if sanctified, can be transformed into articles of worship. I have said earlier that desire, passion, attachment, and so on, are unrefined forms of love, the highest expression of which is worship."

"Don't think of me as your playmate, Shambu. Then you can see Kali in me," Sandhya surprised me with her suggestion.

My aunt lit the brass lamp and set it in the East.

"It's time to begin," my aunt whispered. "Self-consciousness has to go. You can find this in the clothes you both wear," she hinted.

After a moment's hesitation, Sandhya and I stood up and removed our clothes. Aunt Preema undid Sandhya's hair, and it fell to her hips. The moonlight bathed her breasts in a faint, sensual translucence.

"Close your eyes for a moment. The Supreme Spirit is everywhere —it is in you both," I heard my aunt say. "Sandhya is Kali," she intoned.

"Sandhya is Kali," I repeated.

A moment later I felt Sandhya's breasts and belly press into mine. As her hands probed the small of my back, a wave of sensuality engulfed my being.

"I am your Kali," she whispered. At once, the impulse subsided. A fervor sprung in my heart. Desperately, I clung to that ardor and began to work it consciously. I heard my aunt intone,

"Sandhya is your Kali . . . Sandhya is your Kali . . . "

I was aware of my conflict. It was one thing to philosophize that my playmate was Kali, but to practice this felt weird.

"Sandhya, you are my Kali. You are my Kali," I declared with increasing fervor. I shivered as she fondled my back. I slipped my palms under her buttocks. I felt a brief, sharp spasm jar her body. It aroused my passion immediately, and my breathing quickened. A mighty throb pulsed at my loins.

"Slow down your breathing," said my aunt.

With some effort, I slowed down my breathing. The disconcerting throb faded away. I kept my breathing under control. But with my breath under control, my mind cleared of passion and the feeling of worshipful fervor that I cherished also began to fade. In desperation I cried out, "Kali, show me the light! Kali, show me the light!"

Tears sprung out of my eyes. At that instant, a wave of deep surrender spilled out of my heart. I rejoiced as tides of devotion battered the ramparts of my worldly conditioning. Nothing mattered anymore. "Kali! Transform me into your plaything. I am at your bidding," I prayed out aloud.

The love I felt for Sandhya was so intense that I was without any doubt that my body, mind, and soul belonged to Kali, whom I embraced in the moonlight.

"You are my goddess. I worship you in this body," I slid down her body and kissed her feet.

Aunt Preema led us step by step into the ritual of divine love. We anointed each other with rosewater and sandalwood paste. Sandhya and I touched various parts of each other's body, invoking Kali to manifest. At the direction of my aunt, I broke a coconut and poured the coconut water into a tiny, brass vessel with a curved spout. I cleansed Sandhya's mid-parts with this water and introduced the spout into her. Sandhya sucked the water in. After a little while, she ejected this out, and at my aunt's behest, I partook of a little of this water, as the elixir of Kali, a token of Her grace.

No sooner did I take this in than Sandhya pulled me toward her. In a seated posture, with our calves and heels entwined over each other's buttocks, Sandhya introduced me into herself. My aunt sat by us, pressing our chests into each other.

A throb expanded my loins. Aunt Preema urged me to begin a particular breathing exercise. I chanted my mantra a number of times with each breath.

"Exhale and chant," she urged.

Sandhya was passive for a while. Then she gyrated her groin against me. The exquisite sensation overcame the self-control that I had achieved through breath-control.

"Every drop is a hibiscus flower. May your passion be transformed into flowers of worship," I heard my aunt whisper repeatedly in my ear.

I visualized red hibiscus flowers with each chant of my mantra, and I offered them to Sandhya. I felt Sandhya grip me tighter, spasmodically constricting about my groin.

I was elated, for I knew that she was in ecstasy.

Sandhya broke out of my embrace and she pushed me down on to my back. I felt my aunt guide our bodies down. Sandhya lay on top of me, but her heels still dug into my buttocks, now that the weight of our bodies pressed upon her heels. Then I surrendered to her. A childlike voice whispered in my mind.

Sanguine passions transformed as flowers,
Are drawn high by Devotion's angelic fervor;
Billowing forth love's ecstatic streamers,
They embrace Kali, my Divine Paramour.
O! Heart! Surrender your passions into Her;
O! Ardor! Arouse my beloved's sleeping power.
This life, Desire's child from past incarnations,
Is transmuted to worship by our divine teacher.
Her eternal love, like tendrils of streaming light,
Probed empyrean spaces and stygian voids.
In space-time's endless streams, though set adrift,
She searched us out from beyond the Great Rift.
Separated for ages, she brought us together,
And collecting our karmas, she set them afire.
This ritual now warms my beloved's sacred pit
And the serpent awakens from eons of slumber;
Ascending our spines with serpentine slither,
She bestows on my beloved a heavenly splendor;
Like a falcon she soars with all bonds sundered,
Into celestine realms where no passions can enter.

# CHAPTER ELEVEN

# Descending Darkness

It was a perfect summer, and our lives brimmed with joy as Sandhya and I explored our feelings for each other. Under Aunt Preema's guidance, we experienced a blissful flowering of our youth. Our emerging sexuality, and the mutual attraction that we experienced, was tempered by our knowledge of who we had been in our previous lives. In our earnestness to offer us to each other's awakening, our spiritual practices found great vigor and added purpose. They took on a new meaning in the context of our blooming karmas.

Aunt Preema was privy to the sexual twist to our spiritual practices, but no one else in our household knew. The informal confidentiality of the tasks of a preceptor and the apprentices, and the privacy of our mystical practices, kept everyone away from us. Aunt Preema had great clout in the family and in the village, and she wielded this influence to shield our mutual ardor from the public.

My aunt frequently exhorted us to make strong attempts to experience the spirit behind the physical body. The spirit is the only constant in the changing stream of life, and in the cyclical process of transmigrations. She warned us that sexual activities undertaken just for pleasure would only entrench our obsessions with the physical body, thus mooring our awareness in matter, rather than in the spirit.

Several times, she alluded to our childhood experience in the hills—the vision of the band of mystics that we had belonged to in our previous incarnations as astral beings, and of Sandhya and me who had fallen out of the band, driven afar by our sensual desire for each other. She often reminded us of the evanescence of our physical forms, and said that at this young age it was easy to be caught in the stream of physical desire and pulled into the grip of bondage.

"Intent is like the unseen undertow in a stream that propels the whole body of water, including the little leaves and twigs," she said early one afternoon as we sat by the rice fields. It was summer vacation: I had then completed my tenth grade examinations, and Sandhya, her eleventh grade. Aunt Preema took a dry leaf and threw it into the rill that fed the paddy. It was at once carried away by the flow.

"Now, if the surface waves slam into one of the leaves, then the leaf will be pushed away by the waves." She dropped a leaf upstream, while rhythmically slapping waves across the rill downstream. As soon as the leaf entered the choppy area, it collapsed beneath the waves and was deposited in the mud.

"In the course of time, these waves develop into a strong current with a direction of its own. In this case, the current may even have the power to propel a portion of the body of water away from the main undertow, thus taking it away from the general direction of the flow." She paused. I looked for the leaf, which by this time was buried by the silt and mud that constantly shifted about like little sand dunes underwater.

"You were like this leaf flowing in the general current of the combined intent of your band. But your desire for each other developed a strong force, and became a karma unto itself. This force deposited you both in this life, and now this karma is awakening. You must fulfill this karma; that is the law of cause and effect. It is the law of desire and its fulfillment. But you must be cautious not to spawn new desires that will draw you deeper into life's mesmeric meshes. You should participate in the zestful fulfillment of this karma by being humble and by worshipping the Divine in each other. But never give in to lust, or guilt. Lust is an act of violence, and guilt depreciates the joy that life is, and will lead to mental problems."

"I understand that both lust and guilt lead to bondage," I said.

"Correct, lust feeds your self-importance, which draws you into the hands of the demons. Guilt weakens your mind. It splinters the mind, making it feeble and unfit for the pursuit of freedom. An odiyya acts without guilt or remorse, without desire or lust; but he or she acts with intent. This is done with complete surrender."

"How can an odiyya have an intent of his own, when he has surrendered?" Sandhya asked.

"When self-importance is surrendered, all that remains is unlimited awareness and one desire—the desire for freedom. Intent emerges out of these two, Sandhya," she replied.

"How does lust feed self-importance, Aunt?"

"Well, when sexual activities are carried out purely for self-gratification, a person tends to use his or her partner without much regard for the partner's happiness or fulfillment. This is a form of subjugation that feeds a person's ego, thus reducing a sacred and joyful activity into a one-sided experience and an unwholesome one to boot. And very soon, such a mentality becomes an addiction."

"Is sexual desire the cause for everyone's reincarnation, Mother?"

"The minds of most people are filled with very many desires, including sexual desire. All of these contribute to a perfect body-mind that is ideal for the fulfillment of these desires. But you both have been sublimating most desires, and have been focusing your minds to the exclusive goal of freedom for many lives. In the foreground of such a clarified intent, this desire for one another stands out as a clear deviation from your collective goal. That is why, in your case, it was sexual desire alone that pulled you away from your journey to freedom. There were no other deviant desires to pull you away." She paused, then placing both her hands on Sandhya's shoulders, she spoke softly: "Sweetheart, desire for anything is not wrong or sinful. The mind can have desire only for those things that exist. And everything that exists, including this universe, is an aspect of the Divine Mother. Therefore, desire for sensual pleasure is an indirect desire for the Divine Mother, for freedom. It is a long, long way to freedom, though."

Aunt Preema looked about her. Noticing a piece of dry twig, she picked it up and began to clear leaves and litter from the sand before her. She then scored two X marks on the sand with the twig.

"The easiest way to get to this X from this is along a straight line," she said, drawing a straight line connecting the two. The journey gets frustrating if we were to develop a desire to deviate from this straight path to visit a place here, for example," she said poking a dot perpendicular to the line.

"Soon the original goal is out of sight as you begin to eye other places to visit. But visiting those extraneous places is not wrong or sinful. It is just a waste of energy and a misdirection of intent. Desire, lust, human love, and Divine Love are different expressions of the same power, all aimed at achieving complete happiness. It is just that lust happens to be at the bottom of the scheme of things, and a long way off the goal," my aunt said.

She advised us not to approach each other with lust alone. Our worship of Kali was to permeate even those momentary lustful thoughts. When lust coursed through our minds, we were not to suppress it, but to feel it fully. But along with these thoughts, we were instructed to offer mental worship to each other. The simplest way, my aunt said, was to visualize lust as a collection of hibiscus flowers that could be offered to each other. Thus, in the beginning, lustful moments would be associated with acts of worship. Eventually a feeling of supreme surrender and love would permeate the mind every time lust intruded.

Though we both practiced hard and with sincerity, this method took a long while to work. We frequently fell for each other's sensuality when we were alone together. But I had no guilt, thanks to Aunt Preema's counseling. Aunt Preema's technique of sexual sublimation worked wonders with my fantasies. The culturally ingrained association of the hibiscus flower with Kali worship conjured the face of the image of Kali whenever I thought of the flower.

I frequented the desolate temple ruins as an escape from everyone. This isolated place benefited my body, mind, and spirit. It was a sanctum where I could leisurely and uninterruptedly examine everything, including the teachings of Aunt Preema. By nature I was endowed with a questioning and doubting mind that flourished during debate, or a session with Aunt Preema. But the energy at the ruins helped me to fuse all aspects of a subject and perceive things with dreamlike clarity.

Aunt Preema's method of instruction was most unobtrusive, appealing to the intellect and the heart, and her love and welfare for me were indubitable. Although her arguments enlightened me, and I always left her presence uplifted in spirit, a few hours later my mind would examine her thesis. This invariably happened when I spent time alone at the ruins. The ruins and the energy they contained provided a safe haven for my intuitive mind as it probed a subject from all angles.

I kept this place a secret from all, and although Sandhya and Aunt Preema knew of my frequent visits, they never asked me to take them there. My occasional surreal encounters with the goddess at these ruins intrigued me. I wondered if she was a being from my spiritual past.

One evening, I asked Sandhya if she was interested in going with me to the ruins.

"You really want me to see your secret place?" Sandhya was surprised at my offer.

"It is not a secret place," I protested. "I have no secrets from you."

"I wondered if you would ever take me to your place. I know that you have been there many times," she said.

We took off after tea; I led her past the Shiva temple, into the cemetery. Sandhya was uneasy walking there. She pulled me close to her as we moved past numerous hoary edifices to the dead.

Reaching the western perimeter, I located the familiar break in the dense vegetation. Sandhya stopped dead in her tracks, as she squinted at the seemingly impenetrable mass of vegetation before her. I could not help break out into a smile at her discomfort.

"What are you smiling at?" asked Sandhya, brows furrowed. I laughed aloud and her annoyance grew proportionately.

"I'm amused to see you behave exactly as I did the first time I came up against these woods. I am not making fun of you," I assured her. "Here, I will go in first, and you follow me." I stepped into the barely perceptible gap in the undergrowth, Sandhya following close behind me.

"Don't go so fast," cried Sandhya. "Wait for me, Shambu," I slowed down immediately. Taking her hand, I lead her in a more leisurely pace.

"There is a thorn field ahead, Sandhya," I warned her.

"What? Can't we find some other route to the ruins?" she asked, dismayed.

"I am sorry, the thorn field is extensive and I have never tried to skirt around it. But since I have cut through it several times, I can lead you safely," I assured her.

A half-hour later, we broke free of the lush undergrowth and came up against the thorns. Here we paused to catch our breath. I watched Sandhya as she surveyed the area. Her eyes opened wide as she took in the formidable barrier of thorns extending on either side beyond our line of sight. Mirth bubbled up inside me, but I dared not smile.

"This way, Sandhya. There is a path of sorts," I said tugging her arm, barely containing my amusement. But she stood rooted to the spot.

"Path of sorts!" she exclaimed.

"I assure you, with a little care we can get through this," I argued anxiously. "I told you, I have gone through this several times, Sandhya."

She shaded her eyes with her right palm and surveyed the forest on the far end of the thorn field.

"Can we see the ruins from here?"

"They are inside that jungle."

"I thought so," she sighed. "All right, where do we go from here?"

I led her to the right, to the familiar spot where I made my frequent entry. Every step Sandhya took was precarious. Frequently the spikes tangled her long skirt. And then there were thorns that pierced her sandals; I pulled them out as she stood on one leg, while she held on to me.

Almost an hour later, we crashed through the last of the abominable bushes and entered the forest. Considering what we left behind, this was easy territory. So I proceeded to plunge into it, when Sandhya grabbed me. Amid gasps for breath she demanded, "Was that the easiest route through those thorns?"

"Yes, I discovered it after many. . . ."

She cut me off and began to beat me all over with her fists. At length, I managed to hold her still. She pulled away from me, saying, "I am covered with scratches—you are going to work on them when we get home, my friend."

I let Sandhya take the lead through this forest. I frequently indicated to her the right direction, knowing that we were drawing close to the ruins, and the dramatic breach in the foliage was imminent. I walked behind her in excitement, eagerly waiting to catch her visceral reaction on seeing the ruins. Then she pushed aside the final curtain of creepers and vines. Her body propelled forward as her unprepared mind expected more foliage. She careened into the open space in a dramatic tumble. I followed close behind.

"Oh! Kali . . . Bhagavati!" she cried, her face beaming with wonderment.

It took her a while to assimilate the surreal scene before us. Each time I came here, this place had a fresh impact upon my senses and mind. It took my breath away every time. Sandhya kicked her sandals into the bushes. She came close to me and, holding my arm, began to lead me toward the ruins. We walked along the colonnade, past the fallen columns and beams, and we came to a pause at the brink of the pond. The late afternoon sun cast a bright yellow sheen over the granite structure.

"Let's go around the temple," she whispered. I was fascinated to note that this place inspired the same awe and hush in Sandhya as it did to me. Sandhya hesitated at the threshold into the sanctum. Her arms fell limp by her sides.

"Why do you whisper?" I asked in a whisper myself.

"There is a presence in this place, I can feel." Saying that, she sat down inside the threshold. Her eyes had a glazed look and her skin looked pale. I was concerned. Yet I knew my own first experience of this temple had not been dissimilar.

Sandhya sat silent for a long while, her gaze rooted upon the obsidian cube that once supported an icon. My mind quieted and presently I fell into a deep meditation. An overwhelming sense of sanctity pervaded my heart—a sense of fullness, of complete suspension from all thoughts.

When I opened my eyes I saw Sandhya kneeling beside the obsidian cube, her forehead upon it. Presently, she stirred out of her posture and came toward me. She bore a grave countenance. Squatting in front of me, she whispered, "Open your legs . . . here, around me . . . like this," she said as she pulled my legs to straddle her. She held me close as she chanted her mantra. I held her in my arms as I chanted with her.

We sat chanting for some time, holding each other in a close embrace. After a while, I became aware of the flickering reflection of the golden sunlight upon the walls. The sun was setting and I was anxious to get back. Sensing my distraction, Sandhya pulled away. Then she, too, noticed the gathering darkness.

"Let's go back, Shambu," she whispered.

The west was aglow with the rays of the setting sun. They drew alternating bands of light and shadow as they passed through strands of high clouds. Over the jagged rim in the east there hung a lovely full moon. On our way back, I asked Sandhya about her perceptions of the ruins, but she was taciturn, refusing to elaborate her experience. But just by the way she was withdrawn, I knew that she had some serious realizations at the ruins.

Passing through the thorn field made Sandhya even angrier than before, and she complained like a child. We were still an hour early for evening prayers, which gave us enough time to take a quick bath in the pond and prepare for worship. After our family worship was over, Sandhya sought me out and reminded me of my promise to work on her bruised body. She cast the burden of all the aches and pains on me, insisting that it was I who made her tear through the thorn field.

The night was filled with the shrill sounds of the cricket and occasional croaks from frogs. Shafts of moonlight pierced through the foliage and dappled the earth. Sandhya and I skittered nimbly through the palm glades, and approached the open expanse of the family pond. I brought a banana leaf with some soothing balm made from the fresh extract of cucumber, rosewater, and red sandalwood paste.

We stood on the bank of the pond. Behind us, the reddish glow of the fire flicking through the kitchen door marked the house, which nestled amid the gloom of the trees. The clang of utensils and the high-pitched, intermittent chatter of my aunts as they prepared dinner filtered through to us. There was not a wisp of wind to stir the stagnant warmth of the air. Down below, the still waters of the pond caught the silvery reflection of the full moon. I felt the secret excitement thumping within me, uncontainable. The scene before us was aphrodisiacal, adding to the urgency of our mutual passion. The image of the hibiscus flower kept appearing in my mind.

On the far side of the pond was a thick cluster of bamboo. A few bitter gourd creepers took advantage of the bamboo and climbed profusely over the shoots. The shadow beneath was very dark in contrast to the silvery sheen cast by the moon.

"We could settle beneath that," whispered Sandhya, seeing me look at the spot. I nodded, and pulled her with me as we plunged down the sandy slopes, tracing a spiral trajectory toward the shadowy nook. With no patience for a decent landing, we tumbled upon the dry bamboo leaves and sharp spikes in an untidy heap, startling a lizard that scurried out of harm's way.

Gently I applied the cool, fragrant balm over her bared limbs and torso, and her breathing deepened gradually. Each stroke of my palms upon her acted like wind from the bellows, fanning the fires of her passion. I felt Sandhya convulse ever so slowly, and then she began to mutter her chants. At once, the image of a hibiscus flower presented itself in my mind. As I stroked her, I chanted and mentally offered the flower to her. But in a short time, my passion leapt up into an all-consuming conflagration.

The sweat from our convulsing bodies picked up sand and dry leaves. We were two creatures locked in a mating ritual. The loose sand started a tiny sand-slide, which hissed its way down the steep slope into the water below. This sound signaled us to stop. As the sand-slide progressed, the ground beneath us eroded, and I hoisted myself up from Sandhya's chest. In the darkness, the white skin of her face stood out against her billowing dark hair. For a few moments, I was aware of our heartbeats as they drummed against each other.

A faint breeze blew a cool swath past us, and I turned my cheek to it. Just then, a movement to the left caught my attention. The slopes on the left were terraced with palm logs. At the bottom, about fifteen feet away from us, two semi-submerged granite slabs lay in the water. A young girl stood upon one of the slabs, and with her right foot she played with the water by sloshing it in the pond. Her sari was brilliant white in the moonlight. I stared at her mesmerized, but apprehensive that she might be someone from our family.

An involuntary gasp escaped me when she lifted her face to the moonlight and stared at us. Her features eerily resembled that of the goddess from the temple ruins. Sandhya was instantly alert and her sudden movement threw me off balance. I heard her give a muffled cry as I struggled to scramble up the sliding sand. I hauled myself up in time to glimpse the girl disappear over the embankment.

"She looked like Lavanya! She has seen us," whispered Sandhya in dismay.

"Are you sure that is Lavanya?" I asked, puzzled.

"I am not sure."

"We should find out who she is. I am sure that whoever she is, she did not recognize us. We were in the shadow. Let me go and look for her now. Sandhya, you stay here for a while and then go home."

Saying that, I sprinted over the embankment in the direction the girl had gone. It had only been a few moments since her disappearance, and I was confident of finding her. I searched all around the grove for fifteen minutes, but the girl in the white sari was nowhere to be found. Though it was dark beneath the palms, patches of bright moonlight filtered through profusely, and her white sari would have easily given away her presence. This mystery left me uneasy.

When I entered the communal meal room, I noticed Sandhya seated on the floor among my cousins. I joined them in the row opposite Sandhya's. We ate noisily with our backs to the wall. Two oil lamps threw weak puddles of flickering light from their perch upon upturned cans. Giant shadows flitted across the soot-stained walls and vanished amid the dark rafters. Aunt Bhanu approached, serving steamed rice onto banana leaf plates spread on the floor. My mother followed behind her, with a bucket of vegetable curry. As I watched them, a piece of fried chili struck my banana leaf.

It was not uncommon for one of my cousins to fool about when the elders were not watching. Sandhya's waving hand caught my eyes, as she frantically drew my attention in the other direction. There was Lavanya, serving an eggplant dish. She wore a dark blue sari, not a white one as the girl at the pond did. She smiled at me without a word and poured the vegetable onto my leaf. I was now sure that the girl at the pond had not been Lavanya.

After supper, I discussed with Sandhya the possibility of the girl being the goddess. Aunt Preema had always avoided being drawn into the discussion of the identity of the goddess of my visions. Twice before I had approached her with this query and both times she rebuffed me mildly, saying that it was something I would have to find out myself.

"I must agree to such a possibility, now that we have ruled out Lavanya," Sandhya said.

"That is fantastic! She appeared to both of us, which means she is real! She is not my imagination!" I exclaimed. I was happy beyond words.

It had been several weeks since we finished our final exams at school and everyone expected to hear about the results in the forthcoming days. I was apprehensive. One afternoon when Uncle Jaya returned home from his duties at the village school, he began calling out to Reevati, Sreedham, Chitrabhanu, Sandhya and me. As we ran out to meet him, he waved a sheaf of papers at us.

"Your exam results," he announced.

Some of the elders who happened to be home gathered around Uncle Jaya. I waited the few interminable minutes for my uncle to sift through the sheaf of papers. Then he looked at us and said, "All five of you passed your exams."

I breathed a sigh of relief. But he continued, "Shambu, you barely made it through. But you passed." My sigh of relief became tinged with gloom. Sandhya did very well in her exams, but she was quick to sense the melancholy in me.

"I am glad you passed, Shambu. That is all that matters." Saying that, she gave me a big hug. I had expected bad grades. All through the previous year, I was avidly exploring various mental phenomena—especially anything to do with the mystical—and I had not been concerned with my studies at school.

The elders discussed with us what we planned to do, now that we had passed our exams. They promised to support us if we wished to further our studies. However, I sensed their anxiety as to whether our choices would support the household.

Uncle Aravinda, Aunt Ananda, Uncle Damodaran, my father, and Uncle Raghavan sat with us on the back verandah after lunch that afternoon. My father asked Sreedham what he wished to do.

Sreedham, who passed the tenth grade with me, was the second son of Aunt Ananda. He opted to work in our household. Since all the households in our village subsisted on agriculture, there was a steady need for young bodies to take on the tasks of the aging elders. Sreedham's decision was welcome to my family.

Reevati, the second daughter of Aunt Gauri, wished to continue to study temple worship, as her aspirations were to be a priestess at the main temple. She had so far proved to be exceptionally adept at traditional rituals, and she possessed a clear, melodious voice for chants. From her childhood days, I remembered her showing a keen interest in liturgy, and she had apprenticed herself to Aunt Bhanu.

Chitrabhanu was the oldest child of Aunt Bhanu. He wished to study herbal medicine at an ayurvedic school. The closest school was in Kottor, a town fifty miles to the north of our village. Uncle Damodaran threw a fit when he heard Chitrabhanu's plan. My uncle asked his son if he thought about how he was going to support himself.

"Father, the School of Ayurvedic Medicine has a work-study program. A student can work in the school's arboretum and herbariums for a nominal wage in exchange for free room, tuition, and meals."

"Oh, so you have thought all about it in advance, eh?" Uncle Damodaran asked with barely veiled sarcasm. Listening to his tone, my father squirmed with uneasiness.

"Yes, I inquired about it in advance. I did not want to be a burden to the household. That was the only reason. Is that against the rule?" Chitrabhanu was belligerent. I felt that this afternoon's get-together was not going to get anywhere at all. With his reply, Chitrabhanu had deftly checkmated his father's attempt to use financial dependence to control him. Uncle Aravinda interjected at once, "Chitrabhanu, since you will be working as well as studying, I assume it will be longer before you graduate."

"Yes, this is an extended study-plan," Chitrabhanu answered curtly. He was still simmering.

"If young men like you have your own agenda and run away from home, how are we going to manage all the hard fieldwork? Can't you see that we are growing old?" Uncle Damodaran was indignant. His authority was challenged and his arguments rebuffed. The old man was not going to give in without a fight, I thought.

"Planting and harvesting rice is what you like to do. I want to study ayurvedic medicine," Chitrabhanu replied coolly. Sandhya elbowed me in the ribs with a smile.

"So you think that working in the fields is beneath your status?" With that, Uncle Damodaran rose from his seat. "The food you eat is the result of my sweat and blood. Don't you forget that," he admonished his son. Clearly, his ego was bruised, and he worked up a groundless argument.

Chitrabhanu sprang up and said, "I am deeply grateful for the hard-earned food from the sweat of your brows. I want to work hard like you—but I want to become a waidya and help the sick. It has nothing to do with status."

My father intervened immediately, appealing to Uncle Damodaran. "Allow him to pursue his dreams. In a few years he will be back, and then he can help us," he said, throwing his arm across Chitrabhanu's shoulders.

"It is not as if every one of our boys has left us, and we are without help. Besides, as a waidya, he will be an asset to us. Mother Paru is the only one who is proficient in ayurvedic medicines. So far there is none to take her place," spoke Aunt Ananda in Chitrabhanu's support. Aunt Preema knew the use of herbs. But her expertise was more with the mystical and arcane uses of herbs than with medicine.

"Will you come back to us, Son?" asked Aunt Ananda.

"Yes Aunt, I will return home after my studies and I will be home every holiday I can get," assured Chitrabhanu.

"Son, you do what you have to do with your life. It is just that your mother and I are growing old and we are unhappy to see you go." Uncle Damodaran stepped forward and hugged his son. "You have to be a father to know what a father feels," he added.

I caught Sandhya flicking a tear from her left eye. I was amazed. A little while ago, she nudged me, snickering at Uncle Damodaran, and now she shed tears for the same man. Women are inscrutable, I thought.

"If Grandma Paru could teach me this knowledge, I would gladly stay here and learn, Father. But she is old."

"No my son, your grandma needs rest. She has done all she could for us. You should go to the School of Ayurvedic Medicine. I want you to be the best waidya there is."

All were happy at the favorable turn of events.

"What have you decided to do, my son?" My father's question broke into my thoughts.

"I think I will continue my Sanskrit studies," I answered vaguely. I had no clue as to what I wanted to do in life. I was quite happy exploring my spiritual origins. Now I realized that I was on the brink of another change.

"Sanskrit studies!" exclaimed my father, "Are you thinking of becoming a Sanskrit teacher? You may be able to teach in our village school, like Jaya." He assumed my interest was to teach, but my true aim was freedom. However this pursuit was considered impractical—

even though the elders parroted the scriptures profusely in their daily life. I kept my true quest to myself.

"Shambu is a hermit," Aunt Ananda affectionately categorized me. "He is my little monk," she said, tousling my hair.

"It is okay to be a hermit by nature, but a man has to earn a living," said my father.

"Well, can't one earn a living through teaching Sanskrit?" Uncle Damodaran surprised me by coming to my defense. "We need young people like Shambu to keep our traditions alive, and most of our scriptures are in Sanskrit," he argued.

"Hey, listen to this man," spoke my father turning to Uncle Aravinda, "Just a moment ago he opposed Chitrabhanu's decision to be an ayurvedic doctor." Then he asked, turning to Uncle Damodaran, "Shouldn't someone keep our ayurvedic medicinal traditions alive, too?"

"Now, what is the point? We are here to help our children choose their paths in life. Let's not fight among ourselves," Aunt Ananda admonished them. Then she spoke to me, "If you want to pursue Sanskrit, then do so. You have our blessings."

I was relieved and thankful to Aunt Ananda for averting another confrontation. My father did not pursue his line of questioning. How true Aunt Preema was when she said that unlike most women, most men had a hard time handling change, as their egos were rigid.

Now it was Sandhya's turn to tell her father what direction she wanted to take. Everyone expected her to continue her studies since she did so well.

"I don't want to continue with school, Aunt." Turning to her father, she declared, "I am done with school, Father. I prefer to study the scriptures, as I continue to help at home."

"But you have a brilliant mind, my little babe!" exclaimed Uncle Raghavan. "I don't want to see you end up being a clown like me." he added winking at me. Sandhya sprang into his arms saying, "You are the greatest clown, Father, and no one can beat you."

Sandhya's decision not to pursue her education puzzled me. She had a brilliant mind. Even though, like me, she quested deeply for freedom, I thought that she might seek to become a teacher or follow some other occupation that allowed her to pursue her inner quest unobtrusively. But Sandhya was Sandhya.

The meeting was over. Sandhya walked with me, and when we were out of sight of everyone, she said, "Listen, Aunt Ananda thinks you are a little monk. But I know you."

"What do you know?" I asked, frowning.

"That you are a little monkey," she replied, giving me a quick little punch in my groin.

I grunted, as I stooped gasping for breath. She waited around, but finding that I remained stooped, she became concerned. I decided to pay her back and acted as if I was in agony. I sat down without a word, clutching my groin. She sat beside me remorsefully and rubbed my back. I could not maintain my deceit any longer. When she realized that she was being taken in, she pushed me down and slapped my rump as I howled with laughter.

"Now I know for sure that you are a monkey." With that she ran toward the kitchen, almost knocking over Grandma Chandra coming round the corner.

"Sorry, Grandmother!"

"My great Kali! Slow down girl," muttered Grandma Chandra. Then seeing me on the ground, she asked, "What happened to you? Did she knock you down, too? Girls during my time would never run that fast."

"Yes, Grandmother," I answered laughing.

"She is strong, isn't she? If girls are too strong, they will have a hard time finding husbands," she commented as she ambled out of sight.

▼ ▼ ▼

Some of the elders had aged, and the three matriarchs took less part in the affairs of the family. They and their husbands immersed themselves ever more in prayers and meditation. A sublime gentleness enveloped the character of the otherwise austere Grandma Paru. But in my heart I felt an uneasy foreboding.

It was July, three months after the Night of Kali festival. The last days of summer were very hot, and the monsoon rains were a few weeks away. The water level in the well sank deeper, and my folks began looking heavenward, anxious for relief. As was the custom, we made preparations to receive the monsoons. The extra spaces in the cowshed were filled with every piece of dry wood we could scrounge. Dry fibrous husks of coconut were piled high in a corner of the shed. Rows of pancake-shaped, dried cowdung were arranged in another section. Extra torches were prepared and stored suspended as bundles in rope hammocks. When the rains came, everything outside would be damp and fuel for cooking would be very scarce.

One night, the household relaxed in the courtyard after supper. It had been incredibly hot, and the air remained warm well into the night. With their grass mats and sheets spread out on the clean sands of the courtyard, the elders engaged in small talk. Four oil lamps hung from the rafters of the surrounding patio, providing meager light. Some of my younger cousins were running about, playing some game or another, appearing for brief moments in the pools of light. Their high pitched, excited voices rang out above the din of chatter. All of a sudden, I heard the loud rapping of brass rings on the doors of our north entrance. Instantly, a hush fell over the entire household, and the comfortable and relaxed social evening was plunged in an eerie stillness.

"Jai Bhagavati! Open the door. Jai Bhagavati!" someone cried from outside.

The household was galvanized into action; a couple of my cousins sprang up from their mats and rushed to the doors, as others stood up. The moments seemed interminable as my cousins drew the heavy crossbeam timbers, and heaved the screeching doors open. A little later, Cousin Gopalan ran back announcing the arrival of Bharata from the House of Puttuparambu.

"It's Grandma Bhavani! It's Grandma Bhavani," Bharata gasped out. He appeared to have been running hard across the fields. Bhavani was the eldest matriarch of the House of Puttuparambu.

At once, my aunts gathered around him, and Aunt Tara and Aunt Preema held him by his arms and led him toward the south patio. The rest of us followed close behind.

"Grandma died a half hour ago," he muttered.

"Ambae Bhagavati! Ambae Bhagavati!" A murmur rose from all around. Someone had awakened the matriarchs and our grandfathers, for there was a commotion behind me as the family made way for them. My father walked ahead with an oil lamp, leading them toward Bharata.

"Light the kuttuvilakku," Grandfather Vasudeevan instructed me. Cousin Siddharth and I hastened to the central shrine. Within minutes we threw the shrine doors open and brought the big brass oil lamp into the patio.

The elders mobilized the household in a pandemonium of instructions. In a short while, a party of my uncles and aunts headed out toward the House of Puttuparambu. I ran out of the house to our cowshed, and fetched a large bundle of palm-leaf torches. These I gave to each of my uncles and aunts as they filed out of the entrance and walked into the night. Bobbing fires in the distance indicated a similar party making its way to the House of Puttuparambu.

The handful of elders left behind urged us youngsters to get some rest. However, I found it hard to sleep. The courtyard was unpleasantly vacant. The presence of death, though a distant specter, cast its shadows upon my household. I sought out Sandhya, who welcomed my presence. A group of us got together. Thus Sandhya, me, Reevati, her sister Ragini, and Sreedham lay together in a semicircle, each of us on our bellies, with our chins propped up on our hands. We exchanged a good amount of ghost stories. It was well past midnight when we fell asleep.

Aunt Ananda woke us up early the next day. Sandhya and I did our early morning prayers together. On our way back from the temple, we saw the elders return from the House of Puttuparambu. They had been busy the whole night helping the household of Puttuparambu make arrangements for the funeral rites to be performed this day.

It was mid-afternoon when we started out toward the House of Puttuparambu. The matriarchs led the way, followed close by the grandfathers. My uncles held a palm-leaf umbrella over their heads, shading them from the intense heat. A very small group stayed behind, the rest of us joined this procession.

At the entrance to the House of Puttuparambu were Kastoori and Malini, two elders of this house. They were grief-stricken, and cried seeing my matriarchs. Matriarch Paru laid her hands tenderly on the cheeks of Kastoori and Malini.

As was customary, both Kastoori and Malini offered water to our matriarchs, and led them into their house. Uncle Raghavan directed the rest of us to the back of the house, where most of their property lay as an extensive grove of fruit trees and coconut palms, much like our own.

A few hundred yards from the house, a large group of men gathered under the trees. I moved forward into this group, and before me was a massive funeral pyre made of logs. Men from neighboring homes constructed a leafy canopy over the funeral pyre. Water was sprinkled on the sand around the pyre to keep the dust down, and some men drew various auspicious designs around the pyre.

"The Shava Shuddhi begins! The Shava Shuddhi begins," someone shouted from the house. Almost at once the men started back. During Shava Shuddhi the corpse is bathed with water and other unguents, such as sandalwood paste and rosewater. After the eldest son dresses the body in new cotton raiment, the eldest daughter performs the rites of passage. Uncooked rice, sesame seeds, and tulasi leaves are placed in the corpse's mouth. Tufts of kusha grass (Poa cynosuroides) are placed on the arms and legs of the corpse. Elders proficient in funerary rites and incantations direct all these activities.

The pall of gloom was palpable the moment I stepped within the house. I heard piteous wails from the women, as they sat in their rooms and grieved. Just as in our homestead, the House of Puttuparambu had an extensive central courtyard. The body of Bhavani lay on a grass mat in the middle of this courtyard. The head was pointed to the south, to orient the departing spirit on its journey into the realm of the dead, and onto its next transmigration.

I stared at the dead face in morbid fascination. It lay there with its mouth half-open, one eye almost closed, the other partially open, its lifeless gaze directed to realms beyond. A large palm-leaf canopy protected the corpse from the fierce afternoon sun. One of the elders tended a large kuttuvilakku, keeping the cotton wicks clean and burning.

Presently a small group of vallichappads issued out from one of the rooms, followed by Heemavati, who would be the next-senior matriarch, and Elder Krishnan who was the karanavar of the house and eldest son of the deceased.

The Shava Shuddhi began within minutes. The senior vallichappad directed Heemavati and Elder Krishnan in this rite, while the others helped pass various items back and forth as they chanted the appropriate funerary chants. The vallichappad then ordered the dead be wrapped in the grass mat that it lay upon. This signaled the end of the rites.

Some men of the household brought out Bhavani's rope cot and lifted the body onto this. Six of the oldest sons of the household hefted the cot onto their shoulders, with Elder Krishnan in the lead. At once the women setup an ululation, marking the final journey of the dead in this realm. A cacophony of wails and chants rose from all around. The corpse was taken out of the house through the south exit.

All of us followed the procession to the funeral pyre, where the body was positioned on the wood. Additional logs were placed upon it. Buckets of ghee were poured all over the logs. Elder Krishnan pushed a few packets of camphor into the logs to assist the flames. The funeral torch was lit with a lamp brought from the family shrine, and amid chanting of Vedic hymns, Elder Krishnan walked around the pyre and set it aflame all around.

Soon bellowing flames enveloped the pyre. The pyre collapsed on one side, tumbling the blazing logs onto the ground. The men hastly stepped back as intense heat singed those who stood close to the pyre. They used long poles to push the logs in as they crashed out of the pile. Clouds of blue smoke climbed and mushroomed beneath the canopy of leaves. The air smelled from burned wood, flesh, and ghee. Bits of ash sailed through the air and settled everywhere.

A loud report from the pyre startled me, and I saw a greenish blue flame spurt as if consuming some combustible gas. This was followed by another sharp crack. An elder who stood by me commented that this was the skull cracking open in the heat. Soon the flames brought down the temporary canopy, tumbling it into the pyre.

Within an hour, the entire pyre burned down to a mound of ashes and embers. Some of the women of the household brought out cauldrons of tea. As was the custom, none who were near the pyre were allowed to enter the house before a cleansing bath in the pond. I helped myself to a mug of tea, but decided to have my bath back home in our pond.

The mound of ashes remained undisturbed during the ten-day period of transition. It took ten days for the spirit to fully disengage itself from this realm. On the tenth day, Heemavati performed bali kriya, the final ceremony that assisted the spirit of the dead to leave this space-time. I was allowed to be present during this ceremony. It is believed that during these ten days the spirit becomes increasingly disoriented, as its subtle senses lose touch with this physical world, while not yet oriented to the Realm of the Dead. To add to the confusion, the spirit retains its memory of the places and the people it knows yet it is unable to communicate with them because it has lost its physical body.

Guided by a vallichappad, Heemavati collected the burned remains of her dead mother, mostly charred bones and some ashes, using a pair of tongs, into a clay urn. She chanted invocations that drew in her ancestors, who would assist the spirit in its passage into the Realm of the Dead. Pinda, or rice balls, prepared with black sesame seeds were offered to these ancestors who arrived in the guise of crows. With the conclusion of the bali kriya, the spirits of the ancestors departed, taking the spirit of Bhavani with them. The clay urn containing the ashes would be interred during the Night of Kali the following year, in the cremation ground behind the Shiva temple. Until then the urn would hang from a rafter on the south side of the House of Puttuparambu.

On the sixteenth day after the funeral, the elders of our house were invited to the adyantaram, which was an elaborate feast given by the household of Puttuparambu. That morning the family of Puttuparambu performed a special worship at the main Kali temple. Since they had invited families from many households, the men of the House of Puttuparambu built a temporary dining hall out of bamboo and woven coconut leaves to accommodate these guests.

Bhavani died before she could perform the ceremonies to yield her seat of matriarchy to her eldest daughter Heemavati. Thus the House of Puttuparmbu was without an ordained matriarch. After the bali kriya ritual and the sixteenth-day feast were over, Heemavati was ceremoniously ordained the reigning matriarch, with Kastoori and Malini as the co-matriarchs. All of us attended this ordination, which was performed by some of the vallichappads and presided over by a number of matriarchs from the neighboring houses. At the conclusion of this ceremony, Grand-elder Gangadharan, the husband of the late Bhavani, stood up and waved for everyone's attention.

"Listen everyone," he cried. Immediately the clamor died down.

"I have decided to join the vallichappads," he paused, "now that my beloved wife has gone on to her afterlife." He wiped his eyes with the edge of his vest. All of us sat still, our voices hushed by the poignancy of his words. His son, Elder Krishnan, moved to his side and held him close, and Vallichappad Agnimitra threw his arm across his shoulder. I heard a few muffled sobs. Some woman began to wail and had to be rushed off to her private quarters.

In my heart, I felt the old man's loneliness. The passing of our close neighbor drove home the inevitable finality of death. No matter how many relatives and friends Grand-elder Gangadharan was surrounded by, he was alone this day, and his grief was not a whit lessened. In spite of his children's protests, Grand-elder Gangadharan stood firm in his resolve. Very soon he regained his stoicism and asked the vallichappads to confer the traditional yellow raiments of their Order.

That evening, we returned home somber and silent. Especially silent were the matriarchs and their husbands. For days afterward they cloistered themselves, recluses in their own home. Once a day the youngest matriarch, Chandra, would come to the kitchen to fetch food for the rest. When questioned as to why the matriarchs and grandfathers were closeted, she replied vaguely that they were praying for their departed friend. Bhavani was their close friend, and they grieved her death. But we suspected that something more than plain grieving was going on. The clouds of change loomed over our household. I could feel them.

On the fifth day of her seclusion, Grandma Paru sent for Aunt Gauri. Cousin Nala and I were helping Aunt Gauri to tie a clothes line between two palms in our backyard. Aunt Gauri asked us to carry on, and rushed to the matriarchs. Twenty minutes later, Aunt Gauri called out for Aunt Tara and Aunt Bhanu. They were with the matriarchs for almost an hour. When they came out, they called Nala to them and spoke to him in a whisper. Nala nodded his head and at once took off toward the temple. I felt a tense excitement.

After hanging the wet clothes to dry, I helped Sandhya haul pots of water from the well. As she brought empty pots, I filled them with water. At the entrance to the house, Sandhya exchanged these pots with cousin Radha for empty ones. Sandhya hastened toward me, saying, "Just now, Nala came home with Vallichappad Agnimitra. Radha saw them in the courtyard."

"Well, something is going on with the matriarchs," I commented as I filled her pot. Sandhya was about to lift the pot onto her hip, when Radha called out, "Hold that. I think we should go in—the household is gathering."

We put our pots down, and hastened into the house. Among the household, whoever happened to be home had indeed gathered in the courtyard. I overheard that Vallichappad Agnimitra was in private conference with the matriarchs and their husbands. Somebody seemed to have sent word to my uncles and cousins at work elsewhere; presently they hurried in, their faces tense with the expectation of some bad news. The household milled about in the courtyard. My mother and Aunt Preema brought in a large vessel of tea, and soon we were lining up for a cup.

An hour later, the matriarchs and the grandfathers left their room, followed by Vallichappad Agnimitra. I watched their faces for some signs. They seemed extraordinarily calm and serene.

"They seem to have reckoned with their grief," said Sandhya.

"Yes, I think so," I said.

At that moment Grandma Paru made an announcement. She declared her decision to ordain Aunt Gauri the senior matriarch, along with Aunt Tara and Aunt Bhanu as the two other matriarchs. But these elders protested, pleading that they would do all the work and that the matriarchs should stay on and guide them.

"The wisdom and compassion with which you have guided us can never be replaced," Aunt Gauri pleaded.

"Of course. And the crocodile can shed tears, too," I muttered under my breath.

"Don't say that," Sandhya whispered.

"Sathya, Chandra, and I have shouldered this heavy mantle for years," Matriarch Paru said. "It is time to lay aside this weight and begin our undivided quest for God. That is our way."

"The death of our dear friend Bhavani has reminded us of our final task in this life," said Matriarch Chandra.

"But, you can live with us and perform spiritual practices," entreated Aunt Tara.

"It is our dharma to take up tapas, and live an austere life. If we break this tradition, it will only lead to the ruin of our matriarchy. Do not put obstacles in our way," advised Matriarch Sathya.

"Years from now, when your own time comes to take up this dharma, you should do so without delay or hesitation," Vallichappad Agnimitra advised the elders. "Your matriarchs do not want death to snatch them away before they can fulfill this phase of their lives," he added.

"The ceremonies of matriarchy will be performed tomorrow when we will have an astrologically significant window available. The monsoon is close at hand. If we delay this ceremony, we will not have an auspicious time for this until after the rains have stopped," cautioned Grandfather Shankaran. The vallichappad left, and the matriarchs, along with the grandfathers, retired to their rooms. Though we dispersed after tea, the restlessness was intense.

The next day, in the presence of some vallichappads and a few elders from the neighboring homes, Grandma Paru ordained Aunt Gauri as the senior matriarch. A large wooden canister, called the Parra, was filled with raw, unhusked rice. A few tender coconut flower clusters were stuck in this rice. Four large kuttuvilakkus were lit around this. This ensemble, representing prosperity and auspiciousness, was the centerpiece of the ritual.

The three soon-to-be matriarchs, wearing cream-colored raw silk saris, sat facing east in front of this arrangement. They wore their hair down, as per the custom. Aunt Gauri was in the center, with Aunts Tara and Bhanu on either side. When the appropriate mantras to Kali were chanted, the three elder matriarchs poured small copper pitchers of turmeric water over the heads of these women. The household cheered the three new matriarchs, while the elder matriarchs handed them each a new white silk dress, bordered with gold and silver embroidery. Vallichappad Agnimitra led them to our family shrine where he made them repeat the oaths of righteous management of our matriarchy in front of Kali, the divine matriarch, after which he blessed them.

Vallichappad Agnimitra initiated the elder matriarchs and our grandfathers with a fire ceremony. The elder matriarchs exchanged their household garments for the yellow robes of the vallichappad clan. One by one, each of the retiring matriarchs unhooked their jewelry and presented it to their successors. They wore strings of lotus seeds, and rosewood beads. The former matriarchs and their husbands filed out of our homestead, led by Vallichappad Agnimitra.

These elders, now inducted into the vallichappad community, would live as novices for a year, during which time they would be guided to relinquish all connections with their former lives. Husband and wife teams would dissolve their long-observed marital vows and would thenceforth live as kindred spirits, living out their final years in the common pursuit of true Freedom. At the end of a year, they would be given new names, marking the beginning of intensified spiritual practice, and ushering them into the stature of full-fledged vallichappads. But the House of Madatara lost six of its most experienced and benevolent elders, whose mere presence had driven the household in their daily tasks.

# CHAPTER TWELVE

# Storms of Anguish

It had been three weeks since the death of Bhavani. All day long we watched dark gray thunderheads, laden with rain and roiled by the jet stream, mushrooming in the west. The entire village was in a state of excitement at the impending monsoon. Everyone was busy carting in jars of pickled mangoes, bitter-gourd, preserved lemon, while others gathered the chilies, jackfruit peels, and medicinal herbs left drying in the sun.

I helped dismantle all outside clothes lines, and tied them in the patio that edged the courtyard. Although there were speculations as to the exact moment of the first rainfall, we were sure that the rains would hit in the next twenty-four to forty-eight hours. Everyone seemed to expect a storm, some with joyous anticipation, others with unease. The cattle were restless and mooing intermittently from the cowsheds. The raucous crows were quiet and unusually demure. As I assisted others in clearing gutters and making a final shoring of earth around the cowshed, I saw a flock of mynahs fly in from the west. They flew toward the cowshed and settled under the awnings.

"Look at them! They are shaking water off their bodies!" exclaimed Cousin Gopalan. "They must have been through the rain in the west," he added excitedly. The mynas were wet and miserable as they shook water from their feathers.

"Don't get too excited," I cautioned. "They might have taken a dip in the pond, hot as it is."

"But if Gopalan is correct, then I think that the rain is only a few hours away from us," surmised Uncle Bala, who directed our work.

"What? Then why is it still hot? If the rain is only a few hours away, we should be getting some cooler headwinds," I argued.

Uncle Bala leaned on his hoe and scanned the west. "There is a warm wind from the highlands blowing into the west," he mused aloud, throwing a pinch of dust in the air. "This wind is bucking those clouds. Look how the cloud top is pushed up and is curling over toward us," he said, pointing out the formation.

"I think that the storm is closer than we think. Those clouds won't make much progress with this wind slamming into them, and it can be neutralized only when the land cools down," he conjectured.

"You know what that means?" asked Uncle Bala with a conspiratorial expression on his face.

"Yes—tonight," spoke Gopalan, as he nodded with a smile.

"That's right. It's going to happen tonight. It's close to evening now. Two to three hours of darkness will cool the land sufficiently and that would still this warm westward wind. Those clouds will be overhead a little past midnight," my uncle predicted.

Toward late evening, a great cacophony of croaks and snorts filled the air from hundreds of frogs and toads. Great flocks of swallows appeared high overhead, diving and chasing one another. Much higher, eagles flew to the northeast, in pairs, or in small formations, eager to escape the oncoming storm. In spite of the brooding clouds in the west, the night was hot and humid. As usual, the courtyard was our sanctuary that night. I spread my grass mat on the sand and lay down to sleep.

Someone shook me awake. I opened my bleary eyes with a start. At once I felt a few large drops hit my face and arms.

"Wake up! It's raining!" cried Cousin Chandra. Raindrops splashed my sheets and the sand around me. I made out the outlines of people rushing about in the darkness. The courtyard was filled with the strong, musky odor of wet sand and rain. I rolled up my mat and sheets, and scrambled for shelter like the others.

▼ ▼ ▼

It rained all day long, turning the grove and the rice fields into a vast sheet of water. I could hardly see through the gray curtain of rain. Lightning ripped across the grim sky, followed by ear-splitting thunder. The household went about its business, the family went out into the rain and returned from their chores, and the front patio was lined with umbrellas, dripping water into puddles. Someone frequently swabbed the cement floors, made wet with mud and water. I wanted to stay huddled on my cot all day.

There were brief lulls in the storm, when the only sounds were the constant drip of water from the leaves, and the chortle of hundreds of brooks. Even the crows were gloomy. They sat on branches, wet and limp, snorting an occasional complaint as they fruitlessly preened their wings and underbellies dry. Up in the air, the clouds swiftly moved eastward while masses of new ones rushed in to fill the spaces. The clouds appeared to be so close to the ground that I felt that I could have struck them with the tip of a tall bamboo pole. The more these clouds pressed in upon me, the gloomier I became.

During these breaks in the storm, some of the men hastened to the rice fields to inspect the dikes and mud embankments. They had to keep a close watch on the water level in each of the vast rice plots. In a few days, the fields would be ploughed and small sections would be set aside as nurseries for the new paddy.

Numerous times during the following weeks my cousins and I helped my uncles clean litter from the water channels that carried excess water off these fields, and we piled silt and mud on earthen embankments that were eroded by rain. The embankments and the waterways were constantly repaired. While we were busy maintaining the integrity of the fields, the women-folk seeded the nurseries with paddy. Others yoked the water buffaloes to ploughs and began turning the waterlogged earth. Groups of herons and crows swarmed behind each plough, looking for worms and maggots that turned up with the soil.

We had been experiencing two months of torrential rains and storms. The water table was so high I could lean over the well's retaining rim and dip the brass pot into the water. The monsoons usually lasted for four months, with the bulk of the storms lashing down in this last half of the rainy season. We frequently wished for the warmth and light of summer that only a couple of months ago we were anxious to put behind us.

So far, electrical storms had wasted five coconut palms, and two palms were blown over into the pond. We hacked the trunks into sections and piled them by the side of the house. Then we dug out the massive fiber-root systems, and dragged them out of the pits. We planted coconut saplings in the pits, replacing the dead ones. The roots would be left in the rain to be washed, and the following summer they would dry in the sun, to be used as fuel later. Sections of the trunk would be tooled to replace some of the woodwork in the roof.

During the first half of September, the new matriarchs performed an elaborate Amavasya Kali worship. The village worshipped Kali at the village temple, as this officially marked the beginning of the rice planting tasks of the season. Sandhya and I woke up very early. We completed our chanting and meditations together before first light.

After partaking of a hearty breakfast and some black coffee, I left for the fields with my cousins, while Sandhya went about her chores at home.

My cousins and I walked out under an overcast sky into a chill, windy drizzle. Though the clouds appeared to be spent, more pushed in from the west, and gathered against the mountains in the east, shrouding them in a pall of gray. I shivered in the dismal gloom.

After a quick inspection of the dikes, drains, and embankments, we joined some of the women pulling weeds that grew in profusion in the ploughed and fertilized fields. We spread out the length of each plot and worked our way to the other end. Others stooped their way through the nursery fields, already bright green, and thick with growing paddy. It took keen eyes and dexterous fingers to discern the weeds from the paddy shoots, as both looked like grass. We left small bundles of weed behind, which the men carried home to feed the cows and buffaloes.

The wind picked up strength, and the rain came down in sheets. I was working my way through the ruts in the field, a little ahead of the others, when I heard a yell from behind me. Looking back, I saw my cousin Sumati running toward us. She stopped by Chandra, who was a few hundred yards behind me, transplanting paddy into the weeded ruts. I saw Chandra point me out.

"Shambu! Come home, quick!" She cried as soon as she was within earshot. "Sandhya is sick. They brought her in, just now. She is not moving," Sumati stammered out.

My heart began to thump wildly, and I was seized by uncontrollable anxiety. I could faintly hear others shouting the news to one another across the fields.

"Aunt Preema wants you home, now!" Sumati insisted.

Then the reality of the situation hit me, like a slow hard knock on my head. I dropped the bundle of weeds and ran. I sprinted past Uncle Bala and Aunt Bhadra, who were walking home briskly, trying not to slide down the slimy embankment. I ran through rain that came down in waves with visibility restricted to forty or fifty feet. Suddenly shapes loomed dead ahead. A couple of my aunts were racing along the mud embankment clutching their wet saris knee high with one hand, and with the other they hung on to a coconut leaf head-cover as they ran toward the house. I had no chance to shout a warning between gasps for breath. I slid past them down the slimy embankment and ran through the paddy. Within our grove, the rain obliterated all canals, turning the ground into a vast surging stream.

I pushed through the crowd of my female cousins gathered around Sandhya as she lay in the women's room. Kneeling down beside her, I took Sandhya's right hand in mine.

"Sandhya! Sandhya! Do you hear me?" I spoke anxiously into her right ear.

"No my son, she is not responding. I tried," I looked around to see Uncle Raghavan massaging Sandhya's feet.

Sandhya lay there moaning with her eyes closed, breathing fast and shallow.

"What happened, Uncle?"

"All I know is, she was helping Gauri in the kitchen. She stepped out to the cowshed to pull out some logs for the kitchen fire," Uncle Raghavan replied.

"When she did not return, I went out to look for her. I found her on the floor," said my mother, who stood distraught behind Uncle Raghavan.

"I think something bit her," said Uncle Raghavan, raising Sandhya's left foot gently by the heel. "Take a look at this."

I leapt to his side and peered at her foot. A tiny red puncture marked the outer edge of her foot. A broader ring of bluish bruising surrounded this incision. Close to it was a clean gash, as if someone had sliced the tissue with a sharp blade. From the blood-stained rags that lay around, it looked as if someone had squeezed out a lot of blood.

At that moment, Aunt Preema came in followed by Aunt Gauri. Aunt Preema brought in a copper basin filled with a hot greenish liquid that steamed with a strong herbal aroma. She smiled at me weakly.

"Here, soak this in this water and hold it to her foot," she said taking a cotton bundle filled with aniseeds from Aunt Gauri.

I applied the warm compress to her foot as Uncle Raghavan held her heel up for me. In a few minutes, several of my cousins and uncles trooped in and anxiously asked about Sandhya's condition. Then, I noticed that Sandhya had been lying in her damp garments. I pointed this out to Aunt Preema, who asked everyone to step out while she changed Sandhya into dry clothes.

"Stay here and help me," Aunt Preema ordered as I stood up to leave.

Between the two of us, we removed Sandhya's damp clothes, wiped her dry and clothed her in fresh dry garments. The small room had a dank smell from so many of us having been in it with our wet clothes.

"Shambu, change your clothes and come back. I will stay with her," instructed my aunt.

When they brought Sandhya in from the rain, they laid her upon the floor on a grass mat. When I returned from changing my clothes, Aunt Preema asked me to bring a cot into the room. Uncle Raghavan and I brought my cot to the women's room. Between the three of us we got Sandhya onto the cot and covered her with warm blankets.

While I was caught up with helping out my aunt, my mind did not have a chance to worry or grieve. After we had done as much as we could, I lit the small clay lamp in the niche in the wall and I sat by Sandhya's side. Then, my anxiety and grief got out of hand. I sobbed as I massaged her temples and shoulders. Uncle Raghavan sat by her feet, rubbing them under the blankets. When I could handle my anxiety no longer, I laid my cheek on her chest and cried. Aunt Preema came up behind me and gently rubbed my back.

I heard our cows mooing and the short snort of the water buffaloes. Through the window, I saw my cousins leading the animals onto the back porch. From my mother I learned that while some of the elders and my cousins returned to the fields to relieve those who had to keep on planting the tender rice, a few others moved the animals. They moved things around in the cowshed, trying to discover what had bitten Sandhya. This was important in order to prepare the right medicine for her.

I spent the rest of the day by Sandhya's side, sometimes talking to her, sometimes just rubbing her arms and shoulders. Periodically, I resurrected the dying flame in the clay lamp with more oil. The wind and the rain raged outside, the room frequently lit brilliant by flashes of lightning. While the water buffaloes snorted with joy, the unhappy cows mooed their displeasure.

Sometime during that period, I fell into chanting. I invoked Kali, and beseeched Her to return Sandhya to health. The day waned, and the slate-gray sky blended into the bleak blackness of the night. Aunt Preema brought some dinner for me, but I had no appetite for food, and just sat there. A kettle of a special herbal concoction, and a brass pot of water sat upon a wooden stool by the cot.

Sandhya loved jasmine. In a desperate attempt to arouse her, I got my brother Padman to bring in a basket full of jasmine blooms. I placed this by the head of Sandhya's cot.

I held Sandhya's hand in mine as I sat chanting. Then I felt a faint squeeze. I was alert instantly. She lay there, her eyes open for the first time in hours.

"Shambu, water," she murmured.

I reached for the waterpot, and hoisted Sandhya into a semi-recline. Propping her up onto my chest, I brought the waterpot to her lips. Sip after sip, she swallowed between heaves for breath. She nodded to me, and I laid her head back on the pillows.

She asked me to take some of the blankets off.

"I am sweating. It's too warm," she complained.

"That is a good sign, Sandhya. Your body is getting rid of the fever," I commented, rejoicing. I took some fresh towels and wiped the sweat off her, then helped her to change her position on the cot.

"Ah, that sweet, jasmine smell!" she said, scanning the room. I reached over her head and brought forward the basket of jasmine flowers.

"If nothing else, I felt that you might wake up to this," I said.

She raised her hands to my neck. I lowered my face and she kissed me, "Thank you, Shambu. This fragrance lifts up my spirit."

Uncle Raghavan peeped through the doorway, and rushed in upon hearing Sandhya's voice.

"Oh! My little pugee, are you feeling better?" he chortled to her, cupping her cheeks in his hands. Sandhya gave a weak but amused smile.

"Yes Father, but I feel weak."

"Shambu, please call Preema," entreated Uncle Raghavan.

I did not have to go far to fetch my aunt. I caught her coming out of our family shrine with my mother, with the kamakshi deepam in her hands. I was pleased to observe that during this emergency my mother had developed an empathetic camaraderie with my aunt. I wondered if my mother sensed my deep bonding with Sandhya, in spite of the secrecy of our intimacy.

That night, Sandhya sipped a little of the overcooked rice and vegetable goulash that Aunt Gauri prepared for her. When the time came for the household to retire for the night, Aunt Gauri ordered me to go sleep in my room; she said the women's room was no place for a young man.

I was in a dilemma. I desperately wanted to be by Sandhya's side, and she clung to my arm, pleading that I stay with her.

"Aunt Gauri, I must stay with her. It's important. I will sleep on a grass mat on the floor," I pleaded.

"There is nothing you can accomplish that any one of us can't," she retorted.

I looked at Aunt Preema, who was obviously distressed and uneasy. So I nodded to her, and giving Sandhya's hand a gentle squeeze, left for my room. Aunt Gauri had begun her matriarchy with an iron hand

and a hard heart. With these restless thoughts churning up my mind, I slept in my room. But outside the storm had abated, and the night was still. I fell asleep eventually.

A gentle hand shook me awake. I sat up with a start.

"Shambu, roll up your mat and go to Sandhya. Be with her," I heard Aunt Preema whisper into my ears.

"But, won't I get into trouble with Aunt Gauri?"

"Your Aunt Gauri's mandates are the least of our worries. You will have plenty of time to settle matters with her. Sandhya needs you now," replied my aunt cryptically.

"How is Sandhya, Aunt?"

"Go, be with her. When Uncle Raghavan wakes up, tell him that I have gone in search of Ahalya Mata. Also, ask him to call Elder Vallichappad Kaliprasad. He may know what to give Sandhya," she instructed me in haste.

"But who knows where Ahalya Mata is, Aunt? How will you find her? Besides, it's past midnight!"

"If anybody would know, it will be Aghori Narayani," she replied.

With that she walked out of my room. I swiftly rolled my grass mat and sheets, and took them with me as I followed her out. She threw a coarse burlap sheet across her back, drew it tight around her, and disappeared into the chilly darkness.

I tiptoed into Sandhya's room, which was in total darkness. A strong smell of burned wick pervaded the room. The tiny clay lamp had run out of oil.

Sandhya's forehead was hot to the touch, and she was awake. She grabbed my hand and whimpered, "I am cold, Shambu."

In the darkness, I probed the foot of her bed for an extra blanket. But there was none. I hastily unrolled my mat, and threw all four of my sheets upon her.

Her feet felt ice cold under the blankets, so I sat by her feet and rubbed warmth into them. After a while, I heard Sandhya breathe evenly. She was asleep.

I sat there in the darkness, undecided as to whether I should light the lamp or be in the dark. On one hand, I felt uneasy having broken the mandates of Aunt Gauri. But on the other hand, I felt that this was the right thing to do, to be by my friend.

The wind picked up outside. It howled through the coconut palms and trees in our backyard, producing weird whines, whistles, and screeches, as it forced itself into the room through the cracks in the planking of the window.

I felt Sandhya shiver under the sheets.

"Are you still cold?" I asked.

"Yes, Shambu, I am cold."

On an impulse, I lifted her sheets, and curled up beside her, hugging her close to me. She shivered for a while, and frequently tossed about. I slept with her for a little while, albeit a fitful sleep, often snapping awake, afraid that I would be discovered. But, eventually, Sandhya fell into a deep slumber.

I eased myself carefully from beneath the sheets, and sat on the cot. I sat there, dozing on and off, until first light.

▼ ▼ ▼

I conveyed Aunt Preema's message to Uncle Raghavan, who came in to take over the watch. After washing and having some breakfast, I came back to relieve him so he could fetch the vallichappad. Moments after Uncle Raghavan left, Aunt Gauri came into the room.

"How do you feel, my dear?" Aunt Gauri asked Sandhya.

Sandhya did not say a word, but laid there in a semi-sleep. Then looking at me, Aunt Gauri said, "I heard that Preema has gone off looking for Ahalya Mata, and Raghavan is out to call the vallichappads. Doesn't anybody realize that we matriarchs should be informed before they decide to do things on their own?"

I did not reply, but her tone of sarcasm was evident. Obviously, she found these activities to be too independent, and felt that her seniority was questioned.

"You are not planning on sitting here the whole day, are you?" she asked me. "Your help in the rice fields will be greatly appreciated."

"I will be staying with her until Aunt Preema comes back," I replied respectfully.

"And why is that? What extra benefit will Sandhya accrue from you that she cannot get from us?" she demanded, as she stood, arms akimbo, glowering at me.

This early morning altercation had not gone unnoticed. Somebody had the presence of mind to call in Aunt Tara and Aunt Bhanu, the other two matriarchs. They trooped in posthaste, followed by my mother and Aunt Ananda.

"The medicine Aunt Preema made is not working. I think she wants somebody who knows better remedies," I conjectured.

"Yes, better remedies indeed! Would anyone expect an infant killer like her to have the power to make any medicine? Now, there is nothing here for you to do that we cannot do," she snarled. Hearing her accuse Aunt Preema, my fingers curled into fists. Anger infused a spurt of strength in me.

"It is obvious to me that you weren't here with Sandhya last night, to give her the help she needed. I comforted her when she lay here shivering," I retorted. I was bothered by Aunt Gauri's continued accusation of Aunt Preema as an infant killer, but I kept quiet.

"Where did the son of Leela learn to speak back to his elders? Besides, I thought I made it clear that this is the women's room." Aunt Gauri was wrathful, and her choice of words began to acquire a tone of insult. I knew that this had not gone unnoticed by my mother.

"I am just obeying my preceptor's instructions. And last night I was here only a few hours," I said, trying to pacify her.

"Your Aunt Preema is not the matriarch. She is not in charge of this household," snapped Aunt Gauri. "And you, make sure that you get to the rice fields and earn your share of food," she said.

"No he won't!" my mother screamed. I was taken aback. Sandhya stirred in her sleep. "I am giving my share of food to my son today, so he can stay with Sandhya," asserted my mother.

"Gauri, it is perfectly all right with us if Shambu stays by Sandhya. You know that most of the work was completed yesterday," said Aunt Tara, the second matriarch. Aunt Bhanu and Aunt Ananda supported her.

"Oh, Kali! I think this house is going to pieces," Aunt Gauri remarked, beating her palm upon her forehead. She then turned around and walked out. At that instant, I felt that the split in the family was deep, and Aunt Gauri's irrational demands had widened it further. I wished that Grandma Paru were there. She was a perfect figurehead, who let everyone take the initiative to do what was needed.

▼ ▼ ▼

The sky cleared and we were favored with a brief period of sunshine. About midmorning, Uncle Raghavan brought in Vallichappad Kaliprasad. The vallichappad felt Sandhya's pulse and immediately began preparing medicine. He concluded that a poisonous snake, the dreaded krait, had bitten Sandhya. I stayed with Sandhya through the day, with my mother and father assisting me with Sandhya's needs.

When Aunt Preema returned that afternoon, the elders called a council meeting with the vallichappad. The elders met for a long time. Before she went to the meeting, Aunt Preema told me that she was successful in sending word to Ahalya Mata, but I noticed that my aunt was unusually withdrawn. When I told her of my argument with Aunt Gauri, my aunt became more solemn. My inner turmoil grew by the hour.

It was past midday when Uncle Raghavan came to the women's room. From Uncle Raghavan, I came to know that Aunt Gauri had chastised him and Aunt Preema at the meeting. But I felt some relief knowing that Aunt Gauri met with vigorous opposition from many members of our family who remembered her previous baseless accusations. I left him at Sandhya's side, and went out to the fields for a walk.

I felt that Aunt Gauri's attitude was despicable. It was clear that it was more important to her to consolidate her power than tend to human suffering. Even though my mother insisted that I eat her share of the meal, I could not. I ate nothing that day. My feelings were deeply hurt by Aunt Gauri's words. For the first time in my life, I felt alienated. Maybe, I was too comfortable at home. Maybe I was losing sight of the Supreme Objective. The Divine Mother's ways are mysterious. She breaks up complacence and attachment and urges Her children toward Her. The question why Aunt Gauri insulted Aunt Preema, calling her an infant killer, kept creeping into my consciousness. A confusion of thoughts stormed through my mind as I walked along the edge of the rice fields toward the mountains. On the fields, patches of sunlight alternated with shadows from the clouds. I prayed as I walked. It was early evening when I returned home.

Sandhya had lapsed back into a fever, and she was delirious. I took turns with my mother applying a wet rag soaked in camphorated water to her forehead. I worked on her for about fifteen minutes, when, without any warning, an ancient lady walked in, followed by a large band of disciples, who waited outside. I was first taken by surprise, but then recognition dawned on me. This was Ahalya Mata. She wore a vermilion-colored sari, and on her head was the crown of the whitest hair, billowing out like a halo, just like I had seen her almost eight years ago.

"Ahalya Mata!" exclaimed my mother, prostrating at her feet. I did the same.

She gathered me into her arms. "My son! May Kali bless you." Then, she turned to my mother, "Leela, I came as fast as I could." She blessed her with her palm on my mother's head.

Ahalya Mata asked for some myrrh, and requested that we all leave the room for a while.

As we waited outside, we heard her chant periodically. Then we heard her speak to Sandhya. I became hopeful.

After a little more than an hour, she came out and asked to meet with Aunt Preema, Uncle Raghavan, and the vallichappad, immediately. I went back to Sandhya. To my great joy, she was seated semi-reclining on the cot.

"How do you feel?" I asked, as I gave her a hug.

"This body feels better, now," she said.

"This body feels better now! When did you turn into a philosopher?" I teased her. I was amused by her reference to her body in an impersonal way.

"Ahalya Mata has given me energy. The mists in my mind are clearing. I understand the mystery of life better," she declared.

"Now that you feel better, you must be hungry. Let me fetch you some gravy," I said, and brought her some well-cooked and unspiced food. Little by little, I fed her with a small wooden spoon. After five or six mouthfuls, Sandhya pushed the spoon away.

"I want to pee," she whispered.

"I'll get the pot for you. Don't move," I said, laying her gently back on to the pillows. I closed the door, and swung both her legs on to the mat. With Sandhya seated on the edge of the mat, I held the pot in place. Sandhya relieved herself in fits and starts. Exhausted, she began to lean back. I swung her back on the pillows, and covered her with blankets. Her eyes closed in sleep. I watched over her for a few minutes, and then slipped out of the room to the courtyard.

The elders sat in council for a long time. About two hours passed before Uncle Raghavan came out of the meeting. He appeared uplifted, though not overtly displaying his relief. He threw his arm around my shoulder and said, "I want to tell you something, Shambu. After twenty-three years of marriage to your Aunt Preema, I must confess that it is only today that I know her a little better."

"What do you mean, Uncle?" I was puzzled.

But my uncle became solemn and silent as we walked toward the women's room to be with Sandhya. Then turning to me, he said, "You have been learning from Preema all these years. Even though I am her husband, you have been luckier than I have. You have her as your preceptor," he sighed. "I played and buffooned with her these many years, not realizing her greatness." He shook his head in remorse. I felt a great compassion for this man. On an impulse of pity, I threw my arm across his shoulder.

"Aunt Preema is a great sorceress. I found this out after a long time, Uncle. She is not the type of person who would advertise herself. I trust her completely."

We entered the women's room where Sandhya lay. She was awake, and my uncle hugged her, holding her close for a long time without saying a word. Meanwhile, I emptied the chamberpot, washed it, and threw the window open. It was twilight. Through the foliage, I saw patches of clear sky.

"Is everything okay with you, Father? It is unusual for you not to clown with me," Sandhya observed. I whipped around. She had her arms around her father. Uncle Raghavan did not say a word. He sat there hugging her, his head buried on her pillow.

"Father?"

Uncle Raghavan pushed himself up. Looking at her, he said, "As of this moment your mother has a new disciple."

"Who?" asked Sandhya, half rising onto her elbow.

"Any new disciple has to undergo a severe penance," I teased in a solemn voice.

"What penance?" asked Sandhya.

"Willingly done," Uncle Raghavan answered me.

"Any new disciple should be willing to obey the senior disciples of Aunt Preema," I said.

"Who should be obeying whom?" asked Sandhya, who was exasperated at this point.

Just then, Aunt Preema walked in with the Kamakshi deepam, putting an end to our banter. Later that night, Aunt Preema informed me that Ahalya Mata had spoken privately with my mother and father. I had a hunch that Ahalya Mata told my parents about Sandhya and me, and our spiritual bond through many lives. It gave me great relief.

That night, upon Aunt Preema's authority, I slept in the women's room with Sandhya. My aunt slept on the floor on one side of Sandhya's cot and I on the other. At midnight, Sandhya began tossing and turning with fever. She did not call out or complain, but Aunt Preema discovered her plight when she woke up to go to the toilet. My aunt and I took turns sitting by her side.

# CHAPTER THIRTEEN

# *Night of the Soul*

When I woke up, a storm was raging. My aunt was awake. She had closed the window, but the wind squeezed in through the cracks, making fiendish noises. By the faint light of the flickering lamp, I watched her caress Sandhya.

As had been my custom for the last couple of days, I sat by Sandhya and chanted for both of us. It poured outside, while I went about helping the household with various tasks. The planting of rice was completed, and everyone went out in small groups to inspect the fields for flooding, to clear debris from the water channels, and to pluck any new weeds. Work in the rice fields slackened. Now all we needed to do was tend the growing rice and keep the mud ridges and waterways repaired.

I peeped in Sandhya's room several times during the day to check on her. My parents were of great help to me in this task, as were my siblings. My sister Kartiyayini and brother Padman hung out with Sandhya, cheering her up. My sister gave her a sponge bath.

After the evening worship was over, I brought food offerings from the main Kali temple in the village to feed Sandhya.

"I want to sit up, Shambu."

I pulled her up in the cot, and she sat leaning on me. Her breathing became labored.

"Are you all right?" I asked, alarmed.

"Pull me up a little more," she replied. Sitting behind her, I grabbed her by her thighs and hauled her higher onto my chest.

"Feels better," she said.

Minutes went by and Sandhya began to wheeze harder. Her breath came out short and rapid. I became fearful. When cousin Sujata came in, I sent her to look for Aunt Preema and Uncle Raghavan. I held Sandhya close to me and began to chant my mantra. My body trembled with a nameless fear.

My aunt and uncle came hurrying into the room. Within a short time, most of the household gathered around the cot. Seeing them all gathered around us made me feel that I was losing Sandhya, and a knot of panic squeezed at my guts. Sandhya leaned listlessly across my chest, moaning and wheezing hard.

Some of the women were in tears. Uncle Raghavan broke down and sobbed silently. Everyone seemed to realize their utter helplessness. Then Aunt Preema took charge of the situation and asked everyone to move out into the hall. I asked her to open the window to let in some fresh air. The rain fell incessantly. The sky was dark even though it was only twilight. Sandhya squirmed in my arms.

"Take me into the courtyard," Sandhya whispered to me.

"But it's raining, Sandhya!"

"Please take me out," she insisted. I looked up at my aunt.

"What is she saying?"

"She wants to go out into the courtyard, Aunt."

My aunt looked at Sandhya for a few moments in silence. "Well, let's carry her out," she said finally. Uncle Raghavan and I carried Sandhya out into the courtyard. The air felt instantly cold outside the room. Everyone who gathered outside the room was puzzled why we were exposing Sandhya to the cold. But Aunt Preema pacified them. Puddles of water rippled in the courtyard. As we carried Sandhya into the rain, I heard Aunt Gauri send my cousins Siddharth and Gopalan, and my brother Padman, to summon elders from the houses of Tandu, Puttuparambu, Neelamba, and Magha. Uncle Jaya rushed off to the colony of the vallichappads. The rest of the household came forward to help, while the women stood around the courtyard with oil lamps.

Mercifully, the rain abated a little, but remained as a sprinkle. Aunt Preema instructed Uncle Raghavan in the placement of a grass mat on the wet sand. Sandhya indicated that it be placed so she could face the central shrine. While I held on to Sandhya, Uncle Bala spread raw unhusked rice over this mat, flattening it into a rough oval shape. Aunt Preema spread her own white silk sari upon the rice. My father held a palmleaf umbrella over our heads.

As soon as she was seated upon this bedding of rice, Sandhya smiled. I propped her up from behind as she sat facing the central shrine. Aunt Tara had the shrine doors opened and all the lamps lit. The few minutes that we stood in the rain was enough to soak our garments, and I felt Sandhya shiver in the cold. I held onto her for fear that she might lose her warmth and begin to fade. In the meanwhile, the elders directed my cousins as they feverishly erected a small shanty over us. I could hear some woman reading verses from the

Devi Mahatmyam. Within thirty minutes the shelter was completed and Sandhya and I were spared the direct rain.

Cousin Padmini announced the arrival of the vallichappads, led home by Uncle Jaya. Elders from our neighboring households followed the vallichappads into our courtyard. The vallichappads conversed briefly with Aunt Preema and the matriarchs, and then settled down to their death vigil. A knot of fear twisted my gut and I began to wheeze. I could not believe that they initiated the death vigil. Everything began to appear surreal. I held Sandhya close and kept chanting in spite of my chattering teeth.

Sitting under the shanty in the small space around Sandhya and me, the vallichappads began singing the glory of the Divine Mother. The elders from the neighborhood came by to offer their prayers, and walked past us blessing Sandhya. Some of them settled down with their scriptures in the corridors. Then the appalling truth sank into me: The household had given up on Sandhya. Slowly but surely, her life was ebbing out. Strangely, I did not grieve at this realization. Instead, my heart was filled with a strong passion for God. I chanted our mantra, the prayer that Sandhya and I had chanted together all these years. Before us was the brightly-lit shrine, with the image of the Divine Mother.

Imperceptibly, Sandhya leaned more heavily against me. I felt that she was drawing on her last reserves of life, and I became aware of my tears. I prayed desperately. Uncle Raghavan sat at her feet, half within the shelter of the shanty, and half exposed to the night and to the rain. His tears mingled with the rain and his sobs merged with the drone of the vallichappads' chants. He prattled and crooned to Sandhya, calling her his little girl.

Suddenly, Sandhya struggled to sit upright.

"They are here," she exclaimed, "All seven of them," she whispered, her gaze transfixed into the night.

"Who? . . . Who are they, Sandhya?" I asked.

"My path is clear, and I know who this one is," she said, poking her chin at Aunt Preema. Hearing her words, goosebumps broke out all over me.

"Who do you see, Sandhya? Who is she?" I asked her. Then I looked at Aunt Preema. She stood gazing at her daughter's face. By the pale light from the shrine lamps, her face exuded infinite love.

"You will be with us, too, Shambu. With time, you will be with us," Sandhya muttered. "Sit in front of me," she said, tilting her face up to me. "Come in front of me."

232 ▼ *Kali's Odiyya—A Shaman's True Story of Initiation*

Uncle Raghavan moved in to support Sandhya, and I squirmed upon the raw rice and sat in front of her. With some effort, Sandhya lifted her hands up and caressed my cheeks.

"We will be with you. We will make sure that you will not lose your way in the currents of life," she whispered, panting, "We will watch over you, be assured."

I was overcome by a wave of grief and cried.

"Do not grieve for this body," she said. But her words only whipped up a storm of anguish. Seeing me sob, she whispered sternly, "You should be ashamed of yourself. Look at you, weeping like an idiot!" She gazed into my tearful eyes. Then, softening a bit, she said, "You know who I am . . . Yes, you know. Stop crying."

At that point, I began to wail. Seeing me thus, my family broke down and cried with me. Interspersed with the pattering of the rain were muffled sobs and cries.

Sandhya pulled my chin close to hers, "For love's sake, stop crying," she whispered. "Don't you know me?" Then, pointing to her mother, she said, "Look at her." Aunt Preema stood in the rain beside me, her disheveled hair dripping water and falling across her face. Her wet clothes clung to her body, giving her the appearance of a nymph emerging through the surrounding darkness. She was strangely composed, in spite of the lamentations that arose all around. Seeing Sandhya motion to her, she stepped closer. My aunt gazed at her child with love.

"Cease this grief, my beloved. We have always been together," muttered Sandhya in my ear, "and we will always be. This karma may keep us apart for a little while," she said, poking my body. "But what is karma? In the eternity of our togetherness, karma is a mirage," she spoke softly, rubbing my chest.

"This karma will run out of its power, and then we will be together," she said. "I will be waiting," she paused, then sucked in a deep breath. "Chant for me now," clasping my hands, she pleaded, "Watch over me in my hour of transition."

With great effort, I contained my sobs. Suddenly, I felt that her words were mandates of love. I was anxious to obey her. I began chanting aloud. The rain gathered strength and lashed into the shanty.

"Kali! Kali!" cried Sandhya, and her body collapsed in my arms. I held her close to me for a few moments. Then I maneuvered myself behind her and held her leaning against my chest. A great wail broke out all around me. The vallichappads ceased their chanting and cried out, "Divine Mother, let this spirit merge in your love!" One by one, they rose from their seats and touched Sandhya's forehead. They blessed her. They circumambulated us and walked out of the shanty, into the rain. I saw the vallichappads mingle with my family to assuage them.

Uncle Raghavan went berserk with grief. He beat his chest and rolled in the sand crying out to his child. As I sat by Sandhya's body, I saw my father rush forward to comfort Uncle Raghavan, but he was disconsolate. Aunt Preema pulled Uncle Raghavan into her arms and held him. When he seemed to compose himself, my aunt sat him inside the shanty.

As I held Sandhya's body against me, I chanted and waited for my aunt. The pandemonium that broke out barely registered in my mind. With my face in her hair and my arms around her body, I chanted, rocking Sandhya's body.

Aunt Preema brought eight clay lamps to me and told me to lay Sandhya's body upon the rice. I placed the lamps on the rice, around Sandhya's body, and lit them. When I lit the lamp close to Sandhya's head, I noticed a trickle of blood ooze out of her hair in the crown, and spread over the rice. Mystified, I looked up to my aunt. She said nothing as she spread a white silk cloth over Sandhya's body. A surge of emotion prompted me to take her blood on my right palm, and I smeared it on my forehead, my crown, and on my chest. In spite of the rain, groups of people came by to pay their homage and say a prayer, late into the night.

The rain abated, and the neighbors trickled out of our home. But some members of the House of Magha remained with us. Their gratitude to Aunt Preema for her help during their crisis with Rati manifested clearly this night. Most members of my household retreated into their rooms. I sat by my beloved Sandhya, held there by the strongest passion and love. A white silk cloth covered her body up to the chin.

My mother came and pleaded with me in vain to get some rest. I told her gently to leave me. I sat cross-legged and began to meditate. If anything could focus the mind, I realized it was grief.

Around midnight, Aunt Preema brought me some rice and vegetable gruel, but I felt no hunger. I was numb. I sat chanting, with my hands upon Sandhya's body. Aunt Preema sat beside me, and rubbed my back for a while, as she crooned a cradle song. Then, she began to feed me a little morsel at a time, but there was no taste to the food. I was anxious to obey Sandhya's final request to chant and watch over her transition. I had no thought for anything else. With every chant, I visualized protection around her.

About one-thirty in the morning, the trickle of people stopped. The household was at rest. I kept my vigil, chanting by Sandhya's side. Even though the rain had abated, the night was filled with the sounds of running water. Lightning flashed frequently, revealing dark clouds churning in the sky. Uncle Raghavan sat in the rain, his back against the tulasi shrine. My aunt approached him and said something. After a while, I saw him leave. My intense anxiety for Sandhya's safety kept me awake. The lightning, the deafening thunder, and the chill air also helped keep my mind alert.

With her gaze fixed at the dark sky, Aunt Preema sat leaning against a pole near me. She engaged herself in a one-sided, whispered conversation. Hearing her speak to the night air made me fearful. At times, she circumambulated the shanty, maintaining her monologue.

From time to time, people from my household would come by, cowled in blankets from head to foot. They would walk by and observe us from a considerable distance, as if they feared to approach the dead and the sorcerers who stayed awake.

I had my hands on Sandhya's belly under the silk shroud. Sometimes I held her cold hands and fingers. I fancied warmth returning into her body. I took her hand and rubbed her palm vigorously. The motion caught my aunt's attention. She stopped in midsentence, and I sensed her gaze at me. She did not say a word. I stopped rubbing Sandhya's cold fingers. I wondered what thoughts passed through my aunt's mind. If ever compassion and understanding were personified, it would be Aunt Preema.

At times, I felt that time crawled by grudgingly. Around two-thirty in the morning, I got up to replenish the eight clay lamps with oil. Aunt Preema watched me silently. As soon as I filled the last lamp with oil, and deposited the oil reservoir, Aunt Preema pulled me into her arms, rocking me from side to side. Her wet, tousled hair brushed my cheeks.

"My son, I bless you. Sandhya is proud of you," she said.

"Where is Sandhya?" I asked.

"She is here! Right here!"

"I cannot see her, Aunt," I whimpered.

"No, you cannot," she said. I remained silent and dejected. Then, as if sensing my dispiritedness, she pushed me out to arm's length and said, "She is still in her body, but she is safe. The Guardians of the Border are with her."

"Are they the . . ."

"Hush! Listen. Listen now," she urged.

At that precise moment, a pack of dogs let out a symphony of howls, interspersed with modulated baying. My aunt chuckled, "The aghori's people."

Barely did the howling stop, when there sailed in from a distance, the sounds of yelps, and the high pitched whines of wild dogs. I was thrilled, and my aunt clapped her hands like a child, as if encouraging them.

All this howling and hooting woke the household. Matriarch Gauri stepped out into the courtyard just in time to see Aunt Preema clap and laugh.

"In the name of Kali! What is the meaning of this stupidity?" cried Gauri.

"My daughter is with the Great Ones, Gauri. Listen to their song of reunion," said my aunt, and she clamped her palms around her mouth and howled aloud. Instantly, hyenas rent the night with their hideous cackles and discordant yowls. Soon the dogs in the village bayed, setting off a massive cacophony. People who slept in the corridors sat up in terror, crying the name of Kali.

"Oh Kali!" Gauri cried. "Stop this! Have you gone cuckoo, Preema?"

"I am happy for my child, Gauri," placated my aunt.

"Your child is dead. You need to get some sleep, Preema."

I was appalled by her crudeness and a surge of anger flooded my being.

"You don't understand what this means to us. What I have gone through to make this happen!" my aunt said gleefully, and she continued to howl.

Matriarch Gauri stomped her foot in fury, but to no avail. The cackle of the hyenas drowned her protests. She hastened back to her room, leaving us alone. I continued my chanting. Once or twice, my chanting faltered. My aunt shook me instantly.

"Shambu, darling, keep your eyes open. Keep chanting."

"I am sorry, my Aunt," and I began anew with a fresh surge of wakefulness. From my aunt's tone, I felt that she was concerned about Sandhya.

"The guardians are powerful, but Sandhya is still here," she whispered with concern, patting Sandhya's chest. "Don't break your chants, sweetheart. The terrible energies are around," she said, motioning to the dark space outside the shanty with her eyes. As I chanted, I looked around nervously. I had a million questions, but I dared not break my invocations. The questions would have to wait. With some effort, I pushed them from my mind.

I chanted for a long while with my aunt beside me. Then I saw that the space around the courtyard was not so dark. It was early morning, and I heard the household stir awake to a day darkened by clouds and shrouded with grief. Members from the House of Magha were the first to arrive; they joined others from their house who had stayed with us overnight. I saw their deep sorrow at our loss. The karanavar from the Magha household approached us and prostrated before Sandhya's body. One by one, others from his household came by. The karanavar sat before my aunt and said that his matriarch had put all their resources and manpower at my aunt's disposal.

"This is the least we can do for you, Preema," whispered the karanavar.

"Your presence gives me strength," my aunt replied.

The sky weighed heavy with clouds and another downpour was imminent. My mother and my aunts gathered by the shrine. They discussed something with Aunt Preema; it sounded like an argument. My aunt said something to my mother who dashed off immediately. I redoubled my efforts at chanting. With my aunt pulled away into the discussion, I felt I must focus more, to keep Sandhya safe. My aunt came back in a few minutes.

"Sweetheart, we must take her into the hills," Aunt Preema said. I nodded my head as I chanted. Then I saw Uncle Raghavan and my father bring two bamboo poles and a large grass mat. They strung the mat onto the poles like a hammock.

"Is this strong?" my aunt asked.

"Oh yes! It will hold," replied my father.

"Shambu, dear, it's time. We must take her now," Aunt Preema said. Uncle Raghavan and I gathered Sandhya's body, and her shroud, and placed her on the hammock. We tied the ends and the midsection to the poles and hefted Sandhya's body on to our shoulders.

Most of the elders were opposed to Aunt Preema's unconventional ideas. They wanted to cremate the body in our backyard, as per our tradition. But my aunt was firm. She argued that her daughter's death was mystical, and that she passed on with her consciousness intact, exactly as it was enjoined in the Tantric texts. Therefore, she would be accorded the sorceress' farewell. By having us carry Sandhya's body out through the north entrance, Aunt Preema broke one more rule. Scriptures informed us that the spirit of an ordinary person departed via the southern path that leads into the Realm of the Dead. Only illumined souls ascended the celestial realms through the northern path. Therefore, in accordance with the scriptures, the corpse of an ordinary person is carried out of the south entrance of a home to the pyre. Elders like Matriarch Gauri did not see anything extraordinary about Sandhya's life.

None dared to stop my aunt, especially after the previous night's display of her tremendous influence over the denizens of the forest. That day I witnessed the consolidation of the myths and fears with which the people surrounded the being of a sorceress. Very few among my household argued in favor of my aunt and supported her decision.

Though Aunt Preema faced scathing criticism from her own relatives, she enjoyed staunch support from the House of Magha. At the height of the contention, Aunt Preema loomed menacingly, like a mother falcon with her wings arched over the carcass of her dead young. The elders backed off, leaving us to our tasks.

We left behind a divided household when we set out with Sandhya's body for the hills in the east. Uncle Raghavan and I trudged ever upward. We were making our way along the mud ridges of the rice fields when the storm broke out. We carried Sandhya's body, wrapped in a grass mat and suspended beneath the stout bamboo poles. Lashed by the wind and rain, her body swayed from side to side, constantly trying our precarious balance. I could barely make out Aunt Preema, who took the lead ahead of me with a cloth bag swinging heavily from her shoulder. We walked with our heads down, to avoid the rain that flew at our faces. After a while, I learned to pace my breathing to my mantra.

We took several short breaks; it was midday when we left behind several smaller hills and made it to the foothills of the Ramagiri range. It was uphill most of the way, and the forest grew thick. As we gained altitude, the cloud cover got lower. Our visibility was reduced to a few feet in several places. Aunt Preema stopped in her tracks frequently to orient herself. We waded through murky torrents that seemed to have flashed into existence everywhere. With Aunt Preema walking ahead, we came up against what appeared to be a recent tumble of boulders and trapped timber.

"Stop a minute, Shambu," my uncle shouted. I barely heard him above the din of the wind, rain, and the muddy torrents. I halted, at the same time calling to Aunt Preema to stop.

"I must set her down some place, Shambu. I am out of breath."

"Let's lay her on that boulder, Uncle," I suggested, sighting a boulder whose flat top lay at hip level.

"Preema, I don't think I can carry her any further, my dear," said my uncle as he helped me lower the body onto the wet stone. He slid his back down the side of the boulder and slumped upon the wet soil. My aunt hastened to him and sat by his side.

"This is as far as we need to go, dear," she told him.

"I would go further, but I just cannot. I won't make it, sweetheart," said my uncle wearily. I felt bad for him.

"Uncle, I will carry her. You rest here," I said.

"Darling, this is as far as we need to go. Shambu and I will do the rest of the work. I want you to get back home before dark," said my aunt.

"What will you do, Preema?" he asked, tilting his head to Sandhya's body. My aunt placed her hands upon his shoulders. After a pause, she said, "I will send her back to her companions. I will send her back." She looked at Sandhya's body and whispered, "I will send you home."

"I trust you, my beloved. Send my little girl home, safe. My little girl . . ." My uncle was in anguish. Aunt Preema pulled him to her bosom.

"I must do this. I owe it to these two," she said, poking her chin to Sandhya's body and to me.

"Shambu, you bring your aunt home safe. Promise me you will."

"I will bring her home safe, Uncle," I said, reassuring him with a hug.

"Take care, sweetheart. Come home to me," cried my uncle as he turned back downhill.

"Be assured that I will. Take care, going downhill. Watch out when you step on slippery rocks, darling," called out my aunt.

It was some time before he made his way gingerly down the hill and disappeared out of sight.

"Where do we go from here?" I asked.

Aunt Preema looked around. Ahead of us, the land sloped upward, ending in what appeared to be the first of a series of steep crests. To our left, roaring white waters of a torrent tore at a deepening chasm. But to the right, trees grew upon a broad shelf of rock and soil.

"Between the two of us, we should be able to get her into those trees," said my aunt.

"What then, Aunt? There is not a dry twig around to build a fire, let alone a pyre," I bemoaned.

"Why a pyre?" asked my aunt with a hint of sternness in her voice. "The daughter of a sorceress will not be burned upon a pyre like some ordinary human," she declared. "Besides, you would be surprised how much dry wood you can find, if you search."

"Then are we going to bury her? The wild dogs will dig her up!"

"We wouldn't want them to dig her up, would we? Get hold of the poles. We must move her into those trees." Saying that, she grabbed one end of the poles that held the mat bundle. Between the two of us, we heaved Sandhya's body into the trees. Once within the gloom of the trees, we were spared the direct rain of the open hillside. Nor did the chill wind penetrate these woods as fiercely.

We laid Sandhya's body beneath a giant banyan. A thick, springy pile of organic debris carpeted the forest floor. Water dripped from the leaves, making little puddles in the dank humus. But here and there were patches of dry ground, protected from the rain by broad overhangs of branches. My aunt and I settled down on one of these spots. No sooner did I sit down than I began to shiver. She pulled me into her bosom to give me warmth. We sat thus for a while. An incredible weariness began to surface, and I dozed.

I opened my eyes to a weird glow. It seemed to shimmer and exude warmth. In spite of my strenuous efforts to open my eyes, I felt feeble and my eyelids kept closing. I was disoriented and puzzled by the glow. My seemingly gargantuan efforts to arouse myself made me drift helplessly in and out of consciousness.

"Watch over me in my hour of transition," Sandhya's voice intruded into my shifting consciousness. I strained to chant, but parts of the mantra broke up into meaningless jabber in my feeble awareness. Panic seized me, as I feared for Sandhya's safety. I felt trapped in my body. Profound anguish flooded my being and I cried out to Kali.

"Kali, my Divine Mother! Keep Sandhya safe," I sobbed in my sleep. "I cast . . . my astral sheath . . . around Sandhya! I shield her with my being!" I invoked a final feeble force to protect Sandhya before blackness claimed me.

I smelled wood smoke, and in an instant I was awake. I sat up with some effort. It was dark, but a small fire blazed before me. I began to chant immediately. The storm had ceased. The part of my clothes that faced the fire were dry. Aunt Preema sat leaning against the banyan tree, staring at me. Reflections of the flames danced in her eyes, giving them a feral quality. The intensity of her gaze frightened me, and I broke free from her spellbinding eyes. Beyond the ambit of the fire's glow, I saw the vague shape of the mat bundle with Sandhya's body within.

Then I heard a peculiar sound, like that of sand swishing in a metal container. It existed for the briefest time, then stopped. I scanned the perimeter beyond the mat bundle. I heard the sound a second, then a third time. I became very alert, but the blackness of the forest masked the perpetrators. It did not help my vision to look through the flames either. So I scanned the darkness behind me, away from the flames. Vague forms skittered among the trees.

"The night is awake!" Aunt Preema's husky voice jerked me around. "The guardians are here," she said as she continued to stare at me.

"Where are they, Aunt?" I asked as I strained to see into the blackness.

"They are all around us, my dear."

"What do they look like? What do they want, Aunt?" I looked at her. She still had that feral gaze upon me.

"You have seen them before. They want you to free Sveeta." With that she groped inside her cloth bag with her right hand, all the while keeping her disconcerting gaze upon me.

"Sveeta," I was puzzled for a moment. "Yes, you mean Sandhya!"

"Sandhya is Sveeta. You have to free Sveeta."

"How? I cannot even remember Sveeta, let alone keep her bound!"

"Here, take this and cut the body to pieces," she said as she produced a large chopper from her bag.

I sat there transfixed with horror as my aunt held the chopper to me. Then we heard the peculiar sounds again. My aunt whipped around and peeked beyond the rim of shimmering light. Humped shapes seemed to materialize and dematerialize in the jungle beyond. My fear was visceral. The mat bundle moved; something was dragging it sporadically into the darkness. For the first time I felt angry at my aunt. Why was she doing this elaborate hoax? We could have cremated Sandhya at home, thus giving her the proper rites. On an impulse, I sprang upon my feet.

"Why are you playing these tricks, Aunt? Why are you doing this to Sandhya?" I raged at her, my preceptor. All of a sudden, irrational suspicions mushroomed. I began to suspect her integrity. "You did not shed a single tear for her!" I accused my aunt.

"I am not playing any tricks on you, my child. This . . . this is not my power," she said, looking at me with her large eyes, and sweeping with her right hand, to encompass the scene. "This is the power of your karma; our karma, Shambu. This is no trick, my beloved," she explained in a tone of poignant sadness. Something about her voice and her expression made me think. My fury subsided and my legs began to shake as I realized the enormity of my stupidity. I felt faint.

"I took birth for your sake, to guide and shelter you two," I heard her soft voice. "I am not her mother, nor am I your aunt. You cannot 'see' this with your eyes of flesh. Do not be angry with me, Neela." I was perplexed to hear her address me as Neela. Anguish strangulated my heart, but I could not utter a single word. I was ashamed and wished I had the courage to take the chopper and hack my own flesh.

"If it is love that you feel for her, then it should set her free. But, if it is attachment, then it will bind her down to this earthly realm," she spoke softly. "Love knows no grief; love rejoices in the beloved's freedom. Love expects nothing, therefore it is not angered when the beloved passes on. Love has no motive, so in its eyes nothing is suspect."

Painfully, I realized that all my anguish, anger, and grief was the result of my attachment for Sandhya. I stepped toward my aunt. Kneeling before her, I opened my trembling hands to receive the chopper from her. With the chopper in my hand, I placed my forehead upon her feet for her blessings.

"How am I holding her back, Aunt?"

"Sveeta, the astral being, will leave her physical body. That body is Sandhya. Your attachment and love is focused upon that body—not on Sveeta. I will explain the details later. Now, you must set Sveeta free. It has to be done now," she urged. I stood there hesitant, the chopper in hand.

"How is Sandhya different from Sveeta? I thought that they were both the same!" I asked, hoping to delay my gruesome task.

My aunt rose from her seat. Approaching me, she pushed me toward the mat bundle. She pulled loose the coconut fiber knots that held the mat around the body. The grass mat rolled back, exposing Sandhya's silk-wrapped body. A surge of emotion seized my being. I wanted to lie with her and hold her close, to warm her back to life.

"Chop this body to pieces. Now!" ordered my aunt. With incredible speed, she ripped off my upper garment and loincloth, rendering me naked.

"Do not argue with me," she warned, as I opened my mouth to protest. I stood disconcerted for a moment. "Chop up this body now—before the terrible energies get to her," she urged.

My aunt had been selfless toward Sandhya and me. Why would she wish to harm Sandhya, her only child? I must obey my aunt. I must, even though I feel weak. I thought. I closed my eyes and prayed, "Divine Mother, possess me now. Divine Sandhya, you are Kali Herself!"

Tearing the white silk shroud off her body, I laid her naked. Behind me, I heard my aunt begin a chant. I swung the chopper up and slashed down with all my might. Bits of flesh, bone and body fluids flew out. Again and again, I hacked my beloved's body. In the end, there were eleven pieces, and I was covered with gore. The chopper slipped out of my palm and fell to the ground. My head reeled and I felt my knees give. Just as blackness enveloped my consciousness, I caught a vague glimpse of humped shapes hovering over the bundle and tugging at the flesh.

# CHAPTER FOURTEEN

# Supreme Transcendence

"Shambu, wake up! Shambu, wake up!" I heard a high-pitched voice, calling me as if from afar. I felt myself being shaken. But slumber, like the smothering layers of a thick blanket, enveloped me within its languorous folds. Disconnected from my body, I was adrift within sleep's labyrinthine chasms. It was a strange and frightening sensation of being loose within my body, yet awake, but unable to access a toehold in that turbid realm.

I struggled up the torpid gradient of sleep's insentient abyss, and for brief periods, felt reconnected to parts of my body. At those moments, I felt that I thrashed my limbs about, and made fearful noises with my breath, frail attempts to wake up and respond to the urgent caller.

Then I felt the warmth of a hand on my cheek, and a voice asked with concern, "Shambu, are you all right? Wake up, please! It's me, Sveeta!"

That name—Sveeta! It ripped through the fabric of my sleep, scooping my awareness upward. I was awake instantly.

"Sandhya," was all I could utter. She peered into my eyes, kneeling beside me on the forest floor. I sat up, and taking hold of her shoulders, tried to make sense of her features.

"Sandhya, I cut . . . I mean, Aunt Preema ordered me to cut you!" I said, bewildered.

Puzzled, I ran my fingers down her back. I took her hands in mine and held them to my cheeks. They felt warm to the touch. My heart galloped, hoping against hope that this was reality, and her death had been only a nightmare.

"Look at me, Shambu! Look at me," she said, holding me at arm's length. "You chopped Sandhya's body. My former body. This is me, Sveeta."

"Sveeta!" I cried, feeling a terrible disorientation. "Sveeta . . . Sveeta!" I muttered looking down at her feet. I noticed that her feet were suffused with a glow. I touched them in mute fascination.

"You have set me free! I am free," she cried, pulling my chin up to face her.

"Where is Sandhya? Where did she go?" I asked. Anguish surged within me. I inspected her features. She looked so much like Sandhya. I looked about me. The forest appeared the same as before.

"This is a dream," I said to myself.

"No, this is not a dream. You are awake, and this is me, Sveeta. I am here with you," she asserted.

"Aunt Preema?" I wondered aloud.

"Shambu, I am here." A soft voice answered from my left. As I turned, I saw Aunt Preema emerge from among the shadows of the banyan tree. Softness permeated her features, as in a dream. I turned back to Sveeta.

"Were you Sandhya? Are Sandhya and you the same?" I asked, touching her again, and again. She just held me close to her.

"This is wonderful," I muttered aloud to myself. I am so awake in my dream. I must tell Aunt Preema about this when I wake up, I thought.

"You don't have to tell me. I am here with you now," said my aunt.

That was not surprising; she had read my thoughts before. Again I noticed that glow about Aunt Preema, much like Sveeta's. Indeed, the entire forest was lit mildly, as if the very air were glowing.

Sveeta forced my chin around to face her. Again, I studied her features closely.

"Yes, it's me, Sveeta. I am free, and our group is here!" She touched the crown of my head with her right hand, while simultaneously applying a gentle pressure to my navel with her left.

"Our group is here," she repeated. "Amba is here," she whispered reverently.

"The group is here? Amba?" I mused aloud. I was utterly bewildered. Amba! So familiar, yet so distant, I thought. I closed my eyes to extricate my memory of Amba.

"We need to infuse you with power, Shambu. Your perception of the subtle realm is tenuous." Sveeta's voice broke into my musing.

A vibration issued down from her palm onto my crown and coursed through my body. The sensation was exquisite, and I smiled as the vibrant energy throbbed through me. I know this energy! I have felt it possess me before, and I belong to it, I realized.

"Open your eyes—be prepared to awaken some forgotten memories," she warned. Abruptly, she removed her palms from me. I opened my eyes to a gossamer light that filled the nightscape. I had no sensation of the cold that I felt until a moment ago. Sveeta's body was phosphorescent, as was Aunt Preema's.

"Look at your hand," Sveeta said.

I held my arm out. It luminesced. Indeed, my entire body was luminescent. I looked at the trees and was amazed to see them shimmer.

"You are now in the fringe of the astral world, your true world," Sveeta said.

The phosphorescence in the trees seemed to move. I watched the magical light waft among the trees, as the leaves moved gently. The shimmer among a section of the forest canopy intensified and crackled. Suddenly a gigantic radiant form appeared amidst the trees, startling me. Scintillating blue-black light clothed the being. With its head cresting the treetops, it stood well over a hundred feet tall. It grinned at me. A shocking thought struck me—this must be the Amorphous Being! Nishachii!

It stepped out of the foliage and came closer.

"Neela, my little Neela!" The being addressed me as it crouched before me. I was disarmed by its gentleness.

The milky textured light adjacent to this being on either side of the forest crackled, intensified and coalesced into five smaller forms. They were robed in deep-blue luminescence. They emerged from the trees and approached me. As I watched in fascination, I felt Sveeta pull me onto my feet. The five beings walked up to us and stood around me while the giant one positioned itself behind these five. I had a difficult time getting a clear sensory grip on their features. Then all six made way, as if for another. A seventh being appeared in this space. At once, I felt a pulse of energy flood through me, and the features of all seven of them became crisp.

The seventh one, a woman, was fair and radiant beyond description. She beamed an inscrutable smile at me. Tall and slender, she was swathed in folds of golden luminescence, which replenished from the ground up. Her unusually elongated face and her head crowned by billowing tresses, gripped my attention. She held a purplish translucent wand with a coppery lotus crowning its tip. Her presence was tantalizing. Her features were familiar, yet beyond the grasp of recognition. I felt that she was my goddess, the goddess of my heart. The Amorphous Being, who stood behind them, shimmered blue-black.

With fluid movements, the radiant female came to us and pulled Sveeta and me into her bosom.

"My beloved! My soul," she whispered over and over again. My being melted in her clasp, and wave after wave of rapture buffeted me. Indescribable feelings welled in my heart.

"How long till you merge with me? How long?" Muttering thus, she pressed me into her being. I was immersed in ineffable bliss. I felt purified, uplifted, and protected. That instant, I knew that my life was divine. In spite of karmic entanglements, I felt that with her grace, I would become free and soar into cosmic Light.

"Take charge of my life, my Goddess Supreme. I feel feeble without you!" I cried as I clung to her. I prayed fervently—

"My Goddess!
Possess me every moment of my life,
Open my heart to your love at all times.
Dissolve my little self and smear it across,
The empyrean spaces of your divine heart.
Let me merge in your love, and never separated."

As I prayed, I was also aware of the intense feelings that raked my being.

At that instant, a veil dissolved from my mind—a thick warp that had smothered my memory so long was pulled apart. Impressions from a previous incarnation poured into my awareness. The divine being released me from Her embrace, and recognition dawned upon me like a cascade of light. I looked at our teacher, Amba, the supreme sorceress and mystic, who headed our group. I knelt down and kissed Her feet.

In the place of Aunt Preema was Prabha, Amba's oldest disciple. She stood beside Sveeta. I was pleasantly surprised to realize my aunt's true identity, and hastening to her, I took her hand in mine, "Prabha! Aunt Preema! . . . You are Aunt Preema!" I exclaimed.

"Neela, I am Prabha. Yes, I have incarnated as your aunt," she said. "I was mother to her as Sandhya." As I listened to her, bits and pieces of recognition fell into place.

"Neela, you helped us retrieve her from the mortal plane," Prabha said.

"Yes, indeed! Your final act of dismembering Sandhya's body enabled us to consume her mortal essence and release Sveeta into this plane," Amba seconded.

"Consume her mortal essence? You have assimilated Sandhya?" I asked, at once alarmed that all this could be an illusion put up by the underworld odiyyas.

"Neela, do not worry about me. I am free. Look, I am my true being at last. Sandhya was my name when I dwelt in my mortal frame. You will be with us, too. Come, feel my being. I am substantial to your astral senses." With that, Sveeta hugged me and made me rove my hands over her. She was exquisitely tangible.

"So this is no trick by the terrible energies?" I asked.

"No. This is not. Be assured. Come, the rest of our family is anxious to exchange energy with you," Sveeta steered me toward the Amorphous Being, who knelt low for my benefit. She cupped me in her massive hands.

"Neela, I am Nishachii. Don't you recognize me?" At once she became revealed completely in my mind.

"Nishachii! You have carried me in your arms before! You are my guardian. Yes, Nishachii. Now I know who you are. I had pondered over your identity for years . . . so many years," I sighed. Enfolding me in her hands, she carefully lifted me up and held me tenderly against her vast bosom. Lying there upon her chest, I remembered her true identity. This huge sorceress belonged to the yakshini class of beings. She had assumed the role of a protectress to our group.

"I am with you, little one. I may not be visible to you in the mortal world. But rest assured, I am there by your side in the physical realm. I will look out for you until you exit the physical world and rejoin our group," she comforted me as she set me down.

"Oh! Nishachii!" I was profoundly thankful.

"No matter where you are, my essence in the physical world will follow you," she added. She left me on the ground.

Ugra, another disciple of Amba, came close to me. He embraced me saying.

"Beloved Neela, we will keep track of you."

"It feels so good to be united with you all, Ugra!" I said.

"Yes, our energy is full, now that your being is linked to us. But, to be permanent, you must be joined to us as before!" I felt a pang of grief on hearing him. Like me, Ugra always assumed a male form among our group. At that moment, I knew the cause of my present birth. I had succumbed to sexual desire for Sveeta because I had always assumed a male form. My desire reinforced my maleness, causing this birth.

"Ugra, switch frequently to a female form. Look what happened to me and Sveeta. I am sure that my downfall is from retaining a male identity for too long. I think that switching sexual identities will prevent such a disaster," I urged.

"Listen, who is teaching whom?" I heard Phalga, and felt her arms around me. "It's blissful to be joined together. With you among us, our energy feels complete, Neela," she said, as she hugged me.

"Phalga, I am afraid that this feeling of completion will last only a little while more. I know that my tasks in the physical world are unfinished. But it is wonderful to be joined to you now, to feel your pure being inside mine."

"Neela, don't forget that this astral reality is more fundamental and enduring than the physical realm. And even if you can't see us, we are here, on this side of the veil, waiting for you. Do not despair," she spoke, caressing me.

Vibru and Iilava approached me. Vibru had a female form, while Iilava wore a male identity. They were close friends, just as Sveeta and I.

"Keep on switching identities!" They chorused playfully as if reading my unspoken concern.

My mouth fell open, expressing my surprise, when Amba said, "Neela is right. It's wise not to fall into an identity rut. Sexual identity, especially, is the strongest force that can create such ruts."

Instantly, Iilava assumed a female form. "Call me Iilavi," she said. I stared, enchanted, at her beautiful figure. But before I could recover from this surprise, Vibru transformed herself into a handsome male, announcing that her name was Vibran. Phalga, who stood beside us, became a male.

"Call me Phalgu when I am in this form," he said, strutting before me. I was amused by their playfulness. Here were sorcerer-children at play, assuming whimsical sexual identities. I became wistful and yearned to be with them forever. This was my family, my true world. I held my hands to my chest, and closing my eyes, I prayed, "Beloved Kali, keep me close to you, Amba. Keep me close to you, Amba . . . "

"Neela, change your identity now," said Kanaka, who was a golden being beneath her blue luminescent raiment. She pried my hands apart and began pulling me round and round.

"Come on, now. Be a girl. Neela, change your identity," she egged me on. As Kanaka swung me round, I glanced at Amba and Prabha. They caught my eye, and nodded smiling. Sveeta broke in, joining Kanaka and me running around in a circle, arms interlocked. One by one, Ugra, Phalgu, Vibran, and Iilavi joined us. We swung round and round for a few moments, then I felt our pace was slowing.

"Neela, feel a female form," urged Sveeta.

I closed my eyes and said, "I am female. I am female," but nothing happened.

"Look, Neela, I am Sveetin. Look at me!" Sveeta transfigured herself into a resplendent male. I looked at her godly features and a powerful attraction for Sveetin emerged in my heart. At the same time, a vibrant sensation rippled through my being.

"Neelaa! Neelaa!" they cheered me, calling my female name by elongating the last syllable.

"You look exquisite. Look at yourself," cried Kanaka.

The group stopped moving in a circle. I looked down at myself. For an instant, I felt confused at my gorgeous form. I could hear others cheer me. It flashed in my mind that maleness and femaleness were playful identities, and a compelling voice dinned in my head, "I am a sorceress! I am a sorcerer! I am an astral being!"

"My divine love, now you feel your astral identity," said Amba. I saw my divine Amba come toward me, beaming. "You are one with us. You are one with me!" she exclaimed, hugging me.

"Amba, I feel one with you!" I said.

"Yes, eternal one, our energies are thoroughly linked," she confirmed. I held her in silence. As we stood there in each other's embrace, I felt that my power waned. I was afraid to let go of Amba.

"Neelaa, there is no separation from me," Amba spoke softly, "not for you," she whispered. "Your love binds me to you . . . binds us all to you." As she said this, the rest of my group came around us.

"Neelaa must retain her male form in this incarnation, in the physical world. For that is the optimal form for her to dissipate her remaining karmas," Amba said to the rest.

"Neelaa, you will always be aware of your sexual transcendence, even while being in a male form. We are entities beyond the bondage of sexual dualism."

"Amba, if I have no sexual identity, then how do I look?" I asked.

"Come close to me, children," Amba ordered us all together.

She cupped her beautiful palms together. Bringing them to my lips, she beckoned me to drink from them. The hollow of her palms was empty at first, but as I put my lips to them, a pearly liquid welled within. I drank the tasteless liquid.

She raised her hands, and flung her arms outward. A flash of light enveloped us, and I experienced an extraordinary feeling of awareness. As soon as I wished to look around, instantly I saw everything about me. Everybody was a luminous oval. There were no distinguishing features about us; each one of us was a being of light. I felt them all. I heard them all. We merged and separated at will. With each merging, I felt more fulfilled.

"Awareness is all there is. We were, and are, entities of awareness," I heard from all, including myself.

"This experience is extraordinary!" exclaimed the part of us that was I.

"It feels so because of karmic limitations," we answered. "This is our true nature. This is neither ordinary nor extraordinary. This is how we are," I heard us say. "That fraction of us called Neelaa has karmic residues that make this astral reality appear unusual. We have infused a great deal of astral energy into Neelaa. Due to ages of melding with one another, we are one awareness. There is no separation . . . there is no distance," I heard us explain.

There was a brief reverberation, and I found myself standing in the field of light, held by Amba. I was back to Neela, my male identity. Prabha was beside me, with the rest of my group surrounding us.

"Look down, there," Prabha pointed to the ground by the banyan tree. .

I saw my mortal frame, Shambu, lying by the burned out embers of the fire.

"Children, we must return Neela to his physical body," Amba announced. I felt strength ebbing from me. Turning to me, Amba said, "Prabha will be with you for a little while. But Nishachii will remain with you until you ascend. Are you ready to return?" Amba asked.

I looked at them all, one at a time. Their eyes were indescribable pools of love. Streamers of love wafted out of them toward my being. In spite of my growing feebleness, I felt focused on my purpose. Nothing would make Amba happier than my joyous acceptance of my karmic duties. I felt her gladness, and her pride in me.

"Yes, Divine Mother, I am ready to go," I said. I knelt before her.

"I will fulfill your divine bidding. May this being be surrendered to you, Amba," I prayed as I laid my lips on her radiant feet. Amba pulled me up, and gazed into my eyes. Then, lifting her right foot up, she stepped into my being. She was gone—she vanished inside me! But when I closed my eyes, I saw her smiling face assuring me of her presence in my heart.

Ugra came to me. He gazed into my eyes and stepped into my being. Kanaka, the golden sorceress, followed Ugra. Then came Phalga, Vibru, and Iilava. One by one, they gazed into my eyes and entered my being.

Sveeta walked up to me and placed her hands around the nape of my neck. My being was thrilled to her touch.

"We are inseparable, Sveeta," I said.

"We are one. I am you, and you are me, my beloved," she replied. Sveeta passed her hands over my shoulders, down my arms, and pulled my hands out as if spread-eagling me. With her fingers entwined in mine, she pressed her body against me. Then, as her thighs and feet straddled mine, her belly and pelvis thrust into me, pushing me down. My awareness bobbed in and out of twin realities. I felt her place her lips upon mine; in a few moments, her being slipped into mine. I began to fall backward.

I dove through a sea of misty light, conscious, but disoriented, and unable to get a hold on anything substantial. I struggled up to what appeared to be a rosy hue. I felt something under my head, and soft warmth cradled my cheeks. Opening my eyes, I saw Aunt Preema gazing at me. I lay with my head on her lap. A rosy hue filtered through her curly locks. The light came through the gaps among the branches and leaves above us, grazing the damp humus with a faint light.

"Prabha!" I reached for her face.

"Yes, Neela, you know I am Prabha," she said. I was astonished by her words.

"Then my dream was real!" I exclaimed. "I dreamed of all of us . . . our group, you know . . ." I stammered.

"That was not a dream, darling. You experienced the other world," she said.

I stood up and walked toward the edge of the ravine. The ground was damp from the rain, and floodwaters thundered downhill through the ravine. The hill sloped westward into the valley of our village. Bands of golden-pink light pierced the fog-filled valley. I walked back to my aunt.

"Aunt Preema . . ."

"Prabha. Remember, I am Prabha," she said, laughing, and tousled my head. "Call me Prabha when we are alone, and I will call you Neela."

I was overcome by my recent experiences, and of having to deal with our twin identities. "Oh Kali! It's true! I'm part of this divine group," I muttered. I felt fortunate and was humbled by Her grace. I am part of the divine group!

Prabha came close, and touched my chest. "You have peace, now. You know that your beloved is safe, and more alive than she had been on this earth," she said.

"Yes, I know that Sandhya is Sveeta," I replied, and glanced down the valley. After this wondrous experience of the astral realm,

the thought of going back into my village and facing my kin was unbearable. I wanted to run away deeper into the forest.

"You are not alone, you know. I am here with you," Prabha said.

I knew that I was not alone, yet I longed for the group. I closed
my eyes to resurrect Amba's beautiful face. Her assuring countenance
was clear. I was grateful I had retained her form intact in my mind, in
spite of my passage into this realm. Mentally, I threw a hibiscus
bloom at her feet. One by one, I resurrected the images of the rest of
the group. When I came to Sveeta, I felt her pucker my lips with hers.

I thought of Nishachii. However hard I tried to remember her
face, she did not appear in my mind. Disheartened, I opened my
eyes. Prabha stood by me, mutely observing my introspections.
Something moved in the forest, in the periphery of my vision. I
glanced at it quickly and thought I saw a giant form merge into the
gloom of the trees beyond. Before I could alert Prabha, we were
both startled by an explosive crack. A moment later, a large branch
broke off a tree and crashed upon the forest floor.

"Nishachii! My friend!" I exclaimed, delighted.

"Your doubts are settled. Nishachii is here with us. Do not doubt
your experience any more, Neela. Your old questions are answered,"
Prabha said.

"My old questions?" I asked.

"Yes dear. Ever since Ahalya Mata attempted to exorcise Nishachii, ten years ago, you had wondered who Nishachii was, and what
she meant when she said that Her imprint is upon you."

"Yes, indeed, I now know that it is Amba whose footprint that is in
my heart," I said. Then a revelation hit me: "Amba must be none
other than the goddess I often see in my dreams, and in the temple
ruins. I see myself worshipping her in my dreams, along with others!"

"Yes, that is true. We as a group have linked our love to one another. We are joined, no matter how many realities or space-times
separate us from one another," Prabha said.

"Why do they appear only in my dreams or at the ruins, Prabha?"

"In order for you to perceive them, your astral mind has to be
manifested and your logical mind receptive to it—and the place conducive—for them to manifest to your astral senses.

"Our physical senses have an enormous influence upon our
awareness. The sensory input we experience every moment is formidable; these experiences yoke our awareness to the senses and the
logical mind. But there are a few places, and certain states of consciousness, where the physical senses are made dormant, and our

awareness is free to power the astral mind. The ruined temple is one such place. There is enough power there to subdue the physical senses and scramble the logical mind. Our group comes through to you when your logical mind is dismantled, and your physical senses are laid to rest," she said.

I wondered what happened to Sandhya's body. I looked into the forest, in the direction of the mat bundle.

"What happened to her body, Prabha?"

"Our group took the parts," she said.

"There is nothing remaining? Not even a bone?"

"They transformed every part into energy and released Sveeta from it."

"Go, look inside the bundle," she said, after a pause.

The mat bundle lay underneath the branches. The silken shroud was in a heap a few yards away. I pulled the curled edges open. It was empty—not a drop of blood or a strand of hair remained. A chill went through my spine.

"Prabha, could some jackal or wild dog have carried the parts away?" I asked, still incredulous.

"No, no, no! No dogs or jackals carried anything away," she said emphatically, shaking her head. "There is no reason to burden yourself with absurd logical explanations. The odiyya's willpower can transform anything to anything else. It is as straightforward as that," she smiled, and gave my back a loud slap. My aunt seemed to be in an unusually expansive mood.

"Sandhya is no longer with us, and I feel lonely. Why are you so joyous?" I asked.

My aunt shook her head saying, "Neela, this world is getting hold of you too soon. I am happy because I fulfilled one of my main purposes in this life. I came to earth, and bore Sveeta as my daughter. I raised her as a sorceress. Now, I have freed her," she paused. "I am somewhat relieved," she muttered. I snuggled up to her and hugged her. We sat still for a while.

The sun rose higher and my body shuddered less with cold. Much of the sky was overcast, but sunlight came through cracks in the cloud layers. Like brilliant fingers of light, they sliced broad swaths into the valley below. The contrast between light, the gray overcast sky, and the green fields below was heavenly.

"Bring the mat here, Neela," Prabha ordered.

"Are we taking this back with us?" I asked.

"Yes. We will burn them to ashes and carry them home."

"Why?"

"There will be one question in the minds of all, including Ragha-van's. What did we do with her body?" she said.

"Oh! I see. So these ashes will answer their questions. What if they want to inspect the ashes? Won't they realize these are not human ashes?"

"I don't expect them to question me. But if any of the women do, I will tell them the truth. We are not taking these home to deceive anybody, Neela. People take comfort in traditional death rituals. They will not understand the rituals of the sorcerers. With these ashes, our folks can perform the conventional rituals for Sandhya and rest their hearts in peace."

We gathered dry humus and rolled it in the mat, then set it on fire. Within several minutes, the mat was aflame. I worked the flame over the bamboo poles, until these, too, were rendered to cinders. Prabha made me scrape the ashes and coals off the soil with the chopper. We gathered all the ashes into leaves and tied it all into a compact bundle.

"Neela, let's go home," Prabha said, throwing an arm across my shoulders.

"It's not something I look forward to, at this moment. But I am tired and very hungry," I replied.

"Well, you will soon have a belly-full of delicious food. After that, you may rest," she said as we descended the hill and worked our way to the village. It took us longer to go down the slippery slopes than it took to climb them. Prabha took the lead, and we held a long branch between us. This helped us brace each other as we slid from one tuft of grass to the next. After much slipping and sliding, we made it to the hillocks sloping into the rice fields.

"From this moment on, call me Aunt Preema, and I will call you Shambu," instructed Prabha.

"All right, Aunt Preema," I said, as we entered our village.

I followed Aunt Preema into our home. Walking behind her, I was apprehensive of the reception that we might face. The place felt dark and mournful. At the entrance into the courtyard, we met Aunt Susheela. With a look of surprise, she yelled to the rest of the household, "Preema and Shambu are back! Preema and Shambu are back!"

My brother Padman came out of his room. At the sight of my aunt, he ran up to her and touched her feet. Seeing our soiled clothes, he offered to bring fresh ones for us.

"Get Shambu a change of clothes, Padman," she asked my brother. Turning to me, she said, "Shambu, take those fresh clothes from Padman and get yourself cleaned up at the pond."

My brother came back with a change of clothes. I was eager to put off the initial encounter that we would have with the rest of the elders for as long as possible.

The pond waters were cold, but soothing. My body ached and cried for rest. As I swam in the blue-green water, events and scenes from the past forty-eight hours flashed through my mind—Sandhya's final hours, the night of death vigil, and meeting with Amba and the rest of the group. Incredibly, I caught myself dozing as I floated on my back. I paddled to the corner of the pond where the bamboo grew on the banks. Changing into fresh clothes, I drew myself up the damp, sandy slopes into the dark bamboo bowers.

My steps up the slope were laborious. The undulations in the sand, held in place by the dampness, broke apart into caked fragments under my weight, revealing dry soil a few inches beneath. I stretched out upon the leafy litter, beneath the bamboo grove. With my head under its canopy, I shaded my eyes from the glare of the overcast sky. Within moments, my awareness disengaged itself from my body.

"Deepam! Om deepam!" I woke up to a female voice.

"What hour is it?"

"It is dusk, Shambu," said Aunt Sujata. She waved the kamakshi deepam over me. I was lying on my rope bed in my room.

"Ramachandran and Bhaskaran brought you in from the edge of the pond," she said, answering my perplexed expression. "Get up for prayers, Shambu. You have slept the entire day and have eaten nothing! After prayers, have your meals, and then you can rest again," she urged.

I jumped out of bed and dashed to the well to douse my face, hands, and feet with water. Then I entered the family shrine. The entire household was assembled for the evening worship, and as I made my way to the front, my cousins and elders patted me, whispering words of welcome. I drew great comfort from this. My peace of mind was strengthened when I saw my mother and Aunt Preema performing the ritual worship. Looking at my aunt waving the lights, I felt she was superhuman, even in her human form.

For days we were visited by people from the neighboring homes. Aunt Preema and Uncle Raghavan were especially besieged with condolences. Some of the women came to my mother, asking her whether I was coping well. She mumbled some reply, to which they would offer trite philosophical consolations. Copious quotation from the Bhagavad Gita, and the Anushasana Parva of the Mahabharata, were frequently drawn upon to bolster their words of solace.

During this period, I noticed an amazing transformation in the relationship between my parents and their conduct toward Aunt Preema and Uncle Raghavan. I found them taking walks together along the rice field ridges. My mother empathized with Aunt Preema's loss of her only daughter, and knowing my aunt's deep affection for me, she let my aunt decide things for me. The kinship between my aunt and my mother grew. I found them together more often at the temple rituals.

As the family tragedy strengthened old friendships, it also deepened a polarization in the household. Matriarch Gauri used tradition to bolster her fledgling power as the head of our household. Aunt Preema, an outlandish nonconformist, did things in unpredictable ways, apparently in order to challenge Aunt Gauri. There were those who supported or opposed Aunt Gauri to varying degrees. More of those who opposed her dared not speak out. I felt that it would take a while for the elders to get used to being ordered around by someone who had been their peer for so many years. It became clear that this split in our household came to light with Aunt Gauri's emergence into power. When Grandma Paru reigned as matriarch, I remembered that Aunt Preema was as independent as she was now. Unlike Aunt Gauri, Grandma Paru trusted everyone. She delegated tasks to be performed, but did not insist on knowing every step or sequence in the process of a task. While keeping track of the general direction of life at our homestead, Grandma Paru let everyone feel pride in taking responsibility and using their talents to their best. She let them enjoy the euphoria of success that resulted when their creative energies were put to work.

It was ironic that our family was caught in a double upheaval—for adjustments were required of us by the change in the power structure, and in the loss of Sandhya.

Days after we returned from the hills, my elders consulted the vallichappads about the proper funerary rites for Sandhya. The bundle of ashes hung from the rafters of our shrine. No one had asked for it to be opened, nor did anyone question how Aunt Preema and I managed to cremate Sandhya on a rainy day all by ourselves. Aunt Preema's subtle influences worked like magic once again.

On the tenth day, under the guidance of Vallichappad Agnimitra, Aunt Preema, Uncle Raghavan, and I performed the funerary rites. Aunt Gauri initially opposed my participation, saying that I was not the immediate kin of the deceased. But Aunt Preema argued that as our preceptor, I had become a son to her over these years. Vallichappad Agnimitra seconded her, saying that a teacher becomes a spiritual parent to his or her initiated students. In our case, Aunt Preema not only initiated us but also gave constant guidance to Sandhya and me.

The materials for the bali kriya ceremony was arranged in our back yard facing the south. Vallichappad Agnimitra led us through the invocations that invited the ancestors, and received them as divine guests. As we offered rice balls to the ancestors, and the spirit of Sandhya was invoked to depart into the Realm of the Dead, I had an irresistible urge to laugh at the proceeding. Sandhya as Sveeta, had ascended to the astral realm, a realm higher than the Realm of the Dead. I could not mouth those invocations without a smile. Aunt Preema poked me in my ribs and ordered me to concentrate on the ritual.

On the sixteenth day after Sandhya's death, the elders performed the adyantaram ceremony. This included a feast in honor of Sandhya, for which the neighborhood households were invited. As the days and weeks went by, we put behind us the calamity that unsettled our family, and our household swung back to its peaceful state. Even though I knew that Sveeta had ascended into the astral realm from Sandhya's body, I missed her. Every nook and corner of the house reminded me of the happiness that we had shared together. I busied myself with chores in an attempt to lift myself out of my occasional indulgence in sadness.

# CHAPTER FIFTEEN

# *Exegesis*

The rains were infrequent during the closing months of the year. Sometimes I took refuge in the temple ruins and meditated for long hours. It was during these periods at the ruins that I began to question the mechanism of the transition of the astral being from the physical body at the time of death. How had the person I knew as Sandhya become Sveeta? Why did Aunt Preema, or Prabha as I knew her now, ask me to dismember the lifeless body of Sandhya? What did Aunt Preema mean when she said that this was the only way Sveeta could be freed from the physical plane? What specifically were the "terrible energies" Aunt Preema was referring to before I hacked apart Sandhya's body?

One Friday morning, Aunt Preema and I walked home together from the main Kali temple. Fridays, full moons, and Amavasyas, were occasions of special worship at the temple, as these times were considered particularly auspicious for the worship of divinity as the Divine Mother. I broached my questions to Aunt Preema on our way home. She agreed to spend time with me to clarify my doubts and answer my questions. First, she insisted that we have lunch. After lunch we both made our way to the family pond.

At the edge of the pond, we sat upon a couple of coconut fronds woven into mats. The rains of the monsoon months had filled every well and pond to the brim, so the water was only a few feet from where we sat. Even though it was a sunny afternoon, there was a cool and refreshing breeze that rustled the palm leaves and agitated the water mildly. We had begun to experience the tropical winter, making the early mornings cold and the day warm, but comfortable.

The afternoon was tranquil. Neither of us spoke for a while. My aunt sat rocking herself, her arms around her knees. My gaze fell upon the gentle ripples on the water. It occurred that this was the first time my aunt and I had met, since Sandhya's passing on. I fell into a state of melancholy. I missed Sandhya. However much I tried,

I could not escape the gathering avalanche of grief. I pulled my knees up and brought my chin to rest upon them. I felt my aunt's hands upon my cheeks. She drew my face to hers, and for the first time in my life, she kissed me on my lips.

"I miss her, too," she said. "Yet, I know that she is closer to me than ever before. Neela, they are all inside your being. No physical barrier can separate you from Sveeta or Amba," she added. My turbulent sadness subsided in her embrace as we sat still for some moments.

"Amba has been with us for ages," my aunt revealed.

"We have been alive for ages?" I was surprised to hear that.

"Oh, yes! The astral realm is a non-material realm. Entities there are not wrapped in bodies that decay with time as we experience here," she said.

I looked up at the canopy of coconut leaves. The leaves above parted as the palm heads swayed in the breeze, exposing us to sunlight now and then.

"Astral beings live in that realm for a long, long time. Odiyyas and mystics from this world often come up to the astral realm. They eventually give up their contacts with this physical world," Aunt Preema continued.

I looked her over. As she explained this, I felt fortunate to experience both worlds. The realization that I was with this woman who was my aunt, but at the same time my friend and co-disciple, Prabha, was stunning. I was no stranger to the philosophy of reincarnation and the theories of karma, but experiencing these memories felt incredible. I felt the urge to address my aunt as Prabha.

"Prabha, this is mysterious and wonderful!" I said, taking her hands in mine. "Relationships such as mother/father, brother/sister, aunt/nephew, or husband/wife are utterly meaningless now that I remember my astral identity," I said, sighing. I felt a tremendous loneliness as I said this.

"You see now, Neela, what I meant by social conditioning, how these reinforce the veil that covers our truer identity. You realize that to be a sorcerer, you have to decondition yourself. You have to assimilate the veil and set free your identity. Indeed, you realize this now, my beloved friend, Neela. The impact of direct experience is more powerful than a million discourses."

"Prabha, I understand the enormous burden of knowledge that you have been carrying in your heart. You knew who Sandhya was and who I am. But you were alone, with nobody to share this knowledge with. So lonely! Sandhya and I couldn't even understand you," I said, and paused to stifle a pang of sorrow. "I took you for my aunt! And you have to play the role of a wife, mother, aunt, and be subordinate to Aunt Gauri and others!"

"Prabha, you had to incarnate into our family before Sveeta and I were born! When you were a little girl, did you know why you incarnated?"

"No, I did not. Your grandmother Sathya drew me out and began teaching me things, just as I did to you."

She sat silent for a while, staring as the wind whipped water in the pond. She seemed far away. Then, twitching sand with her right index finger, she continued, "My memory awakened when your grandmother Sathya initiated me in the forest, just as I did Sandhya and you. From then on I knew who I am, and what was to come," she said.

"But you were all alone with your memories! Prabha, your greatness is beyond my comprehension," I cried.

Prabha threw her arm around my shoulders and drew me close. "Neela, our beloved teacher Amba was always with me. During my childhood, She came to me almost every night in my dreams. She would carry me away into the astral realm, to be with our group and nurture me. She would return me in the morning." I was thrilled on hearing this and felt my hair bristle. My body trembled out of control.

"Prabha, were Sveeta and I still with the group then?" I asked, trying to grapple with this magical mystery.

"Just before I incarnated, you were both whisked into the intermediate regions of murky awareness, where all souls who are about to reincarnate wait in spiritual stasis," she replied.

"What region is that? Why is awareness murky here?"

"The Realm of the Dead, I have described this plane to you before. It is a region where souls stay who reincarnate cyclically as humans, a realm where awareness is right for the karmas that will be activated in an upcoming incarnation to gather and form the incipient personality. Souls here are in spiritual stasis; therefore their awareness is not lucid. For some souls, it is a stage of quasi suspension of awareness. But for more advanced souls, it provides opportunities to learn, to do penance, to pray and so on. No one can ascend into the astral realm from the Realm of the Dead without eliminating all human karmas."

"What do you mean by that?"

"Souls have to descend into the physical realm, and die enlightened to some extent, in order to ascend into the astral plane. In the

Realm of the Dead, beings continue their identities and relationships from previous lives in this physical plane," she explained.

I felt a shudder course through me. With my eyes closed, I prayed to Kali to keep me safe.

"But, before you both were pulled in, I promised you that I would be in this world to receive you. Amba agreed. For that is the quickest way we can retrieve you both and prevent cyclical reincarnation."

I took her hands and placed them upon my head. "You are divine! Only divinity has such compassion and strength! My dearest Prabha, you are a goddess! I am grateful to you forever!" I touched the dust of her feet and applied it to my forehead. I felt that I would do anything for her. I now had a glimpse of what divine love was. "Love without expectation, Love for love's sake," Prabha's words to me before I dismembered Sandhya's body, now rang in my ears.

"Prabha, is part of that realm hell itself?"

"No! No, my dear. Hell is a region in the plane of subhuman awareness called Naraka. But regions of the Realm of the Dead adjoin hellish regions."

"Is subhuman awareness equal to animal awareness?"

"No. Animal awareness is different. Entities in the realm of subhuman awareness are disembodied human beings. They live to experience fear, rage, and self-gratification. Upon reincarnating in a human body, they experience these karmas. These are beings whose awareness is given over to the demons. Their awareness is trapped in dense karmic vortices. The weight of their karmas is appalling; their lives are run by demonic karmas."

"You mean the demon possessed?"

"Yes. Beings with a great gulf between their personality and their conscience," she said.

A tender coconut bud fell off a palm and hit the water with a loud splash. It bobbed up and down in the center of the ripples that it generated in the pond.

"The scriptures have identified thirty-four hells in Naraka to fit all types of subhuman mentalities. But the Realm of the Dead is a higher world," she said. I sighed with relief.

"Prabha, your parents, Grandmother Chandra, and Grandfather Madhavan must have been kind to you when you were a child. Did they have any idea of your true identity?"

"They knew a great deal indirectly, through my birth chart. Kurukkal Angavattacchan had made detailed hoary writings on my chart. My chart was described to be insubstantial—nihsattva yoga. As per the chart, I should either die as a child or grow up to be a mystic," she explained.

"There were no karmas to support a material life—how thrilling!" I exclaimed.

"Your Grandma Sathya knew many mystical practices. As soon as she knew of my birth-chart predictions, she took a strong interest in me," Prabha said. She moved her arm from my shoulder and ran her fingers through my hair. "Just as I do for you and as I did for Sandhya," she added affectionately.

"Was it difficult to lead your life the way you needed to?" I asked.

"Our society is wonderful. All are Kali worshippers. Before I was born, there was already a strong trend toward female preceptorship in our community. That allowed Aunt Sathya to be my preceptor and guide me, and Sandhya and you, through me. Besides, our beloved Guru Amba, with the rest of our group, influenced situations in subtle ways."

"How, Prabha? For example?"

"Take my marriage, for example. I am married to a man who is sweet and humble. He is always cheerful, sexually content, and tame," she said, laughing. She fell silent for a while.

"But in spite of his buffoonery, he is quite evolved. There is a mystic lurking in him. Poor man! His relationship with me makes it difficult for him to accept my guidance. I must set him on his path," her voice trailed away, as if she mused.

"Prabha, how long were Sveeta and I lost?"

"From a human standpoint, for long, darling. You both disappeared for 350 human years," she said. I felt my legs tremble.

"When I was growing up, a few years before I was married, I would often wake up with a start in the middle of the night. I could hear you both call to me, 'Prabha! Prabha!' But when I was awake and sitting up, the voices would be gone. Only an intense feeling of both your presences remained. I would not sleep the rest of the night. Lighting a lamp, I would pray and meditate, to try and reach you both wherever you were," she said. I was stunned by these revelations; I felt sapped.

"I have no memory of any of this. None at all," I said.

"I would be distraught for several days, knowing that you both needed me and I could not be there for you. I prayed and chanted, and practiced disciplines that Aunt Sathya taught me. That would assuage my distress," she said.

"How did you know of my identity in this body? Did my parents know any of this at all?" I asked.

Prabha became solemn. "I continued to hear both your voices through the first few months after my marriage. But, just after I was pregnant with Sandhya, these voices stopped." My aunt fell silent. Clouds gathered and disappeared in the sky. The sun moved imperceptibly to the west.

"Neela, there is something that you must know," Prabha said, but she sighed and sat quiet.

"What is it?"

"It will be difficult for you to hear this, Neela." I felt a strange chill. My anxiety mounted as Prabha continued to hesitate.

"Almost a year after I gave birth to Sandhya, I became pregnant again. After a few weeks of being pregnant, I found out that I was carrying you."

"What!"

"It's true, Neela. Amba revealed this to me in a dream."

"Oh, Kali! I am your son!"

"In a manner of speaking," Prabha said. She swiftly pulled me into her arms and holding me tight, said, "This is the hardest part, Neela. I aborted you soon after." I felt listless.

"Why? Of course, I know why?" I murmured while she held me.

"As soon as Sveeta entered this realm you became anxious. Your karmas would not have been fulfilled if you were born as her brother. I had to act quickly."

"I understand, Prabha. It was my folly. My folly, Prabha. I am appalled at what I put you through. I am ashamed even more for having suspected you. I was your second child, your lost child! Aunt Gauri is wrong to call you an infant killer. Please forgive me, I have brooded over this, you know."

"I know, Neela. When you run through the thorn field to get to the ruined temple, won't your eyes look out for your feet, to watch out for spikes? Won't your hands guard your eyes from twigs coming at them? Amba, Sveeta, the rest of our group, you and me are one consciousness, bound together for a period the length of which is difficult to calculate. We are one illumined cluster of souls, inseparable by any force. Like the limbs of one body, we protect each other. Don't worry."

"Prabha, I know that you faced terrible criticism from Aunt Gauri and the others. I don't know how you endured all this."

"It was difficult, Neela. But, you know, Amba always showered me with Her love. That sustained me. Knowing that I am Prabha, and not this body they call Preema, helped me through rough spots. After I aborted you, I worried endlessly as to your whereabouts. I prayed to keep you close to our family. Then one night, several days later, I had a fascinating dream. In my dream, I saw Amba throw a ripe mango at Leela, who caught it and began eating. Amba then turned to me and said, 'Take care of the seed.' The dream ended there.

"The following day, I told your mother about my dream. But Leela had no clue what it meant, and I did not elaborate. Days later she became pregnant with you."

"Prabha, why did you make me cut up Sandhya's body? You know, that was one action I have been unable to make peace with."

"I have to give you some details before I can answer you.

"A human being has a personality powered by two forces: jiva shakti, or biophysical energy, and prana shakti, or astral energy. Jiva shakti comes from food consumed and transformed in the body, while prana shakti is drawn from the astral continuum through the astral body.

"When a person dies, the astral being leaves the dead body. In a normal human, upon leaving the dead body, the astral being is cloaked by a body composed of two abstractions—a residue of the personality that was formed while living in the physical body, and the karma stharam or karmic strata."

"What is a karmic strata?"

"Karmas sedimented from past transmigrations lie in wait to be kindled. This is karma stharam.

"Self-identity with the old personality is strong in ordinary people. After death it takes a long while to wear this down. But, only after it wears down can the astral being reincarnate into another identity and generate a fresh personality."

"How long does it take to wear out this residue?"

"On the average? Five hundred human years."

"Oh Kali! Where does the astral being spend all this time?" I asked.

"In the Realm of the Dead. But this is for normal humans, though. A personality is an aggregate of active karmas. So it stands to reason when a person dies, the moment of death is the completion of a batch of karmas. You see, a batch of karmas from the karmic strata shakes loose, activating a new personality, and propels the astral being into reincarnation. Thus each incarnation is a manifestation of karmas that collectively project a personality in life. Are you with me?"

"Yes, yes. It's fascinating, Prabha!"

"Upon the fulfillment of a batch of karmas, the body falls. I have told you before that pure awareness collects around every active karma. This awareness is astral energy, prana shakti. Active karmas also draw biophysical energy around them—jiva shakti. Thus a batch of active karmas, by drawing these two energies around them, develop a body-mind tailored to their fulfillment."

"The act of fulfilling these active karmas is life!" I said.

"Correct. Over a lifetime, these karmas generate many impulses and drives, and the ever-active free will creates new desires, which spawns new karmas that will be sedimented in the karmic strata. Over a period of time, many impulses will be absorbed into drives, and some of these drives will be assimilated into an incipient intent of sorts.

"While a batch of active karmas burn out over a lifetime, and the body perishes, the personality that had been collectively projected by these karmas drives the astral being through the Realm of the Dead. This is the residue that carries over into the afterlife, cocooning the astral being. This cocoon keeps the astral being in the Realm of the Dead. After a few hundred human years, this residue is worn out and a new batch of karmas emerges from the karmic strata—impelling the astral being to reincarnate again. In this way the astral being transmigrates back and forth between the Realm of the Dead and the physical realm. The karmas that are activated with each incarnation help form a body and personality, and drive the being through life."

"It seems to me that the personality lives a while longer than the physical body. But how long does the astral being live, Prabha?"

"The body lives a hundred to a hundred and twenty years in this physical plane, and the personality lives five hundred to a thousand years in the Realm of the Dead. But the astral being lives until the end of a kalpa."

"A kalpa?"

"A long time, dear, from a human standpoint, a period so long that it will sound incredible."

"Give me an idea. Is it ten thousand years?"

"Four thousand, three hundred and twenty million human years. This is one day of Brahma, the overseer of this universe of unlimited space-times."

"That long!"

"Yes, it is very long from a human standpoint," she said laughing as she rubbed the wrinkle of disbelief that appeared on my brow. "Indeed, it appears to be very long from the human perspective. But human eons pass in the blink of an astral eye. Life in the astral realm is blissful," she added.

"At the close of each day of Brahma this universe of space-time is retracted into Brahma's mind, and all beings lose their physical forms. Indeed, matter itself is withdrawn into Brahma. This action is called *pralaya*. Then, the night of Brahma begins; it lasts as long as the day of Brahma. During this period, astral beings, who have evolved to the highest refinement, discard their astral sheaths and pass beyond the realm of Brahma, into the abode of the Divine Mother. Less evolved beings are suppressed and confined to seed-forms.

"At the beginning of a new day of Brahma, a new and reconstituted universe of space-time explodes into being, with the seed-forms regenerated as new astral beings who continue their ascent. They evolve to take the place of those who have gone beyond."

"How long does Brahma live?

"Well, one hundred of Brahma's years," she replied. That did not clarify the time in human terms. Watching me strain to compute, Prabha picked up a rib from a coconut leaf and began scratching numbers on the sand. After several minutes, and having worked over a large patch of sand before us, she declared,

"You want to know what one hundred years of Brahma is? It is . . ." She took a moment to glance at the figures on the ground, "three thousand one hundred and ten trillion, forty billion human years—the life span of one Brahma,"

"Oh, Divine Mother! It's an inconceivable amount of time!" I exclaimed.

"Yes, that's one mother of a lifetime." Prabha said laughing.

"The dying throes of Brahma signal the beginning of universal dissolution, or Maha-Pralaya. Even time ceases to exist. Unlike at the end of a night of Brahma, when the reconstituted universe emerges, there is nothing to emerge. All realms of awareness are obliterated. With the death of Brahma, a period of inscrutableness exists. I use the word 'period' for want of a better term. Nobody knows what it is as there is no space-time. This is the Transcosmic Void, the Para Brahmanda Shooniyam."

"I understand that matter, energy, and all space-times cease to exist. But what happens to all the beings in all the realms?"

"All beings cease to be. They lose their sheaths—the annamaya, manomaya, pranamaya, vijnanamaya and anandamaya koshas—all are obliterated. What remain are the souls, naked and sheathless. These merge into the Void, to be the paramatman, the Supreme Self."

"One hundred years of Brahma constitute one menstrual cycle of the Divine Mother. During each menstruation several eggs float out into this great void. Each such egg is a Brahmanda or cosmic egg, the precursor to the mighty being of a Brahma. This discussion is taking us on a tangent. Let me explain to you why it was important to cut Sandhya's body.

"The personality, projected by a batch of active karmas, is given a name at birth. For example, Sandhya was the name given to the personality projected by the karmas that cloaked the astral being Sveeta.

"After death, the astral being lingers over places and near people of its past association. It stays close to its body for ten days. This is partly caused by loved ones clinging to the body and the personality of the astral being, thus binding it here with their astral energy. After the tenth day, the astral being, cloaked in the residue of its human personality and the rest of the karmic strata, floats away into the Realm of the Dead."

"Why ten days?"

"The bone collecting and the shrardham rituals done on the tenth day sever all remaining ties the astral being has to this place and time. The ancestors invoked by the kin accompany the astral being on its way into the Realm of the Dead.

"The being lives in the Realm of the Dead until the residue wears out and a new batch of karmas vibrate to activity. Look upon the residue as a shroud that sits as a barrier between the karmic strata and prana or astral energy, diffusing into the Realm of the Dead from the higher astral realm.

"This was one of the problems we were worried about after Sandhya's death. Sandhya's personality remained, and we did not want Sveeta to be cocooned by this shroud. That would have forced Sveeta to migrate into the Realm of the Dead and be lost for several hundred years. To compound the problem, both Raghavan and you clung to Sandhya's personality with such tenacious attachment and love that this only strengthened the residue, or the shroud. Your attachment for Sandhya gave her personality coherence.

"We carried her body into those hills so that we could distance her from these surroundings. She had a strong bond with everything here from her birth," said Prabha with a sweeping gesture at our homestead.

"By making you cut Sandhya's body to pieces, I managed to demolish your hold on her personality. The place we were guided to was a power place. Did you know that?"

I shook my head in negative.

"Well, that helped the astral being Sveeta to assert herself. Amba and the rest of our group finished off Sandhya's remains, thus annihilating her body and the residue of her personality, which would otherwise have taken hundreds of human years to whittle away. Timing was crucial, which was why I could not explain all this to you then."

"What was your second worry, Prabha?"

"The bhaikari odiyyas."

"The terrible energies you mentioned?"

"Yes. They would love to get hold of Sveeta's energy and assimilate her."

"Prabha, what could they have done to us?"

"Do you know how much energy Sveeta has?"

"No."

"Sveeta's energies can power the consciousness of a thousand young suns of this space-time."

"I understand now," I murmured. I closed my eyes and to my great joy, the faces of Amba and Sveeta resurrected within my being.

"Traditional funerary rites are perfect for normal people," Prabha's voice intruded into my visions. "They take into account the personality residue of the dead, and even reinforce it around the astral being. Invocations manifest the ancestors around the newly deceased and help propel the being into the Realm of the Dead.

"This funerary rite is not for Sveeta, nor is it for you, my dear. I did what I did to prevent our well-intentioned family from committing Sandhya's body through a traditional funerary ceremony."

"This gives me much peace of mind, Prabha," I said.

Prabha then explained that the personality residue, along with the karmic strata, makes up a body around the astral being that is suitable for habitation in the Realm of the Dead. She called this the yatna deha or effort body.

The Realm of the Dead adjoins regions of great happiness, called Swarga, which lie close to the astral realm. There are also regions of the Realm of the Dead that adjoin regions of dense darkness, worlds of perpetual gloom—thirty-four regions collectively called Naraka. These regions are forlorn cinders of darkness wherein dwell beings whose personalities are as dense as the night that shrouds their worlds. Entities endowed with horrific cruelty, possessed by greed, deranged by unreasonable lustfulness, and pursued by a ceaseless fear of annihilation roam these worlds.

"An astral being in the Realm of the Dead is driven into Swarga or Naraka by the nature of its personality as well as by a fresh batch of emerging karmas. Its journey through this shadowy realm of variegated experiences helps wear out the residue of its human personality, and activates a fresh batch of karmas from the karmic strata.

"Desires create and destroy karmas. The process of living shapes a personality. The awareness with which a person lives determines if karmas strengthen or undermine the karmic strata. If the karmic strata is undermined, enormous awareness is released to help strengthen the intent for freedom," Prabha remarked.

She explained that, on the other hand, if the karmic strata is strengthened, divine intent is undermined, causing the being to loop back into the birth and death cycles that beset normal people.

"Tea is served. Come in, you two," Reevati called from the back verandah. We waved to her, and Prabha was about to erase the calculations on the sand when I held her hand, "Prabha, please! I'd like to copy these numbers," I requested.

"I will write them down for you later. If you copy these scribblings now, they may confuse you." With that, Prabha pulled me into a hug and stood up. A day later, she slipped a paper to me with elaborate calculations on the scheme of Hindu cosmology.

▼  ▼  ▼

I had spent so much time with Sandhya that her passing left me lonely even in the midst of my extended family, despite the fact that I enjoyed numerous acts of kindness and tender support from most of the elders. Prominent among the elders who were solicitous to me were my mother and father, Uncle Raghavan, and Aunt Preema, and Aunt Ananda and the matriarchs Tara and Bhanu. Of my cousins, Reevati began to get close to me. She was Matriarch Gauri's second daughter, and this appeared amusing in the context of her mother's antagonism toward me. But I could not forge friendships as profound as the one I enjoyed with Sandhya.

I engaged my time in the business of helping my family carry out the daily chores. Early mornings and late evenings, I practiced my meditation alone. It was during these periods that I experienced the need to leave all these behind and go away. There were times when I dove inward, cocooning myself. Everything here reminded me of Sandhya—even though she had become Sveeta! I needed to get in touch with my astral self. I had to get to some place where I could practice and gather enough power to ascend into the blissful astral realm. It was only in the astral realm that I could be with Sveeta.

Then something happened that helped me decide what to do. I was resting under a mango tree after I washed down the cows and cleared dung off the floor of the cowshed. I had been dozing for awhile, and was awakened by a light tap on my shoulder. I saw Aunt Preema and Uncle Raghavan crouched before me.

"Is this a good time to talk?" asked Aunt Preema, beaming me a smile. I sat up briskly.

"Yes . . ." I was about to address her as Prabha, but caught myself. ". . . Aunt Preema. I was just resting," I said.

"Hey, I am the senior disciple by age! You should be greeting me," joked Uncle Raghavan. Then I noticed he was wearing a dhoti and upper cloth dyed in light ochre.

"What's with this outfit?" I asked, unable to suppress my mirth.

"I initiated him this morning," said Aunt Preema softly.

Uncle Raghavan grinned and comically fell at her feet chanting aloud, "Om Bhairavi Ambae Bhavani!"

"Is that your secret mantra?" I asked him.

"I told you not to chant it within earshot of others!" admonished Aunt Preema with a mock frown.

"Now that I have introduced myself to you, Junior, I shall leave you both alone," Uncle Raghavan said, and took off.

"I am your junior by age. But don't you forget that I am the first disciple, Uncle Raghavan," I teased, shouting after him.

"Shambu, Raghavan and I are planning a pilgrimage to various places sacred to the Divine Mother. We will be gone for a long time. You must make up your mind about what you would like to do for the next few years."

I felt a pang of fear, hearing this.

"I have the urge to go away . . . some place. Maybe do some tapas," I replied.

"Austerities! No. You are young. You need to study first. Then the Divine Mother will guide you to your next goal," she said.

"I want to tune myself more into the astral world, and only austerities can bring me closer to my astral self. What good is worldly education when it fortifies my ego and draws me away from my spiritual goals?"

"Before we left the presence of our divine Amba, you made a promise that you would joyously accept your karmic duties in this plane of awareness. You must keep this promise. Do not nurture any preconceived loathing toward your duties."

"I do not want to fall away from the divine path. I want to get back into our group. This is my constant anxiety, Prabha," I implored.

"I have faith in you. You should have more faith in yourself. Your experiences in life will lead you higher and higher. My spirit will be with you. Nishachii is with you. You must be alert at all times; but you must drop your anxiety," she said. Then she wiggled closer to me, and laying a hand across my shoulder, said, "I took this birth to lift you both up. After all that I have gone through, do you think I will let go of you now, and watch you drop away? If you see the divine everywhere, wherever you land will be divine. But you won't fall. Be assured. Neela, I have other ways of knowing that you do not have yet."

"I don't know where to go. I don't want our family to incur any expenses on my upkeep, Prabha."

"I know somebody who can help you. Kurukkal Andhra Swami comes from an ashram where temporal learning is mixed with mystical training. That would be a good place for you to live and study."

"Where is this hermitage?"

"Beyond Karimala, roughly six hundred miles away. But first we must discuss this with Leela and Bhaskaran, and get the advice of Ananda, Tara, and Bhanu," she said. My anxiety drained away as she laid out a basic plan for my future.

Later that evening, I met with the elders and convinced them of my determination to pursue a higher education. Matriarch Tara pointedly questioned me on my goals. Taking my cues from Aunt Preema, I avoided any mention of my quest for the astral self. I informed the elders of my growing interest in acquiring knowledge in the sciences while pursuing mystical knowledge. Surprisingly, my plans met with no opposition. Unlike the meeting a few months ago, where the elders vehemently opposed youngsters' plans to leave our community, my family seemed drained of the will to hold on to me.

The meeting focused on the formalities that needed to be pursued in order to gain admittance into the ashram. Aunt Preema suggested approaching Kurukkal Andhra Swami, who would be the best source of information.

The next day Aunt Preema, my father, and I petitioned my cause to the revered kurukkal. We entered the enclosed, communal buildings of the vallichappads and were immediately escorted by a yellow-robed novice to a courtyard where lay people waited for an audience with the seers. Yellow- and red-robed members of this mystic community, young and old alike, tended herbs of various kinds in the vast, wooded grounds. I wondered if my grandmothers Paru, Sathya, and Chandra were among them. Did they know of Sandhya's passing on? Probably not. In their final stage of their life's journey, they were beyond worldly cares.

We passed several granite statues of deities before being ushered into a small well-kept courtyard, whose fine sandy ground was traced with wavy patterns from the movement of a broom. We tried to walk as lightly as possible to avoid disturbing the exquisite tracings with our footprints.

It was morning, and though the courtyard was lit partially by the early light, the rooms and recesses were dark. We stood in silence by a few steps that ascended onto a verandah leading into an open door-way. Fragrances from incense and flowers hung in the air. I was tense in spite of the serene environment. My gaze drifted onto a line of tiny black ants that raced back to back carrying bits of white fluff over the green, moss covered stones. I heard a shuffle, and when I looked up, I saw a movement in the darkness beyond the doorway. A small wiry man emerged, draped in a rose-colored dhoti. He appeared to be in his 90s. A younger vallichappad followed close, helping him over the threshold. The younger man whispered into his ear. This was the legendary kurukkal, seen very little by outsiders like us. But he emerged from this hermitage each year on the evening of the Night of Kali and took upon himself the Shakti of Kali. So much power in such a frail body! I felt overawed.

A smile spread across the kurukkal's face, "You from the House of Madatara?" he asked.

"Yes, revered one," replied Aunt Preema as she stepped closer and touched his feet. My father and I prostrated before him. I placed our offering of rose-colored silk at his feet.

"Aayushman bhavanthu!" He blessed us and gave the silk to his attendant.

"What brings you to this hermitage?" the kurukkal asked.

"Shambu here wants to join the ashram your reverence comes from," my aunt replied.

"At such a young age!" he muttered, peering at me. Then he added, "Yes, the younger the easier it is for the mind to be trained. What propels you to join this ashram?"

"I want to follow the path of yoga and live the life the ancient sages did, as well as study the material sciences," I replied.

"Hmm," muttered the kurukkal. He gazed at me in silence.

"Most people join an ashram because they are burdened by grief, or because they are penniless, or because they are too old like me," he said, breaking into laughter. My heart sank. The old man gazed at me for a few moments, then he smiled, "It's refreshing to see one so young choose the inward path. I will write a letter to the mahant, while you wait." Saying that, he stepped back into the room.

I was relieved and happy. A few minutes later the younger valli-chappad came out to us with a sealed, saffron-colored envelope. As he handed it to me, I noticed the name "Swami Vimalagiri" scrawled across its face. The man advised me to enclose the letter in a larger envelope, along with a copy of my tenth grade certificate, and to send it to the ashram. We returned home with blessings, and much happiness. With the help of Uncle Jaya, my father and I wrote an application and mailed this along with the letter from Kurukkal Andhra Swami, to Swami Vimalagiri, the mahant of Dakshayini Ashram.

Several weeks went by; we looked forward to each week's mail. Then, one overcast afternoon, Aunt Bhanu hastened to my mother with an envelope.

"This is for Shambu, Leela," she said handing the brown envelope to my mother. My mother took the letter to my father. My father gingerly slit the envelope. As he unfolded the ochre hued paper and began reading the contents, a gleam of joy broke on his face.

"You are accepted into the ashram, Shambu! You are accepted!" He shouted, gathering both my mother and me into his arms. I snatched the letter from his hands and read it, then reread it. I ran with the letter to Aunt Preema. Within a short time, this news spread throughout the household and numerous cousins and various elders congratulated me. I was happy and profoundly sad at the same time.

Late that night, after supper, Aunt Preema and I sat on the sands of the courtyard. We spread our sleeping mats close to each other. She explained that academic education at the ashram began with seventh grade and proceeded to master's degrees in various sciences and arts. The ashram had separate quarters for celibate initiates as well as for householders.

"The best part is, many itinerant mystics stop at the ashram. You know what that means?" she asked.

"I can learn from them," I replied.

"Right. And that means the ashram is not rigid in their philosophical perspectives."

"I wish Sandhya were here to witness this good news, Prabha."

"If Sandhya were here, then you would still be here with her," she said.

"That's right."

"You know that Sandhya is Sveeta. And she is here," she said, tapping my heart. I lay back and pondered over what she said.

"Jai Jagad Ambae! Sleep well," she whispered.

The ashram took in fresh recruits in the month of February, so I had only a few weeks left at home. On January 14th, Aunt Preema and Uncle Raghavan bid farewell to me as they set out on their pilgrimage. This was the second time since Sandhya's departure that I felt my life was slipping away from me. In spite of my experiences of astral reality and knowledge of the enduring nature of the human soul, I felt intense pangs of separation. I walked with them for a few hundred yards along the rice fields, as they made their way out of our village. At the outskirts of the village, on the edge of a large pond, Aunt Preema stopped.

"This is as far as you will accompany us," she said. I touched Uncle Raghavan's feet.

"May the Divine be with you always, Shambu. Preema, I will walk ahead slowly. You may catch up with me after you talk to him." So saying, Uncle Raghavan walked ahead.

"Aunt Preema . . ." I muttered, trying to contain my grief. "Prabha . . ." I prostrated at her feet. She pulled me up.

"Be strong now. The divine unites us both; space and time are no barriers for us." Saying that, she pulled me close and blew sharply into my ears. "There, you will always hear the divine. Go now." She walked away.

▼ ▼ ▼

With two weeks left until my departure to the hermitage, my folks helped me prepare for the journey. Words of advice poured in. My aunts gave me tips on what to eat and how to cook. They dinned into me to eat well and keep my health good. My mother said prayers and pledged offerings to all local gods, goddesses, and serpents, soliciting their divine grace on my behalf.

My aunts scoured empty bottles from the kitchen storeroom, washed them, and put them out in the sun to dry. As the days went by, they filled these bottles with pickled mangoes, sticks of fried jackfruit, banana chips, salted lemons, and fried bitter-gourd slices and lined them up on the courtyard verandah.

Uncle Damodaran rummaged about the attic of the dining hall and brought down an old iron chest, which he cleaned and repainted for my use. He tinkered with the old lock, and with the help of a few drops of coconut oil, nudged the rusty levers into action. My female cousins packed the bottles of pickled and fried food into a smoke stained wicker basket.

It was past twilight, time to say farewell and to take stock of things. In spite of the impending transition, I experienced numbness. I visited every nook and corner of the house. Stepping out into the darkness, I walked toward the cowshed. Lakshmi, the piebald cow, mother of several generations of calves, grunted at me through the semi-darkness. It seemed that she sensed my pangs, for she stopped her incessant chewing and swung her drooling muzzle toward me in a slow arc. I said farewell to the cows and the buffaloes. I walked over to the pond and sat under the bamboo bowers. I scooped up sand into my palms. Many sweet memories lay scattered among these sands. A great wave of sentimentality swept over me. Anguish wrenched my heart and suppressed emotions raked my body. I bid farewell.

# Glossary

**Adyantaram:** The sixteenth-day feast thrown by the kin to celebrate the ascension of the spirit of the Dead into the Realm of the Dead.

*Aghora Rahasya:* A manuscript authored by Narayanan Namboodiri, a great grand uncle in the matriarchy of Madatara. This manuscript, in addition to describing in detail the mystical techniques of mastering different states of awareness and the cosmology of the mind, also describes, in gruesome detail, the methods of harvesting live fetuses through the use of occult violence to pregnant women—a feat that marks the underworld odiyyas from the benign ones. The people were only too familiar with this technique by being on the receiving end, and they remembered Narayanan Namboodiri to have dealt with black sorcery during his time. The matriarchs of my family hid *Aghora Rahasya* out of fear and respect for this ancestor. They were afraid because once a person becomes an odiyya he or she is not bound by space-time and thus is beyond the clutches of death. An underworld odiyya could thus still cast his malevolent energy upon the household. The matriarchs wished to keep the existence of this manuscript a secret from the general public for fear of reprisal for harboring such a document.

**Aghori:** A mystic, like the *odiyya*. Lay people perceive the aghori as one who has transcended horror, fear, disgust, and loathing. An aghori practices rituals that appear bizarre to lay people.

**Ahuthi:** An ancient technique of exorcism, which reveals the entity that invades a human being.

**Akshatam:** Raw rice yellowed with turmeric powder, used during divine worship.

**Alowkika Anubhavam:** When the physical senses are absorbed into the astral senses and consciousness is withdrawn into the dream mind, a person experiences parts of the subtle realm while still retaining a sensory grip on the physical. This experience of the dual realms is called *alowkika anubhavam* or transmundane experiences.

**Amavasya:** First day of the first quarter of every lunar month when the night is moonless.

**Ambika:** A manifestation of the Divine Mother in the form of a young virgin.

**Ammuma:** An endearing term for grandmother.

**Anandamaya Kosha:** The sheath of bliss. This sheath is encased within the sheath of divine intelligence. Within this sheath of bliss is the atman or soul. From the human body to the sheath of bliss there is a dramatic lightening of the sheaths.

**Angavastra:** A rectangular piece of cloth, sewn together at the width; worn by women with the upper end above the breasts and the rest of the cloth fitting loosely about them.

**Annamaya Kosha:** The sheath shaped with food and physical sensations. The human body is the gross sheath encasing the soul. Though it is primarily the seat of the unconscious mind, the logical mind works here, and to a lesser extent the dream mind. The human body is the instrument with which the human personality interacts with the physical realm. Annamaya kosha encases the mental sheath.

**Anushasana Parva:** A portion of the great epic *Mahabharatha,* wherein Sages Vyasa and Vidura instruct the grieving King Dritharastra and his household on matters of life and death, karma, the path of the migrating soul, and of heavenly regions. This chapter happens after the description of the great clan war and the subsequent annihilation of the Kauravas, the sons of King Dritharastra.

**Ashuddham:** A state of spiritual impurity. In the context of a mystical rite, the time is made pure by choosing an auspicious moment to begin the rite. The place and the materials are made pure through preliminary incantations, but have to be constantly guarded from evil or impure energies through rituals that proceed parallel to the main rite.

**Astamangalya Vidya:** A hoary technique in which the *kurukkals* channeled higher beings to ascertain the cause of a phenomenon when all rational and physical investigations have been conducted without a satisfactory outcome. Its use required the consensus of all the elders of our village.

**Atharvana Veda:** One among the four vedas; the other three being the Rg, the Yajus and the Sama Veda. The Atharvana Veda also contains chants and invocations to spirits and entities, and sections of this veda describe death, the realms beyond death, transmigration, and reincarnation.

**Atman:** Soul, Self; the pure, imperishable, blissful divine representation in each human being.

**Avadhanam:** Recitation of chants from the Vedas by a group of men seated in a circle. The first member chants the first verse; the person next to him chants the second verse, and so on. It is a mnemonic exercise that helped men retain volumes of verses.

**Avyakta Kayin:** Undefined body-mind. A stage in the evolution of a human into a full-fledged odiyya, when the odiyya has enough power to dismantle his or her physical body and retain a coherent and intact awareness without a specific body.

**Ayurveda:** The divine wisdom of longevity and the mystical basis of health. The human body-mind is taught to be a composition of the five states of matter (earth, water, fire, air, and ether), and they generated three preponderences called *vata, pittha,* and *kapha,* which in mutual equilibrium, promoted good health. But in various fractions of disequilibrium, these disrupted the normal flow of *prana,* or life force, causing the body-mind to dysfunction, thus generating gateways for opportunistic organisms to invade. In ayurveda, students explore the use of specialized diets along with various herbal preparations to restore good health. The prescriptions are herbal medicines with specific diets.

**Bali Kriya:** A collection of funerary rites. The gathering of bones from the funeral mound of ashes and sealing them in an urn or a hollow gourd, invocation to the spirits of the ancestors—propitiation, rite to assist the spirit of the recently Dead on its way into the Realm of the Dead, and purification of the house to prevent the spirit of the Dead and other disembodied spirits from returning.

**Bhadra Kali:** Kali the auspicious goddess. A benign manifestation of Goddess Kali.

**Bhagalamukhi:** The eighth of the ten great manifestations of the Divine Mother. She represents the deep unconscious and the underworlds. All ten are called the *Dasha Maha Vidya,* or the Ten Cosmic Wisdoms.

*Bhagavad Gita:* Also called simply the *Gita,* consists of the teachings of the divine being Krishna to Arjuna on the battlefield.

**Bhaikari Odiyya:** Underworld *odiyya.* Predatory sorcerers from realms below the conscious human realm. They plunder human beings whose awareness is in a state of transition. Like vultures, they also gather at rituals to harvest awareness from the ritualists. If they are not alert, even mystics are ravaged by these beings during mystical practices. Some among the bhaikari odiyyas are those who are of human origin, but are drawn into the underworld in the course of their occult practices. Then there are those who are from the underworld originally.

**Bhakti:** Devotion and a sense of surrender to God. A sublime state of mind where the devotee is filled with love and ecstasy.

**Bharani:** The name of a cluster of stars identified in the Hindu astrological almanac and corresponding to 41 Arietis, a star in the star cluster Arietis documented in astronomy star charts.

**Bilva Leaves:** Tri-foliate leaves of the plant *Aegle marmelos* used in the worship of God Shiva.

**Brahman:** That stateless presence that underlies all space-time—also called the *Trans-Cosmic Void*. This stateless Brahman co-exists with its opposing principle Kali, the manifestor, sustainer and destroyer of all space-time.

**Brahmarakshas:** Disincarnate soul of a Brahmin who deviated steeply from his spiritual life in a past incarnation.

**Burfee:** A sweet made with sugar, coconut, cardamom, flavored with vanilla, and cut into small cubes.

**Champakam:** The ochre-orange flower of the plant *Michelia champak*.

**Chit:** Absolute, unqualified consciousness and awareness. An ascription of the *atman*.

**Chitrini, Vajrini:** Chitrini and vajrini are astral energy channels that contain astral energy of similar names. Chitrini energy surrounds vajrini. Vajrini and chitrini energy surrounds *sushumna*. These three form the astral *meru*.

**Chudala Kali:** Kali of the cremation ground. A gory manifestation of Kali, patron deity of some mystics.

*Devi Mahatmyam:* Seven hundred verses in praise of Goddess Chandi from the *Markendeya Puranam*. It is also called *Devi Saptashati*.

**Devi Prasadam:** Food offerings prepared and offered to a deity, which is then partaken by devotees.

**Dhoti:** A rectangular cotton cloth worn ankle length from the waist by men—much like the lower half of a toga.

**Forest Kali:** Forest Kali. The deity in the forest shrine, awakened one night each year.

**Garuda Purana:** A scripture that consists of God Vishnu's discourses to the celestial bird Garuda. It contains topics on the nature of the Self, rebirth, and the afterlife.

**Gayatri:** A mantra from the Rg-veda that a child is initiated into. This initiation confers a spiritual rebirth after which he or she is known as a twice born.

**Ghora Kali, Ghora Bhairavi:** Kali of fierce form. Bhairavi with a fierce form. Using potent chants, the *odiyyas* invoke the power of these goddesses to aid them in their battle against the underworld odiyyas.

**Ha:** The astral force that flows through *pingala,* the right astral channel, and identified as masculine solar astral energy.

**Hiranya Sutra:** Golden thread, or the astral self encased in *sushumna.* And sushumna is surrounded by *vajrini* and *chitrini* energy respectively. Hiranya sutra appears as a shining golden thread. It is also described as a sizzle of lightning. The astral self should not be confused with the *atman* or soul. The astral self, itself, contains the vijnanamaya and the anandamaya koshas within which is the *atman.*

**Homa Fire:** A ritual fire ignited within a special pit. Into this fire the ritualist pours clarified butter with the accompaniment of mantras.

**Homa-kuntta:** A square fire pit used in vedic fire ceremonies.

**Ida:** The left astral channel that carries the *"tha"* astral force—the feminine force of lunar energy.

**Iswara:** Masculine personification of the Supreme Being.

**Jaggery:** Brown sugar made from the molasses of the palm.

**Jeera Water:** Drinking water boiled with cumin and ginger.

**Jiva Shakti:** Life force or biophysical force.

**Jnana Yogi:** A mystic who has achieved Self-illumination through inquiry into the nature of the Self, using mystical reasoning, weeding out the perishable from the imperishable. Such a quest begins outside, but in the end reaches his or her innermost self.

**Kala:** (Pronounced with emphasis on the last <u>a</u> as in Kalaa). The sixteen phases of the moon identified in the sixteen metamorphoses of a Tantric initiate. Each phase of transformation grants the initiate the experience of a specific aspect of the Divine Mother. Just as the moon always exists fully, but appears to emerge into totality over sixteen days, so too the divinity of the disciple is revealed in these transformations. Goddess Kali with her sixteen arms is this fullness.

**Kalasham:** A brass pot used in rituals.

**Kalpa:** One day of Brahma (not to be confused with *Brahman*). This period is 4230 million human years.

**Kamakshi Deepam:** A small hand-held lamp, lit during sunset and taken into every room of a house to usher in auspiciousness before the descent of darkness.

**Karanavar:** The eldest maternal uncle in a matriarchy, who supervises the agricultural and maintenance activities of the men in their homestead. The karanavar, in turn, is accountable to the matriarch. In a matrilineal system however, even though a karanavar has similar functions, he is not subservient to the oldest matriarch, but is on par with her.

**Karma Stharam:** Strata of Karmas. Sedimented layers of karmas that constitute part of the mental sheath. In an embodied being, these strata extend into the deep unconscious. The lower the layers, the greater the compaction of individual karmas. The portions of the strata that reach into the conscious mind are less compacted as the individual karmas here are in a state of activation, projecting, as a result, the body-mind with its personality.

**Kasavu:** *Dhoti* made of raw silk.

**Kashaya:** A bitter herbal medicinal concoction.

**Kula Bhadra Kali:** Benign Kali of the clan of matriarchs; the original 108 priestly homesteads in the village Karingkalchuttoor. The devotees of this Kali are classified as Kaula because the rituals practiced by these mystics and tantriks are peculiar to this village and differ from the mainstream Kali worship among Hindus.

**Kumkum:** A red mineral powder used for Kali worship and related rituals.

**Kundabhisheekam:** Ablution to the sacred pit. A secret Tantric rite during which the dormant divine consciousness in a disciple is awakened by tweaking his or her sexual energy. The disciple is then initiated in potent mystical practices.

**Kundalini:** She who sleeps in the pit. Divine energy that lies curled as three-and-a-half coils clutching the egg of divine awakening. With the tip of its tail, it plugs the astral channel *sushumna*. The astral energy of the root vortex in the astral sheath and sexual energy in the corresponding *mooladhara chakra* in the physical sheath surround kundalini. Kundalini is stationed at the junction of the realm of the unconscious mind and the realm of the conscious mind.

**Kurukkal:** Men and women who are grandmasters among the *vallichappads*. This position comes from the intensity of austerities they have performed.

**Kuttuvilakku:** A large brass lamp lit at dusk and placed at the inside entrance of every home.

**Linga Sharira:** Subtle body or the astral sheath.

**Maha Kali:** Supreme Kali.

**Maha Prakriti:** The creatrix identified as Nature, whose body is this macrocosm.

**Maha Pralaya:** The great cosmic dissolution when all space-time, and even the overseers of each space-time, are obliterated and absorbed into the primal cause, Kali.

**Maha Prana:** Cosmic astral energy. The sea of awareness that penetrates all things and beings.

**Maha Preeta Niskarshana Mantram:** A system of chants used in the extraction of the cosmic spirit that tenents the idol of Goddess Kali in the main temple. This is done once a year.

**Maha Preeta Samkramana Mantram:** A system of chants used in transferring the cosmic spirit of Goddess Kali onto the gory image in the forest—again done once a year.

**Maha Preeta Sammoohanam:** Enticement of the Supreme Spirit. This chant is sung in homes by the matriarchs at the time when the kurukkals work to draw out the spirit of Kali from the image in the temple on the Night of Kali.

**Mahant:** Chief monk of a hermitage, also the administrator of a monastery.

**MaiKumbham:** Solar festival—marking the beginning of the apparent northward movement of the sun. A celebration of light when householders undertake an austerity called *Surya Narayana Vratam.*

**Mailanji:** A shrub, the leaves of which yield a reddish orange dye that the women use to produce cosmetic patterns on their hands and feet.

**Manomaya Kosha:** The sheath of the mind, or mental sheath. This sheath includes the karmic strata, active karmas in the karmic sheath, and the human personality projected by the active karmas. This sheath is the seat of the logical mind, or physical consciousness. Manomaya kosha encases the astral sheath.

**Mantra:** A special aggregation of phonemes and syllables uttered to call forth divine beings and invoke their energy.

**Mantra Vadini:** A woman seer versed in invocations and spells, who is able to manifest supernatural phenomena—a witch. A *mantra-vadi* is her male counterpart.

*Markendeya Purana:* Or *Markendeya Puranam,* is a scripture that details the feats of the Goddess Chandi and her victory over the demons Mahisha, Chanda, Munda Shumba and Nishumba.

**Matrilineal:** In a matrilineal social order, the female owns the property, but the oldest maternal uncle is the true head of the household. In a matriarchy however, the oldest *female* born in the family is both the owner of the landed property as well as the head of the household. Some of them are also elected to the council of Tantrikas in our village.

**Meru and Meru Dandam:** The meru or nerve tube that forms in the fetus between the seventh and the eighth week of its existence is the physical meru. This meru continues to grow to form the spinal axis or meru dandam. Corresponding to this physical meru is the astral meru. The astral meru exists at all times in the astral being. The astral meru is a nine-tiered structure that begins in the *kundalini* in the root vortex, and ends in the highest tenth vortex in the crown.

**Moola Chakra:** It is also called *mooladhara chakra*. It is the physical counterpart of the root chakra in the astral sheath. Moola chakra contains a pit wherein *kundalini* sleeps in unawakened human beings.

**Mudra:** Mystical gestures made with the fingers at different times during Tantric worship.

**Muhoortham:** Auspicious time determined through astrology to perform a ritual, or to do a task.

**Nagas:** Serpent divinities whose earthly brethren are snakes. Just as myth has it that snakes are guardians of earthly treasures, nagas are thought to guard divine treasures. *Kundalini,* the divine serpent, guards the most potent of all treasures—awakening. The realm of the nagas is above the realm of the underworld, but below the human realm.

**Naraka and Swarga:** Realms of awareness that border the Realm of the Dead. Naraka describes a cluster of subhuman realms of horrendous experiences through which some will pass upon death. While swarga are portions of the angelic realms through which others pass on dying in their cycle of reincarnations back into the physical realm. Naraka must not, however, be equated with the unconscious realms or the underworld, as they lie below these cluster of subhuman realms.

**Nihsattva Yoga:** A rare astrological aspect indicating powerful mystical tendencies in a human being.

**Nishachii:** A member of a mystic group where she takes on the role of a protectress because of her massive astral presence. She is from a class of demi-gods called the *yakshinis.*

**Nitya Deepam:** A tall brass lamp in the family shrine wherein a little flame stays lit day and night.

**Odiyyas:** Mystic sorcerers, humans who have transcended the clutches of space-time, mind and body through mystical practices. An *odiyatthi* is a mystic sorceress.

**Paishachii Malayalam:** Language of the ghouls. A dialect spoken by *odiyyas.*

**Pan:** Betelnut, leaves, and calcium carbonate chewed after meals.

**Para Brahmanda Shooniyam:** The trans-cosmic Void. A state (or statelessness) that underlies all phenomena, the manifested cosmos, and even Brahma, the overseer of the cosmos. The trans-cosmic void, however, is on par with Kali, the Cosmic creatrix, as they are the ultimate opposing dualities that sustain each other.

**Parra:** A brass trimmed wooden vessel that looks like a squat keg, used as a measure of paddy. A parra filled with paddy is often part of the centerpiece of a ritual setup.

**Pidi:** A sweet preparation made by encasing a mixture of brown sugar and coconut in a rice tortilla. The ends of the tortilla are pressed together to seal the contents and then steam cooked.

**Pingala:** The right astral channel that carries the *"ha"* or the solar astral force.

**Poornahuti:** The concluding chants and ritual activities of a fire ceremony.

**Poornima:** Full moon.

**Prakriti:** Nature; the Divine manifested as this universe.

**Pralaya:** Cosmic dissolution. As opposed to Maha Pralaya, these are lesser, periodic foldings of space-time, and they occur at the close of each day of Brahma, the overseer of each specific space-time. Space-time is not obliterated, but rather withdrawn into a seed state, to be regerminated at the dawn of each day of Brahma.

**Prana:** Life-force. Also principal among the five pranas that circulate through the astral sheath. The five pranas are *prana, apana, vyana, udana,* and *samana.*

**Prana Shakti:** Astral force. Prana Shakti is awareness drawn into the body-mind from the astral sheath. It powers the mental and astral constituents of the incarnate being. *Prana Shakti* and *Jiva Shakti* together power the body-mind complex.

**Pranamaya Kosha:** The sheath of astral energy, or astral sheath. This is the seat of the subconscious or dream mind, and the astral, or dream awareness. This sheath of astral energy surrounds the astral *meru.*

**Prapanjam:** Space-time.

**Pratha Smaranam Sree Shakti Pitham:** A pre-dawn chant sung to awaken the Goddess Kali in the main temple. The title of the chant means "dawn remembrance of the seat of feminine power."

**Preeta:** A disembodied being, ghost, or the spirit of the Dead.

**Puja:** Ritual worship to a deity.

**Raja Rajeeswari:** Supreme Queen; an epithet of the Divine Mother. Kundalini is also referred to as Raja Rajeeswari.

**Raktha Kali:** Sanguine Kali; another reference to Forest Kali.

**Rudram:** Also known as *Satha Rudriyam*; chants praising God Rudra found in Taittiriya Samhita, which is a portion of the Yajur-veda.

**Samhara Raktha Kali:** The manifestation of Kali who resurrects during cosmic dissolution along with her chief of staff *Vira Bhadra*.

**Samhara Rudra:** A manifestation of God Shiva, who is the destroyer of space-time. He manifests along with Kali during endtimes.

**Samskra:** Impressions from past life. Precursors to current tendencies.

**Sankalpa:** Intent; the purpose behind a certain ritual. In a general sense, sankalpa is imagination.

**Sankalpa Dhara:** The constant emergence and flow of thoughts and images that constitute the conscious mind.

**Schizognostic:** (A word coined for the purpose of defining a vague construct, by combining Schizoid and Gnosis). The manuscript *Aghora Rahasya* describes two paths to freedom. The first path leads the aspirant through methods that are noninvasive, and anchored along such principles as nonviolence, humility, and surrender to God. The second path describes in gruesome detail the methods of the underworld odiyyas in plundering awareness from other beings for the sole purpose of accumulating vast hoards of awareness in a short time, bypassing the foundational stages of cosmic principles. Thus, the author, Narayanan Namboodiri, exposes a mind split by the influences of two opposing paradigms—knowledges and paths that acquire power in both cases, but one leads into the underworld and the other leads to the realm of the angels.

**Scimitar:** A large sword with a curved blade—much like a sickle, but with an elongated handle, most of which is also part of the blade.

**Shakti:** Divine power, cosmic energy, or the conscious power that manifests in the image of Kali.

**Shakti Bhava:** A state of divine ecstasy. A mystic consciousness wherein God is perceived as the Divine Mother. In such a state, the devotee is overpowered by extreme ecstasy and becomes an active receptacle for the Divine Mother for the duration of that rapture.

**Shava Samskram:** Ceremonies related to the cremation of the dead.

**Shava Shuddhi:** A rite done to the dead body before cremation. Invocations guide the spirit of the Dead to relinquish its preoccupation with the body. After this, the body is washed and shrouded before it is burned and dispersed. This assures that the elements are returned to nature in their pure state so that other bodies can be reconstituted from them. By this rite, the kin of the Dead thank nature for lending the astral being such elements to form its body on earth.

**Shivalanga:** Also called shivalangam, is an egg shaped out of stone, crystal, or metal, and it represents the subtle self of the cosmic being. It is also the oval luminescence, or *linga shariram,* that remains when the body is dropped.

**Shoodashaksharii:** The mantra of sixteen syllables heard during the sixteenth transformation of the Tantrik initiate.

**Shrardham:** Rites done on the first anniversary of the death of a relative. It is also an annual rite done to propitiate the Spirits of ancestors, who are invoked and rice offerings are made to them. This also assures the peace of these spirits in the Realm of the Dead. Usually seven generations are invoked.

**Shuddha Pranis:** Astral beings with sublime consciousness. Beings of the boundary between the physical and astral realms. Beings who are naturally odiyyas without any human origins. The *woodland odiyyas* are an example of shuddha pranis.

**Siddha:** An illumined one. An adept in mystical practices.

*Sree Devi Mahatmyam:* **Same as** *Devi Mahatmyam.* A Tantric scripture that celebrates the triumph of Divine Mother over the demons.

**Surya Narayana Vratam:** Mystical austerity undertaken by devotees to propitiate the Supreme Being in the sun, heralding the ascension of light in summer.

**Sushumna:** The central astral channel that begins at the root chakra and ends in the uppermost chakra.

**Talam:** A circular brass platter used in ceremonies.

**Tambulam:** A small brass platter containing betelnut, betel leaves, a vial of calcium carbonate, and some spices.

**Tandava:** Shiva's dance of joy after he sublimates his grosser self.

**Tantra:** An ancient Hindu mystic philosophy espousing that the manifested Supreme Being is feminine—Divine Mother.

**Tantrik:** A mystic who practices tantra. *Tantrika* is a woman mystic of this category.

**Tapas:** Spiritual austerities performed with a specific goal.

**Taravad:** A matriarchal or a matrilineal homestead.

**Teerthayatris:** Kali pilgrims who gather on the Night of Kali from several distant villages.

**Tha:** The astral force that flows through *ida,* the left astral channel, and considered to be feminine lunar astral energy.

**Tulasi:** Also **Tulasi Shrine.** The sacred basil plant worshipped at dawn and dusk. It is planted in a raised brick structure with niches in its four walls for oil lamps.

**Ululation:** A word from the Webster's Dictionary adapted in this book to describe a peculiar cry uttered by women from Eastern cultures on ritual occasions or during ceremonies. The word is onomatopoetic, as the cry can be described as: *Ulu-Ulu-Ulu-Ulu . . .*, and is uttered in rapid sequence.

**Vaisvanara:** Universal Being as fire. The vedic deity, who represents elemental fire, invoked in a fire ceremony.

**Vallichappads:** Mystics who aspire to divine illumination through intense devotion to Kali. They serve the villagers assisting them with rites and rituals. Vallichappads live as celibates in a separate community.

**Vastu Purusha Mandala:** The spiritual science of homestead and temple construction. The layout of manmade structures should reflect the ordered cosmos and the Supreme Being who permeates it. And the belief that the human body, or the microcosm, reflects the design of the macrocosm is the essence of this philosophy. Just as the body that ensheaths the human being is a living breathing form, the house constructed in accordance with these principles is considered a vibrant space alive with ordered life force.

**Vijnanamaya Kosha:** The sheath of divine intelligence. It is the seat of the superconscious mind. It lies encased within the astral sheath. This intelligence guides the human free will in making correct choices at the forks of life's paths. It is the voice of conscience.

**Villambadis:** A *Paishachii Malayalam* term meaning "Children of Kali." At midnight on the Night of Kali, these devotees of Kali strike their heads and undergo a ritual bloodletting.

**Waidya:** A medicine man or woman, proficient in herbal remedies and holistic treatments.

**Woodland Odiyya:** A class of sorcerers who exist in the astral realm. These do not have human origins, but originated in the astral plane. These beings can manifest with ease in this physical realm—especially in those areas on this space-time that have a natural umbilicus into the astral realm, where the awareness from both realms intermixes with least effort.

**Yajur (Vedic hymn):** Any hymn from the Yajur Veda, such as the Rudram.

**Yaksha:** An entity of the astral realm considered a demigod. *Yakshini* is a female yaksha.

**Yamas:** Five principle commandments for a mystical aspirant enjoined by Sage Patanjali in his famous work, *The Yoga Sutras.* These yamas are as follows: Ahimsa—nonviolence, Asteeya—general self-restraint, Aparigriha—elimination of greed, Brahmacharya—being non-lustful, Sathya —being truthful. These inviolable cosmic principles must be the foundation upon which mystic practices and power-gathering rituals are to be structured if ascendancy into the angelic realms is desired.

**Yantras:** Geometric shapes put together in relationship to one another, usually representing the dynamics between the energy of astral beings and the astrophysical dimensions they influence.

**Yatna Deha:** A cocoon of gross impulses surrounding the spirit of the Dead that propels it into hellish regions. The spirit of everyone who dies is not encased in this.

*Yoga Sutras:* A scripture containing terse aphorisms on the science of Self-illumination, ascribed to Sage Patanjali.

**Yoni Kumbham:** The pot of union. A power spot in the hills outside the village of Karingkalchuttor, where odiyya disciples are initiated. This pot represents the female receptacle during Tantric rites.

# Bibliography

*Bhagavad Gita.* Translated by Swami Chidbhavananda, the Secretary, Sri Ramakrishna Tapovanam, Tirupparaitturai, India, 1992. *The Bhagavad Gita,* translated and introduced by Antonio de Nicolás. Nicolas-Hays, Box 612, York Beach, ME 03910, 1990.

*Anushasana Parva of Mahabharatha.* Translated by Kisari Mohan Ganguli. Munshiram Manoharlal Publishers, Pvt. Ltd., New Delhi, 1990.

*Markandeya Puranam.* Kshema Raja Sri Krishnadasa. Nag Publishers, Delhi, 1986.


## SOURCES OF CHANTS

"Agni prajvalitam vandae jata vedam hutashanam . . . " Chants from the *Satapatha Brahmana.* Madhyandina recension, section on techniques and invocations for Agnihotram fire ritual. Nag Publishers, 11a/U.A Jawahar Nagar, Delhi-11007, India, 1990.

"Sradhayam pranae nivisto amrutam juhomi . . .": Section 69, verse 1, *Mahanarayana Upanishad.* Commentary by Sri Shankaracharya, Shankara Dikvijayam, Kanchikamakoti Peetham, Tamil Nadu, India, 1960.

"Ardhram jvalati jyotiraham asmi. Yo aham asmi brahmaaham asmi." Verse 67 *Mahanarayana Upanishad.* Commentary by Sri Shankaracharya, Shankara Dikvijayam, Kanchikamakoti Peetham, Tamil Nadu, India, 1960.

"Triambakam yajamahae sugandhim pusthi vardhanam . . ." Supplemental to Rudram of Yajur Veda of black recension. This verse appears at the end of the third yajus.

"Kali Kali Maha Kali, Bhadra Kali Namostutae . . ." Anonymous composition, chanted by members of our matriarchy.

"Vata vriksha mridu patrakaree . . ." Anonymous composition, chanted among the odiyyas.

# Index

# About the Author

Amarananda Bhairavan experienced a joyous childhood growing up among his extended family on the west coast of South India. When he was 9 years old, his aunt gave him a mystical initiation, and under her spiritual guidance, he began his mystical practices. At age 11, he began to study Sanskrit and learned to chant hymns from the Vedas. Mentored by his aunt, Bhairavan practiced tantra, and in the years that followed, received several initiations in various aspects of Kali worship. Later, he learned fire rituals and invocations to different divinities that he continues to practice in private, and during ceremonial social occasions. He teaches yoga, Sanskrit chants, and lectures on Hindu metaphysics and tantra. He lives in Laguna, California.